# Education, Work and Social Change

# Education, Work and Social Change

## Young People and Marginalization in Post-Industrial Britain

Robin Simmons
*Professor of Education, University of Huddersfield, UK*

Ron Thompson
*Principal Lecturer in Education, University of Huddersfield, UK*

Lisa Russell
*Senior Research Fellow in Education, University of Huddersfield, UK*

First published 2014 by
PALGRAVE MACMILLAN

Palgrave Macmillan in the UK is an imprint of Macmillan Publishers Limited, registered in England, company number 785998, of Houndmills, Basingstoke, Hampshire RG21 6XS.

Palgrave Macmillan in the US is a division of St Martin's Press LLC, 175 Fifth Avenue, New York, NY 10010.

Palgrave Macmillan is the global academic imprint of the above companies and has companies and representatives throughout the world.

Palgrave® and Macmillan® are registered trademarks in the United States, the United Kingdom, Europe and other countries.

ISBN 978–1–137–33592–0 hardback
ISBN 978–1–137–33593–7 paperback

This book is printed on paper suitable for recycling and made from fully managed and sustained forest sources. Logging, pulping and manufacturing processes are expected to conform to the environmental regulations of the country of origin.

A catalogue record for this book is available from the British Library.

A catalog record for this book is available from the Library of Congress.

*This book is dedicated to our children*

# Contents

# Tables and Figures

## Tables

## Figures

# Acknowledgements

First and foremost, we would like to thank the young people who gave their time to share their experiences, hopes and fears. It has been a privilege to gain an insight into their lives. We would also like to thank the many practitioners who gave us their time, providing detailed accounts of the local context and their views on young people not in education, employment or training.

We are particularly grateful to the Leverhulme Trust for supporting the research upon which this book is based, and to the members of the advisory group who gave us invaluable support during the project: Professor Tracy Shildrick, Fay McIntosh, Judith Horsefield, Denise Robinson, Claire Bentley, Mike Hobbs and Liz Singleton.

# 1
# Introduction

## Young people and marginality

This book is about 24 young people whose stories illuminate the experiences of marginalized youth in post-industrial Britain. Drawing on data from a longitudinal ethnographic study of young people not in education, employment or training (NEET), the book charts their experiences, identities and aspirations over a period of more than two years, but also locates their trajectories within a broader discussion of the social and economic context which has shaped the lives of a generation often described as 'lost'. A central part of the book consists of detailed case studies of six participants, which provide an insight into both the nature of the data and particular themes we want to emphasize.

Popular images of NEET young people often evoke pejorative stereotypes of 'hoodies' and 'pramface girls' destined for a life on benefits. In August 2011, when a series of riots erupted in London and other parts of England, politicians and the media seized on these events to portray an increasing threat from out-of-control youth in 'Broken Britain'. Prime Minister David Cameron, attributing the riots to 'social problems that have been festering for decades' (BBC 2011), claimed that Britain had become 'literally de-moralized' and announced that policies to improve parenting and education, and turn around the lives of troubled families, would be accelerated. However, there is another perspective on such stories, and it is necessary to look much deeper than isolated events or the behaviour of a small proportion of individuals and their families. First of all, there is little evidence that a swathe of young people in Britain have become disconnected from the aspirations and values of mainstream society (MacDonald and Marsh 2005). The research presented here, as well as other studies, suggests that disadvantaged young

1

people generally have quite traditional aspirations, for a job, a home and a family life. Secondly, phenomena such as mass youth unemployment or disaffection from education are related to changes in society on a global scale, although the extent to which social problems actually occur is influenced by policy decisions in individual nation states. This book aims to explore the rich ethnographic data at our disposal by locating it within these global shifts in social experience and to enable the voices of young people to be heard as they recount the stories of their lives and ambitions. A central theme is that their attitudes and behaviours are shaped in the same way as other people's, by the conditions in which they live and work, by the challenges they face and by the resources available to them. We also examine more specific facets of their engagement with work, education and training, and welfare, drawing attention to the ways in which the construction of NEET young people within social policy shapes their experience and future prospects.

Negative images of youth-as-trouble, of disengaged young people as a threat to society and a drain on its resources, have always been offset (to some extent) by more caring representations of youth-in-trouble and the benefits to society that would ensue if their talents could be harnessed. This dual representation of marginalized youth was expressed particularly clearly in Tony Blair's foreword to *Bridging the Gap*, a report on NEET young people produced in the early years of New Labour government.

> The best defence against social exclusion is having a job, and the best way to get a job is to have a good education, with the right training and experience...Getting this right offers the prospect of a double dividend. A better life for young people themselves, saving them from the prospect of a lifetime of dead-end jobs, unemployment, poverty, ill-health and other kinds of exclusion. A better deal for society as a whole that has to pay a very high price in terms of welfare bills and crime for failing to help people make the transition to becoming independent adults.
>
> (SEU 1999, p.6)

The reference to social exclusion reminds us that in the last 20 years concerns about poverty have been discursively reconstructed as problems of participation – in education, work and other social contexts. The reason why people and communities are poor, beset by social problems, or both, is because they are excluded from one or more forms of participation, often interacting with each other. Within this paradigm, education plays a central role – in creating responsible citizens, equipping young people with the skills they need to find work and improving the quality of parenting. However, the concept of social exclusion has risen to prominence at precisely the time when the power of nation states to assure a link between participation and prosperity is declining. Globalization, and the intensification of capitalist accumulation, has led to many young people in Western societies being confronted with what Loïc Wacquant (1996) calls *advanced marginality*. Changes to the nature of wage labour, the increasing disconnection of the lowest-paid from the benefits of economic growth and the decline of social infrastructure in certain neighbourhoods all limit the capacity of participation to remove the threat of poverty. Whilst some of these changes are felt most acutely in large cities, their ramifications are also felt elsewhere, and one of the arguments of this book is that marginality is a powerful lens through which to view the experiences of NEET young people.

Within such conceptions of marginality, certain forms of education and training can be seen as particularly problematic, and education as a place to 'warehouse' young people until the labour market has need of them has been extensively critiqued, as a contemporary reconstitution of the reserve army of labour or as part of a 'political economy of youth' in which intergenerational exploitation parallels some aspects of class relations (Ainley 2013; Coté 2013). Even from an instrumental perspective that sees education simply as readying young people for work, such provision has been criticized as inadequate and likely to lead to further marginalization or exclusion. The stigmatization and poor labour market returns associated with low-level vocational provision and condemned in the Wolf Review (2011) is a case in point. As we discuss later in the book, the young people in our research were often reluctant to participate in programmes which they found dull and repetitive, and rarely led to higher-level study or suitable employment.

This chapter sets the scene for the remainder of the book. We first provide a brief overview of the research project on which it is based, and then introduce some of the key concepts we will develop and draw upon later. In addition to tracing how young people who leave education at an early stage have been constructed as a problem group, the chapter also discusses some broader issues of social change, including the debate over individualization, reflexive modernization and structural inequality, and the theorizations of class, gender and race in education which will be needed as we present our data. The chapter ends by outlining the structure of the book and looking ahead to our conclusions.

## An ethnographic study of the experiences of NEET young people

Our interest in conducting research with young people on the margins of education and employment stems from a combination of factors. As social and educational researchers, we have a long-standing interest in social class, inequality and social justice, as well as the relationship between education and the economy more broadly. Working in a university school of education during the mid-2000s sharpened our interest in these matters, as it became apparent that the composition of our student body was changing in ways related to particular conceptions of work, education and learning. Our institution is a large provider of teacher training for the post-compulsory education sector and, for many years, tutors in further education (FE) colleges and similar settings have undertaken programmes of professional development at the university. Over time, however, we saw a distinct change in the intake of these courses. Whilst academic disciplines such as English, history or sociology, and established vocational subjects like engineering, accountancy or construction were declining, there had been a notable increase in the number of 'key skills' and 'employability' tutors. Moreover, whilst some of these practitioners were teaching in FE colleges, many more worked for training providers focusing specifically on work-related and pre-vocational training aimed at NEET young people. At the same time, political and academic debate about social exclusion and its causes directed our attention to youth employment and unemployment, and the role of so-called employability programmes. In September 2008 we began an ethnographic study of young people taking part in Entry to Employment (E2E), a training programme designed to prepare young people outside education and the labour market for the workplace (Simmons and Thompson 2011).

Whilst our E2E research provided valuable insights into the nature of education and training for young people at risk of becoming NEET, it was evident that a more wide-ranging study of the lived experience of marginalized young people would provide a fuller understanding of their lives and the challenges and opportunities facing them. Whilst education is an important site of social differentiation and reproduction it is, after all, only one facet of an individual's broader societal experiences. Our aim of engaging in longitudinal ethnographic research with a group of young people initially outside education and employment became a reality when we were fortunate enough to obtain a research grant from the Leverhulme Trust, which enabled us to carry out the work upon which this book is based. The project, *An Ethnographic Study of the Experiences of NEET Young People*, was conducted between August 2010 and June 2013. Fieldwork took place in two neighbouring local authorities in the north of England between October 2010 and March 2013; 24 young people took part in the ethnography for substantial periods of time although, for various reasons, four of them ended their involvement between October and December 2011. Of the remaining 20 participants, 12 were female; six of the young women were parents or became pregnant during the research. One young man was a father. Ten participants had spent at least some time in care and 15 lived alone. Two young women were of Pakistani descent and one young man was of mixed heritage; the others were White. All were between 15 and 20 years old when the fieldwork commenced in late 2010. By the end of the project, our data included over 280 hours of participant observation conducted in a variety of settings. Seventy-eight interviews were conducted and transcribed, including 20 with practitioners such as Connexions advisers, Jobcentre staff and tutors in training providers; three with employers; and 54 with young people. Other forms of data were collected during the course of the study, including photographs taken by the researcher and by participants; copies of qualifications and certificates of achievement; minutes of practitioner meetings; national and local statistics; and course information literature.

The young people who took part in the research had differing circumstances, educational trajectories and aspirations. However, although one must generalize with caution, certain trends were evident. Some participants had been academically successful at school, but the majority had negative experiences of education and few academic qualifications. In some cases, particularly for those who had been in care, frequent changes of residence had led not only to disrupted patterns of schooling, but being allocated to schools with places available due to lack of popularity and/or high pupil turnover. Perhaps the main common factor in our sample is that they were from largely working-class backgrounds and, in the majority of cases, participants had lived for most of their lives in deprived areas. In many ways, the very richness and diversity of the data generated by longitudinal qualitative research can provide challenges for analysis and presentation. Moreover, when researching the lives of NEET young people, it is important to bear in mind that differences within particular subcategories – such as teenage parents, young offenders and care leavers – can be as great as those between them (Finlay et al. 2010). For this reason, although the book also draws on our data more broadly, the presentation of findings largely adopts a case-study approach. Individual young people's stories are used not only to illustrate key themes emerging from our research but also to highlight patterns of difference as well as similarity. The six case studies represent something of the diversity of the NEET population, with different biographies, circumstances and responses; they illuminate the themes we wish to explore, but in different ways and sometimes by exception as much as by example.

## The normalization of extended schooling

The emergence of the NEET category reflects the normalization of full-time post-compulsory education or training as the initial stage in school-to-work transitions. Whilst in earlier decades the great majority of young people expected to enter full-time employment soon after completing their compulsory education, the decline of youth labour markets associated with de-industrialization in the late 1970s and 1980s confronted school-leavers with a context of sharply reduced employment opportunities, particularly for those with few qualifications. Young people's experiences became more individualized and fragmented, as collective transitions from school to factory or mine were replaced by a diversity of jobs, often with smaller employers, particularly in the service sector, or a place on the much-criticized training schemes developed to absorb the rising tide of youth unemployment. Whilst young people with high levels of educational attainment, particularly those from middle-class backgrounds, were able to take advantage of increasing opportunities in higher education, the majority were consigned to various forms of vocational education or a place on a youth training scheme.

Young people who rejected these options to seek employment came under increasing pressure, and in 1988 their entitlement to unemployment benefit was removed. Effectively, the unemployed young person ceased to exist, and was replaced with a more problematic figure, the young person outside education and employment. This shift exemplified broader trends to individualize social and economic risk, reflecting the emphasis on markets at the expense of collective institutions characteristic of neo-liberalism. The slogan 'Education, education, education' used by Tony Blair during the 1997 election campaign crystallized an approach in which supply-side initiatives, aimed at creating a workforce suited to the demands of post-industrial economies, are seen as more effective and sustainable than interventions aimed at increasing the demand for labour. The global mobility of capital, it is claimed, leaves no alternative, for if productivity and skills are uncompetitive investment – and jobs – will go elsewhere.

The expansion of education and training is an immediate corollary of this argument; if the UK is to compete in a global marketplace, young people must be equipped with the knowledge and skills sought by employers and be prepared to retrain when these skills become out-dated. Youth unemployment is attributed to a lack of skills, not a lack of jobs, and extended periods of post-compulsory education are seen as essential to avoiding recurrent exclusion from the labour market. How-ever, the benefits of such policies have been felt largely by employers, and young people are required to run in order to stand still. As edu-cational credentials become extended to the great majority of young people, the least qualified school-leavers become progressively more dis-advantaged in the labour market (Roberts 2004, p.212). Forty years ago, most young people left school without qualifications; now, 'sixteen-year-olds who insist that they want proper jobs and who try to avoid all alternatives have become a new problem group' (Roberts 2009, p.358).

Introduced initially as a euphemistic term to replace perhaps more emotive descriptions such as 'Status 0' (Istance et al. 1994), the NEET category has framed UK policy discourses on youth unemployment for two decades. Although it has well-known limitations – for example, the diversity entailed by the definition *not* in education, employment or training – the concept of NEET has taken root in many other countries, particularly those dominated by neo-liberal philosophies. Most recently, it has become established in analyses of youth unemployment in the European Community (Eurofound 2012), and although the institutional environment varies considerably between countries which employ the NEET category, its relationship with individualized conceptions of social risk is well established. Furthermore, the scope of NEET has increased considerably as concerns have grown over graduate unemployment and the labour market engagement of other young people over the age of 18. Whilst initially restricted in the UK to 16–18-year-olds, the term now comprises young people under 25 and, in some contexts, extends to the age of 30 or more.

In general, we will avoid talking about NEET young people as a group, due to their disparate circumstances. Generalizations are problematic, and being NEET is not necessarily undesirable for all young people. Occupations such as motherhood or taking a gap year are valued by many, and pursuing activities unrelated to the labour market may be rational in some circumstances. Nevertheless, there is overwhelming evidence that, for the majority, being NEET is likely to have severe consequences in later life. Moreover, both the risk and consequences of early exclusion from education and employment are unequally distributed in society; and from the earliest interest in NEET young people, it has been clear that these risks are structured by gender, ethnicity and – above all – social class.

## Individualization, identity and class

Theorists of late modernity argue that social conditions are experienced in increasingly differentiated ways from person to person (Bauman 1988; Giddens 1991; Beck 1992). According to these accounts, the traditions and certainties associated with industrial societies are supplanted by reflexive modernization, in which the self must confront the multiplicity of choices, risks and dangers encountered in post-industrial times unaided by the prefigured scripts of class, gender, religion and culture which characterized earlier generations. As Kehily (2009) points out, reflexive modernity is often taken to imply the primacy of freely created identities, constructed from the fluidity, mobility and choice offered by late modern social worlds. Phrases such as 'the entrepreneurship of self' (Rose 1998, p.158) or 'choice biographies' provide articulations of contemporary selfhood through recurring themes of plurality, selection and self-narration. However, an alternative reading of reflexive modernization recognizes that, far from ending the inequalities associated with industrial societies, it presents new opportunities for capitalist accumulation in exploiting burgeoning varieties of selfhood. Beck (1992) and authors such as Giddens (1991) and Lash (1992) see individualization as a characteristic feature of capitalism in late modernity. Increased heterogeneity within the middle and working classes (Wacquant 2008), the culturalization of the economy, and the valuing and revaluing of ordinary people as neo-liberal subjects enable the exploitation of labour in both mundane and newly created ways (Skeggs 2004).

What changes is the way in which class relations are perceived. Whilst class-based inequalities have remained remarkably stable in the transition from industrial to post-industrial society, they have been recast in terms of differentiated individual responses to the social and economic risks of wage labour, such as unemployment and deskilling. In this way, the individual lives out the complexity and diversity of the social relations surrounding them, without necessarily confronting them as questions of class. Reflexivity goes only so far, and problems such as unemployment, ill-health and crime are perceived in the light of individual dispositions and failings, or as the price to be paid for freedom and choice. Globalization, the weakening of family and community structures, and the conjunction of technological progress with decreasing confidence in science and authority confront individuals with a variety of options and disrupt their capacity for engaging in collective action. For many young people, marginality or exclusion is a normal part of life or is seen as a stage in their transition to adulthood; it does not immediately strike them in terms of class structures or their intersections with gender and ethnicity. Moreover, activities in which young people engage have, to some extent, ceased to segregate them by gender or class; service-sector employment, higher education and certain forms of popular culture attract young people from many backgrounds. However, although all social groups are affected by the risks of late modernity, structural factors retain their importance. Class, gender and ethnic patterns in youth transitions have by no means disappeared (Furlong 2009), even if the ways that young people deal with decisions concerning education, employment or consumption have diversified and fragmented. Furlong and Cartmel (2007) refer to the apparent contradiction between objective and subjective experiences as the *epistemological fallacy* of late modernity, remarking that 'People's life chances remain highly structured at the same time as they increasingly seek solutions on an individual, rather than a collective basis' (p.5).

Bauman (1988) proposes that identities no longer wait to be assumed as a young person enters adulthood: 'Everyone has to ask himself the question "who am I", "how should I live", "who do I want to become" – and at the end of the day, be prepared to accept responsibility for the answer... Self construction of the self is, so to speak, a necessity.' (p.62). In a longitudinal study such as ours, the location of identity-work within the temporal sphere is a critical condition of analysis, and the development of identity states over time gives rise to contradictions, repetitions and sudden departures, particularly with young people vulnerable to personal and economic crises and in shifting relationships with practitioners, the 'street-level bureaucrats' at the crucial interface between young people and the state (Lipsky 1980). A unifying theme emerging from our study was the expression of what McDonald (1999) has called the *struggle for subjectivity*: the endeavours of participants to establish and maintain a sense of agency in the face of identities projected by the state, or the disruptions of sometimes chaotic personal circumstances (Thompson et al. 2014). Narratives of conflict and resistance

constantly recurred, reflecting disconnections between official conceptions of legitimate activities and our participants' sense of self, belonging
and aspiration.

As we will see in this book, processes of individualization and reflexive modernization have only obscured the ways in which social and
economic structures shape young people's lives, not obliterated them.
Social reproduction, the processes by which relations of dominance
and subordination are perpetuated, continues to operate: the conditions of late modernity have diversified young people's biographies,
but their trajectories remain profoundly influenced by their location
in a matrix of class, gender and race positions. Reflexive practices
re-articulate class inequalities under conditions of 'structured fragmentation' (Farrugia 2013). In times when working-class kids can no longer
be sure even of working-class jobs, it is necessary to reconcile the construction of biographical projects with contemporary realizations of
social reproduction.

## Theorizing social class and education

Theoretical explanations of social class differences in educational experiences and attainment have been central to the sociology of education for
more than half a century. Whilst genetic theories have retained many
adherents throughout this period (see the brief review in Bukodi et al.
2013), there has been no convincing case made to support the idea that
measured cognitive ability is largely biologically inherited. Sociological
theories which focus on cultural processes and inequalities in power
and resources have consequently been more influential, and the work
of theorists such as Pierre Bourdieu and Basil Bernstein informs much
contemporary research into social reproduction. Although class is traditionally conceptualized in terms of the relations of capitalist production,
Bourdieu broadens the idea of capital to include cultural and social
dimensions in addition to economic capital (Bourdieu 1986). These
*forms of capital* are deployed 'in the struggle (or competition) for the
appropriation of scarce goods ... it follows that the structure of [social
space] is given by the distribution of the various forms of capital ...'
(Bourdieu 1987, p.4). Classes are characterized by the shape of their particular distributions of capital, and class struggle may be expressed in
symbolic form, in attempts to maximize the effectiveness of certain elements of cultural capital, as well as through more obvious competition
in the economic field.

For Bourdieu, class relations are embodied within the individual along
cognitive and behavioural axes – the habitus, as Bourdieu calls the

internalized principles which govern our responses to situations, is both the conditioned product of past experiences in the social field and the means by which the field is recognized and known (Bourdieu 1977, pp.82–83). Cultural capital therefore exists in an embodied state, as long-lasting dispositions of the mind and body, as well as being objectified in cultural goods – books, pictures, musical instruments – or institutionalized in educational qualifications. Social capital, which Bourdieu conceives as the resources linked to social networks, depends on the extent of the networks to which an individual belongs, and the aggregated capitals to which these networks give access. As we will see later in this book, many participants had quite extensive social networks; however, the aggregate capital that could be mobilized through these networks was limited.

According to Bourdieu, the function of the education system is to reward those whose habitus, and with it their accumulations of social and cultural capital, are best adapted to the dominant culture of the field, whilst convincing others that their exclusion from this culture is both legitimate and a matter of no great regret. Bernstein (2000) focuses more closely on the discursive structures within the education system itself, and their relationship with distributions of power and control within society. Bernstein places great emphasis on the cognitive and linguistic forms associated with different class positions, and sees the emergence of a new middle class, highly dependent on educational success relative to other groups, as a significant factor in working-class underachievement. As in Bourdieu's account, the dissonance between dominant cultural forms and the cultures more typical of working-class families makes education an alienating experience for many children from such backgrounds. Although both of these perspectives have been criticized for positioning working-class cultures as deficient, they are rich in insights and have been used with great power in many contemporary accounts of social reproduction.

Rather than seeing educational under-achievement as the result of failure to come to terms with dominant cultures, Paul Willis, in his famous ethnography *Learning to Labour* (1977), develops an account of how some young people from working-class backgrounds actively reject the culture of the school in preference to the resistance which they associate with the relations of production in working-class employment. Although focusing on 'the lads' who embrace this culture of resistance, Willis's work also recognizes a different working-class culture, the 'ear 'oles' who aspire to social mobility through educational achievement; Phil Brown's *Schooling Ordinary Kids* (1987) takes up this point in more detail, providing a typology of responses to education which

suggest how a range of outcomes can derive from relatively homogeneous social backgrounds. More recent studies, such as Archer et al.
(2010), deploy the notion of identity to powerful effect, blending class,
gender and ethnicity in an integrated account of urban schooling and
youth transitions.

A somewhat different perspective is provided by the work of Raymond
Boudon (1974). This approach has two components: the first focuses
on inequalities in educational achievement, whilst the second considers
how education translates into achieved social status. As we have already
seen, this second component highlights the important point that large-
scale social mobility requires equally large-scale changes in the occupational structure, particularly if the education system is expanding.
In the first component of his model, Boudon distinguishes between
the primary effects of social stratification – differences in educational
performance between different social groups – and secondary effects,
which concern the choices made by young people from different social
backgrounds but with similar levels of educational achievement. Whilst
Boudon acknowledges that the explanation for primary effects may follow the lines proposed by Bourdieu, he sees secondary effects as largely
deriving from a rational evaluation of the likely benefits of particular educational choices compared with their costs – social and cultural
as well as economic. Because secondary effects are cumulative over a
school career, Boudon argues that they have greater importance than
primary effects. Social class differences in educational achievement are
therefore not the consequence of fundamental differences in values, but
arise from the different evaluations of educational opportunities made
by people occupying different social positions. In our view, Boudon's
approach – which has been better known within the field of social
mobility studies than in the sociology of education – has a great deal
to offer in understanding the trajectories of young people, such as those
who took part in our research.

Educational achievement is only one of many factors operating to
produce social inequality, and particularly in relation to gender and
ethnicity, cultural norms and expectations still help to channel young
people into traditional occupational and social roles, although such processes are significantly mediated by social class. The effects of race and
gender interact in complex ways with those of class. As Terry Lovell
points out, even the concept of class may be subjected to critique in
that gender relations may be concealed by using households and families as the units of class analysis (Lovell 2004, p.37). Similarly, class may
be used to 'analyse away' racial differences in achievement. Although

in quantitative terms class has a greater impact on educational achievement than either race or gender (Moore 2004, p.15), there is a danger that statistical analysis can erase important inequalities by focusing on the largest effects (Gillborn 2010a). Moreover, deterministic ascriptions of life chances to whole sections of society can be misleading, and differences within groups are just as important as those between them.

Recent work in the sociology of education has acknowledged that inequalities of gender, race and class cannot be fully understood in isolation (Gillborn 2010b), and intersectionality – the exploration of lived experience as constructed simultaneously through classed, raced and gendered subjectivities and structures – has been increasingly prominent. These intersectional studies move beyond economic understandings to draw on culturalist forms of class analysis, which provide greater scope for discussing the different ways in which class position impacts on young men and women (Archer et al. 2007). For example, class differences in the performance of 'hyper-heterosexual' femininities, constructed around themes such as heterosexual relationships, romance and motherhood, have been implicated in the resistances to schooling of young working-class women. Cultural analysis has also been used to examine shifts in the representation of working-class life associated with de-industrialization, showing how markers of the 'rough' as opposed to 'respectable' working class have been racialized and feminized to draw on images of young, Black gang members or teenage mothers rather than 'Andy Capp' figures (Skeggs 2004).

## Structure of the book

The book begins with a discussion of the concepts of poverty, social exclusion and marginalization. Although to some extent these concepts have become part and parcel of academic and political discussion, they are also complex ideas which carry a wide range of connotations, meaning different things to different people. They have also been extensively critiqued from a variety of standpoints, and our discussion aims both to review the key features of the debates concerning poverty and social exclusion and to establish our own usage. We also indicate why, in some contexts, we prefer the term 'marginalization' to 'social exclusion', and relate this term to the political and economic positioning of marginalized people. An important feature of contemporary discursive constructions of the marginalized or socially excluded is that their plight can be traced to particular cultures within certain families, cultures which – whilst ultimately having material roots and therefore susceptible to material intervention – are inimical to the work ethic which might enable these families to find a route out of poverty. This type of explanation finds a particularly clear and pervasive expression in the notion of cultures of worklessness, and we begin to draw on our ethnographic data to illustrate and contest some of the propositions contained in cultural explanations of poverty. Within this data, the accounts of practitioners contrast markedly with the attitudes expressed by the young people who took part in our research: whilst terms such as 'three generations of worklessness' and 'breaking the cycle' of deprivation were embedded in practitioner discourse, young people contested these discourses and sought to resist their moral evaluations and attributions. However, we leave it to later chapters to further explore our data and the light it casts on the varied attitudes to work of individual participants.

In Chapter 3, the focus turns to the specific issue of young people outside education, employment and training. In addition to tracing the influence of social and economic change on youth transitions generally, we discuss the conceptual shift away from youth unemployment to more individualized ways of thinking about the labour market vulnerability of young people. Following the introduction of the NEET category as an instrument of policy analysis in the mid-1990s a veritable explosion took place in research, policy initiatives and practical interventions, with the aim of identifying effective ways of moving vulnerable young people into education or training. We draw on this evidence to analyse the structure of the NEET population and to review some of the most significant research findings, including the relationship between becoming NEET and being socially and economically disadvantaged in childhood and adolescence. We also outline some of the evidence regarding the impact in later life of exclusion or marginality in post-compulsory education and the labour market.

Having established the broad nature of the NEET category, we turn in Chapter 4 to the methodology of our research project. Ethnography provides a distinctive approach to social research, and the chapter begins with a discussion of the nature of ethnography and the knowledge it generates. In focusing on a number of young people whose lives were largely disconnected from each other, our project departs in some ways from traditional conceptions of ethnography with their emphasis on single, tightly defined sites. The implications of a multi-site approach are explored, and located within the relationship between geographically and contextually mobile individuals and broader concerns about inequality and power which are characteristic of critical ethnography.

Chapter 4 also explains the origins of the research project and outlines the social and economic context of the towns of Middlebridge and Greenford, where the research took place. The chapter also outlines the process of data collection and the nature of the data gathered, together with an overview of the 24 young people who took part in the research and how we met them. Some examples of ethnographic data are provided, and we discuss some of the practical and ethical issues encountered in the research.

Although most participants were NEET at the beginning of our research, the great majority engaged in various forms of education, training and employment in the ensuing months. Chapter 5 provides the background to this engagement, first examining the structure of the UK labour market and its relationship to the employment of young people, and then taking up the issue of education and training, particularly in relation to those for whom academic learning has been unproductive. This is not to say that we concur with discourses of the 'non-academic' and of differentiated educational systems; rather, we note that there have been successive failures within education to tackle the problem of parity of esteem which has been so divisive, especially in the English system. Within our discussion, we review two forms of provision of particular relevance to the participants in our research: apprenticeships and the various pre-vocational or 'employability' programmes aimed specifically at vulnerable young people. We also highlight some of the labour market experiences of those participants who became employed during the research.

The next three chapters present individual case studies of young people in our research who raise issues of particular interest in relation to the foregoing discussions. We begin with Danny, a young man who perhaps came closest to popular stereotypes of NEET young people. A former young offender, partly estranged from his mother and stepfather, and still engaged in criminal activity such as dealing in soft drugs, Danny resisted engagement in low-level vocational programmes and had strong views on what he saw as their poor quality. However, he saw the value of some forms of education and attempted to use training programmes to develop his literacy and numeracy skills, which he saw as his only hope for progression. By contrast, Hailey was academically successful but dropped out of education after becoming pregnant at the age of 16. Although receiving little support from the baby's father, Hailey aimed to return to education; nevertheless, there were difficulties to overcome and at times her future appeared precarious. Without her mother's intervention, and state support with childcare costs, it is likely that Hailey would have remained NEET for considerably longer than she did. The third case study is of Sean, a young man who dropped out of a catering apprenticeship after experiencing what appeared to be exploitative working conditions. Like many other participants, Sean's experiences were made more complex by family poverty, and at times he also appeared at risk of sustained exclusion. Partly by chance, Sean obtained permanent employment with a restaurant chain, which provided security, reasonable working conditions and opportunities for progression. Sean thrived in this environment, and was still working there when our fieldwork ended.

Although selected for their relationship with education, training and employment, these three case studies also highlight the important influence of other factors, such as family poverty, local environments and early school experiences. Chapter 9 explores the background to these issues, focusing in particular on family backgrounds, neighbourhoods and schooling. Many participants had been in care or had difficult relationships with their families; a high proportion had experienced school exclusion, with almost inevitable impacts on their educational performance. These experiences, alongside the ways in which they are modified by gender and ethnicity, are discussed in relation to the research literature in these areas. The chapter also outlines young people's relationships with the welfare system and their experiences as benefit claimants.

Three further case studies illuminate the ways in which experiences of family, community and welfare interact with labour market participation. For Isla, chaotic experiences of the care system, followed by motherhood and ultimately losing custody of her child formed the backdrop to her struggles to obtain a hairdressing apprenticeship. Saheera, who was at school when the research began, married at 16 and remained NEET throughout our fieldwork. Her resistance to schooling and further education, as well as her identity as a maturing young person in her own right – and as well as a wife, mother and daughter – were shaped by the interactions of class, gender, ethnicity and family. Finally, Cayden – a young man with learning difficulties who simply wanted a job and a family life – illustrates the important but limited role that can be played by voluntary organizations, not only in supporting vulnerable young people but in providing them with work.

This book is about young people whose lives have been profoundly affected by social and economic change: directly, in terms of the contraction and limitation of employment opportunities in a few short years of recession and austerity; and also indirectly, as the outcome of longer-terms shifts associated with de-industrialization and other neo-liberal responses to the threats of globalization. Unemployment, family breakdown and disaffection from schooling do not have merely individual causes. They also stem from broader structural and political factors which undermine social cohesion. Ultimately, the book is also about class; whilst being NEET affects young people from all backgrounds, it has its most serious impact on young people from poor families with the least accumulation of dominant forms of cultural and social capital. Furthermore, the ideological impact of NEET is part of a totalizing discourse which seeks to attribute social and economic ills to an excessive reliance on institutions which provide collective insurance against individual social and economic risk: the welfare state, trade unions and labour market regulation. Whilst this discourse seeks to bolster its arguments by means of moral evaluations which portray the working class as wasteful, disorderly and afflicted by pathology and degeneracy (Skeggs 2004, p.4), the research presented in this book will, we hope, provide a balanced picture in which structural change, ideological forces and individual responsibility can be seen in their proper perspective.

# 2
# Poverty, Social Exclusion and Marginalization

## Absolute and relative poverty

In later chapters, we describe some of the young people in our research as living in poverty, or as being affected by poverty in various ways that reduce their ability to participate in work or education. To people accustomed to thinking about poverty as a lack of material resources, this might seem an exaggerated way of expressing the circumstances of individuals who are neither starving nor without access to material goods that would have been luxuries less than a century ago. For many people, the traditional conception – usually referred to as *absolute poverty* – conjures up distressing images of beggars in the streets of Victorian England or drought, disaster and starvation in the developing world. From a similar perspective, early research into poverty, such as the work of the philanthropist Seebohm Rowntree at the end of the nineteenth century, also focused on the objective conditions in which people lived. Rowntree and his colleagues carried out door-to-door surveys examining the living conditions of thousands of working-class people and calculated the income required to secure the food, fuel and clothing necessary to maintain health (Coates 1966, pp.28–33). People who lacked the necessities of life according to these standards were regarded as being in poverty.

Although the recent proliferation of charity shops, food banks and pay-day loan companies would seem to suggest otherwise, the absolute conception of poverty often leads to assertions that it has been eradicated from contemporary Britain. However, focusing on basic needs alone is inadequate to understanding the material and psychological consequences of deprivation in advanced societies. Although Rowntree's study drew attention to the number of people living in such conditions, conceptualizing poverty in absolute terms can be misleading. Being poor is about more than basic nutrition, clothing and shelter: humans are social as well as physical beings, and being forced to shop around for cheap goods, having insufficient resources to sustain relationships and being unable to participate in a range of social activities undermine human dignity and self-esteem (Nolan and Whelan 1996). Alternative conceptions of poverty have therefore often emphasized its relative nature. Peter Townsend's (1979) seminal study *Poverty in the United Kingdom* shows how relative poverty is a multidimensional concept, which embraces both material and social factors (Lister 2004, p.21).

> Individuals, families and groups can be said to be in poverty when they lack the resources to obtain the types of diet, participate in the activities and have the living conditions and amenities which are customary, or are at least widely encouraged or approved, in the societies to which they belong. Their resources are so seriously below those commanded by the average individual or family that they are, in effect, excluded from ordinary living patterns and activities.
>
> (Townsend 1979, p.31)

Although relative definitions of poverty remain contentious, official statistics in the UK and European Union (EU) have adopted a relative measure. Someone is described as being at risk of poverty if their disposable income (adjusting for household size and redistributive transfers such as income support and child benefits) is less than 60 per cent of the national median figure (ONS 2013d). According to this measure, 16.2 per cent of people in the UK were at risk of poverty in 2011, a *fall* of more than two percentage points since 2008. Although this may seem surprising, it highlights a deficiency in using income differentials to define poverty, as the reduction in poverty rates was largely due to a lower poverty threshold because of reduced incomes overall since the onset of recession. For this reason, official measures also draw on assessments of material deprivation, including a lack of consumer goods such as a washing machine or TV. However, the recognition that poverty is a complex cultural phenomenon has a longer history. Even the classical liberals of the eighteenth and nineteenth centuries accepted this dimension of poverty:

> By necessaries, I understand not only the commodities which are indispensably necessary for the support of life but whatever the custom of the country renders it indecent for creditable people, even of

the lowest order, to be without. A linen shirt, for example, is strictly speaking not a necessity of life... But in the present time... a creditable day labourer would be ashamed to appear in public without a linen shirt.

(Smith 1776, p.691)

Rising living standards mean that items once regarded as luxuries – telephones, central heating and refrigerators, for example – have become the norm in Britain, and those unable to afford such things may well be regarded as poor. Echoing Adam Smith's analysis, Townsend points out that certain customs, material goods and social pleasures represent amenities to which all or most people in a society are entitled. Those who have few of these amenities can be thought of as deprived (Townsend 1979, p.399).

In its relative conception, poverty is therefore both dynamic and contingent; it is only possible to tell if someone is poor when their position is examined in relation to others living in the same society at the same time (Lister 2004, p.22). In Western liberal societies such as the UK, which is both intensely consumerist and highly unequal, people are often defined by possessions, and there is substantial evidence to suggest that poverty is felt socially and psychologically as well as physically. Consumer fetishism can make children and young people vulnerable to bullying, humiliation and ostracism if they do not wear the 'right' label or buy fashionable items (Farrell and O'Connor 2003). It is therefore necessary to go beyond the debate between absolute and relative poverty, understanding that being poor is also experienced in various relational and symbolic ways (Lister 2004, p.36). For many people, poverty denotes inferiority, and this is perhaps one reason why even people living in deprived circumstances are often reluctant to describe themselves as poor (Shildrick et al. 2012a). Whilst 'othering' people in such circumstances has a long history (Lister 2004, p.104), contemporary media images of poor people are particularly lurid. Although open sexism and racism are nowadays unacceptable, it seems to have become legitimate to publicly denigrate poor people (Jones 2012). However, such images of the poor are about more than providing the staple grotesques of cheap TV; the way that poverty is represented in politics or the media influences the way it is understood in society more broadly. For Skeggs (2005, p.968), these representations are part of a complex process in which class, poverty and behaviour are discursively intertwined, valuing and devaluing people in relation to their worth in neo-liberal economies. The threat to middle-class authority and security represented by the rising costs of unemployment and welfare is countered by pathologizing the casualties of flexible labour markets.

In advanced economies, poverty is often thought of as deriving largely from unemployment; however, in-work poverty has received increasing attention in recent years. Although there are difficulties in defining exactly who counts in this respect – part-time work, second earners and redistributive transfers can affect whether a household with working adults is in poverty, irrespective of the gross pay of individuals – it has been estimated that 6.8 per cent of people in work in the UK in 2010 were living in households falling below the poverty threshold (Marx and Nolan 2012, p.13). Taking into account all family members, the number of people in low-income working households grew from around 5 million in 2000/2001 to 6.1 million (4 million working-age adults, 2.1 million children) in 2010 (Aldridge et al. 2012, p.25). The prevalence of insecure, poor-quality work in many parts of the UK means that many poor people are trapped in a cycle of recurrent unemployment and low-paid employment, in which work rarely shifts them out of poverty.

## From poverty to social exclusion

Seebohm Rowntree argued that poverty could be caused both by 'primary factors' such as sickness, old age and irregular work, and 'secondary factors' such as drinking, gambling and other vices – echoing notions of the deserving and undeserving poor. Yet, despite this, Rowntree showed a degree of sympathy towards spending on 'non-essential' items. Defending the perceived extravagances of the poor, he argued that:

> They cannot live on a 'fodder basis'. They crave for relaxation and recreation just as the rest of us do. But…they can only get these things by going short of something which is essential to physical fitness, and so they go short.
>
> (Rowntree 1937, pp.126–127)

Since the 1990s, the debate between absolute and relative poverty has to some extent been superseded by the concept of social exclusion. Whilst British policymakers traditionally used terms such as 'the poor' to describe the disadvantaged and deprived, the roots of social exclusion as a policy discourse lie in the Christian democratic politics of continental Europe, and particularly the French emphasis on social integration (Byrne 2005, pp.52–53). In some ways, social exclusion is an attempt to refine and extend the concept of relative poverty, developing multidimensional indicators of the degree to which someone is able to participate fully in society. Whilst definitions of social exclusion are abundant, Atkinson (1998) identifies three common features: relativity, agency and dynamism. The first of these relates to our discussion of relative poverty, but includes social and political interaction as well as material goods; the second draws attention to the fact that other people or institutions – and not just the excluded themselves – may be responsible for exclusion; and the third relates to the temporal experience of exclusion, including expectations for the future as well as past or present experiences. However, in the hands of policymakers, these features received very different interpretations and emphases, and in practice the concept of social exclusion proved to be highly malleable.

Social exclusion is, of course, particularly associated in the UK with New Labour. According to Ruth Levitas, 'social exclusion and inclusion was central to the creation of the "centre-left" consensus... But if inclusion was New Labour's guiding value... what this meant was far less clear' (Levitas 2005, p.2). In some ways, the very multidimensionality of social exclusion can obscure its meaning, and the concept slips easily back towards notions of the deserving and the undeserving. Under New Labour, it was initially defined as 'a shorthand term for what can happen when people or areas suffer from a combination of linked problems such as unemployment, poor skills, low incomes, poor housing, high crime environments, bad health and family breakdown' (SEU 1997, p.1), but the analysis by Burchardt et al. (1999, pp.231–232) in terms of inclusion or exclusion across five dimensions of participation is particularly helpful. These dimensions are: consumption; accumulating savings or property; engaging in paid work, education or training, or looking after a family; political activity; and engaging in social interaction with family, friends and community. The first of these dimensions is closely related to relative poverty. In the second, the inclusion of caring responsibilities highlights a tension between different ways of conceptualizing the position of young parents which we will return to in some of our case studies. The broader definition of social exclusion compared with poverty brings more people within its scope: using a combined indicator bringing together low income, severe material deprivation and low work intensity, official estimates indicate that 14 million people in the UK in 2011 were at risk of poverty or social exclusion, compared with

10 million according to the narrower definition of poverty alone (ONS 2013a).

Social exclusion has been criticized for suggesting, at least implicitly, that divisions within society occur mainly along a line separating a minority of severely deprived people from an included majority. It therefore disguises the enormous inequalities in wealth and power which can found within mainstream society (Levitas 2005, p.7). Furthermore, although social exclusion can refer to structural inequalities, different emphases have been placed upon the term, and it has often been used as part of a discourse to describe a condition people are in, mainly through individual shortcomings rather than a result of broader social and economic processes. Whilst social exclusion is usually framed in serious analyses as multidimensional and dynamic in nature, it also lends itself to simplistic approaches which see finding a job, a home or a place on a training programme as solving exclusion. Levitas (2005) identifies three discourses of social exclusion: a traditional redistributive discourse, another based upon a discourse of social integration and a more disciplinary discourse which links social exclusion with moral turpitude and benefit dependency. These discourses can, in turn, be linked to particular political regimes. Redistribution, progressive taxation and the provision of comprehensive welfare benefits was, for example, associated with the politics of the post-war consensus and especially the values of the Labour Party during that period, whilst a moral underclass discourse characterized at least part of New Labour policy as well as the Coalition Government's approach. The increasing tendency to describe NEET young people as 'disengaged' derives from a particular combination of liberal individualism and disciplinary moralism which is popular amongst key figures within the Coalition's Conservative leadership (Fergusson 2013).

Like the Coalition, the New Labour governments of Tony Blair and Gordon Brown also embraced many of the central tenets of neoliberalism. However, Levitas (2005) argues that their approach to social exclusion was essentially a combination of social integrationist and moral underclass discourses which placed greatest emphasis on supply-side factors whilst retaining redistributive measures, particularly those which encouraged participation. Although the concept of social exclusion was in circulation before Tony Blair came to power in 1997, it soon became associated with Third Way politics and policy initiatives which attempt to ameliorate some of the inequalities deriving from free market capitalism (Simmons and Thompson 2011, p.33). This was evident in the influential report on NEET young people *Bridging the Gap* (SEU 1999), which presented increased participation in education, training and paid work as central to social inclusion. However, being in work does not necessarily mean that an individual has moved out of poverty. Indeed, low pay, job insecurity and negative workplace experiences can reinforce exclusion rather than alleviate it. The adverse social, economic, psychological and physical effects of such work upon the individual may produce a self-reinforcing cycle, in which people are rendered progressively less able to escape from these kinds of 'poor work' (Shildrick et al. 2012a). We will also see in later chapters that engagement in certain forms of education and training does not necessarily lead to social inclusion.

## Cycles of deprivation, cultures of worklessness?

Explanations for poverty or social exclusion can be placed into two broad camps. One sees them as structural phenomena caused largely by social, economic and political processes, whilst the other emphasizes individual and cultural shortcomings – or, in other words, it sees the poor as fundamentally responsible for their own condition. These two positions are underpinned by competing political and philosophical perspectives and, perhaps unsurprisingly, different approaches to dealing with poverty derive from them. Whilst the former emphasizes the redistribution of wealth through progressive taxation, welfare benefits and other forms of state intervention which attempt to improve the condition of the poor, the latter views the benefit system as one of the chief causes of poverty. Welfare, it is argued, only encourages reliance upon the state.

During the mid-twentieth century, structural explanations for poverty were in the ascendency across much of the Western world and underpinned the establishment of the welfare state in the UK. For many on the political left or centre-left it is tempting to normalize the spirit of post-war Britain, but it is probably more accurate to see structural explanations for poverty and the establishment of the welfare state as diverging from an altogether different norm (O'Connor 2001, p.8). Contemporary Anglo-American understandings based on individual-deficit models of poverty are often associated with the rise of the New Right from the 1980s onwards, but also underpinned the New Poor Law of 1834, the workhouse system of Victorian England and the eugenics movement of the early twentieth century. Although, over time, such views became unfashionable, they were re-popularized with the rise of neo-liberalism in the late twentieth century. Contemporary proponents of individualized explanations of poverty often use the ideas of the right-wing American sociologist, Charles Murray (1990; 1994), and his controversial views about welfare, single parenthood and the underclass, as an intellectual touchstone.

Today's popular notions about the underclass – the idea that a certain section of society is characterized by long-term unemployment and a culture of dependency – are essentially rooted in such beliefs. Many politicians and media commentators are fond of claiming that the welfare system is overly generous and often argue that excessive benefits provide the unemployed with lifestyles better than those of many people in work (Jones 2012).

> There is no point assuming – for example – that everyone understands the intrinsic benefits of work, the feelings of self-worth, or the opportunity to build self-esteem. For someone from a family or peer group where no one has ever held work, the pressure to conform is enormous, underscored by the notion that taking a job is a mug's game. Thus, across generations and throughout communities, worklessness has become ingrained into everyday life.
>
> (Duncan Smith 2012)

Perhaps surprisingly, ideas about welfare dependency are also widespread amongst those most affected by them: although benefit claimants normally deny being lazy or feckless themselves, they are often willing to apply such labels to others in the same situation (MacDonald and Marsh 2005). Shildrick et al. (2012a, pp.221–223) argue that such beliefs are based largely upon myth and hearsay, and most poor people are neither permanently unemployed nor lacking a work ethic. In fact, the nature of the UK labour market today means that many working-class people 'churn' repeatedly between a series of insecure and poorly paid jobs, unemployment and various state-sponsored training and retraining programmes (Shildrick et al. 2012a). Nevertheless, most poor people prefer employment to the boredom, isolation and degradation of unemployment. It is also usual for unemployed people to want their children to have a job and to help them find work (Shildrick et al. 2012b). Even Oscar Lewis, the American anthropologist who first promoted the idea of distinct cultures of poverty, acknowledged that such lifestyles were more a response and adaptation to the conditions of poverty than a set of innate characteristics. Moreover, it is often forgotten that Lewis also wrote about the fortitude and resilience shown by poor families living in highly adverse conditions (Lewis 1966; Lister 2004, p.106).

The idea that unemployment can be explained by flawed cultural values is nevertheless a powerful one. Explanations for young people's behaviour based on cultures of worklessness and welfare dependency were strongly embedded within the discourse of practitioners we encountered in our research. Many of these practitioners described their role in terms of challenging a so-called cycle of deprivation, in which the behaviours and circumstances of poor families are reproduced from one generation to another:

> Some people are better off on benefits...And it's also the culture because with some of these incapacity benefit customers you've got five generations and we see trends where a young person's dad has done alright on incapacity benefit and so that's what they do – they'll say they've got a bad back. So it's to try and break that cycle.
>
> (Jobcentre adviser, 04/02/2011)

> Say I was third generation unemployed: I'd seen my parents and my grandparents get on fine thank you very much without having to get up in the morning and they've got a big television in the corner and all this sort of thing. But, within the programme itself, you've started them off on the beginning of that journey and it's how then to keep that motivation up...
>
> (Partnership manager for 14–19 provision, 30/09/2010)

Whilst the claim that some families have a history of unemployment going back three or even five generations is perhaps an extreme example of such views, other researchers have found it to be widely accepted amongst those who work with disadvantaged people (see, for example, Shildrick et al. 2012b, p.8). However, practitioners do not necessarily accept these ideas without reservation; in our research, accounts such as those quoted above were often qualified with the words 'some young people', and the families cited as having ingrained benefit cultures were contrasted with those seen as typifying a more traditional work ethic.

> So it's coming from a very low income family where it is just benefits and if their parents say that if they don't start contributing they will kick them out and then...they will probably have an entitlement to severe hardship. Now for some young people that's a destination and

so we then have to try and change that culture... [But] the majority
want to do something. They seriously want to do something...

(Connexions Personal Adviser 13/10/2010)

There is a substantial body of evidence that deprivation is transmitted between generations, both directly in terms of a lack of material
resources to support family members and indirectly through the poorer
educational outcomes associated with deprivation and the impact
on family life of socio-demographic risks. The statistical association
between unemployment in one generation and the next is also well
established (O'Neill and Sweetman 1998; Macmillan 2010; Barnes et al.
2012). However, there is little evidence for the existence of a *causal* relationship which might support the notion of 'cycles' of deprivation or
cultures of worklessness.

Whilst cycles of deprivation and cultures of worklessness are closely
related theses, one way of distinguishing between them is the emphasis
of the former on inadequate parenting and anti-social behaviour, irrespective of whether parents are employed, whilst the latter focuses more
on long-term and intergenerational unemployment. The cycles of deprivation theory has surfaced most recently in the discourse of 'troubled
families':

> What came from these families' stories were that they had
> entrenched, long-term cycles of suffering problems and causing prob-
> lems. Their problems were cumulative and had gathered together
> over a long period of time – perhaps over generations... In many
> cases their problems began with their own parents and their parents'
> parents, in cycles of childhood abuse, violence and care which are
> then replayed in their own lives.
>
> (Casey 2012, p.1)

In explanations based on cultures of worklessness, the central idea
is that the processes responsible for persistent deprivation are essentially processes of *learning*. Young people in certain families are said to
acquire values and knowledge from parents and older siblings which are
opposed to the normal values of society. Within these families, knowledge of the benefits system and how to exploit it are developed at an
early age, maintained throughout life and transmitted to the next generation. It has to be said at this point that we found little evidence
amongst the young people who took part in our research to suggest that
their marginality was derived from cultures of worklessness. However,

we did find a few instances which illustrate the kind of behaviours that might be expected if such cultures underpin the experiences of vulnerable young people. One such example is provided by Jed, who insisted that he needed little advice on benefits or the limitations of what he could afford on them. In an interview in November 2011, he talks about his father's knowledge of the benefit system:

> I don't want to move into a council flat but that's where they put you. I just don't want to be on a council estate. But there are things out there which will pay for private rented and my dad's knows about this and he's on it at the moment... He lives on benefits and stuff and he gets about three hundred pounds a week.

Jed returned to this theme three months later, telling a benefits adviser that his father 'lives off benefits' and he would 'learn everything I need to from him'. He also talked about his father's frequent changes of address to avoid bills and debt. However, it is debatable whether this sort of discourse represents cultural acquisition, or is simply a pragmatic response to the circumstances Jed and his father find themselves in. A later interview, in July 2012, illustrates this:

> [My personal adviser] was helpful at first because I didn't know how to apply for benefits or owt like that; I didn't know you had to go to the Job Centre to apply for housing benefit or income support. I didn't know that, but it wouldn't bother me anyway because I would have just phoned me dad or me sister because they've already been through it all.

An interview with Isla and her older sister Sally was particularly revealing. As we will see in Chapter 10, Isla's father (aged 57) had not worked for many years; although he used to be a fork-lift truck driver, Isla could not remember him working and he had suffered from anxiety and depression for a considerable time. Her mother worked in a mill before the girls were born. About to begin a Level 1 hairdressing course, Isla was discouraged by her father; however, the sisters showed considerable resistance to his advice:

> Isla: My mum's very happy but my dad, for some reason, says that there are no jobs and I won't get any work and... I'd be better off staying on the dole. Most parents want their children to get a job but I don't know with him. Mum doesn't really say much, does she?

Sally: It's better to be working. Before, I felt like I was more independent because I were going out working and I were paying rent and
council tax and then when I got told that the café were going to be
shutting down I were gutted.

In our view, and this will become more evident as we develop the presentation of our data, a balanced reading of such evidence is that the
relationship between worklessness within families and the trajectories
of young family members is not necessarily causal and interacts with a
number of other factors. Cultural explanations of deprivation underestimate the extent to which disadvantage is not merely passed between
generations but is produced afresh by the conditions in which each
generation must live. We would not deny that the behaviour of some
participants was at times deeply problematic, often rooted in difficult
family circumstances during childhood and in some cases visibly recurring with their own children as the research progressed. However, as
their stories will show, their attitudes and dispositions were as much a
product of structural and institutional factors as they were the result of
inherited or inculcated behaviours.

Claims about families with a history of worklessness dating back several generations have little empirical support. Whilst the number of
households in which no working age adults have ever worked increased
from 178,000 in 1996 to 362,000 in 2011, this number has since
declined and in percentage terms has never been particularly large.
In 2013, these households numbered 297,000 – representing 1.5 per
cent of all households, and reducing to 224,000 when student households are excluded (ONS 2013b). In fact, the overwhelming majority
of workless households have some experience of employment, and as
can be seen in Figure 2.1, which shows trends in both 'workless' and
'never-worked' households, the prevalence of worklessness is associated
largely with economic conditions. Households containing two generations of the same family who have never worked are even less common:
Gaffney (2010) estimates that such families constitute approximately
0.5 per cent of all households. As McInnes (2012) points out, there is
a crucial distinction between families experiencing multigenerational
workless – in which more than one generation are *currently* without
work – and families where no-one has ever worked. In our research,
the former was not unknown; but we have yet to meet a young person from a family which had *never* worked. More generally, over the
last 20 or so years the number of children living in workless households has declined substantially, from 2.4 million in 1996 to 1.6 million

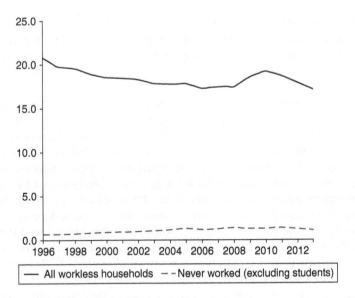

*Figure 2.1*    Workless households in the UK with at least one member of working age, 1996–2013 (% of all households)
*Source*: (ONS 2013b).

in 2013 (ONS 2013b). Even amongst the NEET population, parental worklessness – whilst undeniably an important risk factor (see Barnes et al. 2012, p.34) – is not the norm. For example, Barham et al. (2009) found that just 26 per cent of NEET young people aged 16–17, the majority of whom were living with their parents, lived in a household where no-one was working. Our own research found that around half of participants had no parent working; whilst the circumstances of participants often made it difficult to ascertain the exact work history of their families, very few of these parents, if any, had *never* worked.

In our research, several participants were concerned about the stigmatization brought about by stereotypes they encountered in the media or in their everyday lives; they framed their discussion around specific terms of opprobrium, such as 'benefits scrounger' or 'teenage mum'.

> I'd work in McDonalds or something like that. It's a job. I'd do anything. No cleaning; I don't do cleaning... All I ever get told is that I'm lazy and... sit on my arse all the time... It's not that I'm lazy because I'm not lazy. I do everything I can but if... I could get a job

I'd do it but there are no jobs around here. A lot of people don't understand that. Those people that are out earning think that people are on benefits for no reason.

(Vernon, interview 19/05/2011)

I wouldn't say I was a teenage mum because the other teenage mums either leave their kids and go off every night doing drugs…Because that's what people do identify teenage mums as. They think they're irresponsible. But I have responsibility; I look after her twenty-four seven and if I weren't responsible I wouldn't be here; I'd be out dossing it up or whatever…I don't think it's fair at all. But when you're on a bus you still get stared at because you're young with a baby.

(Hailey, interview 18/11/2011)

Drawing on cultural understandings of social class, Skeggs (2005) argues that binary oppositions based on notions such as respectability and worth, which served to evaluate the working class in industrial times, have been reconstructed to reflect the changing valuations of prole-tarian labour power in post-industrial societies. The operation of class as a 'process of evaluation, moral attribution and authorization in the production of subjectivity' (p.976) constructs some behaviours – even those formerly regarded as vices – as marketable and consistent with an entrepreneurial self. Others, such as teenage motherhood or refus-ing to engage in low-quality work, do not generate worth. Discourses of welfare dependency provide the moral framework for such evaluations, requiring the continual reassertion of subjectivity by those affected.

## Exclusion or marginalization? Being young and poor in post-industrial Britain

Although nearly half of the young people who took part in our study had parents in work, these parents were largely engaged in ordinary working-class employment, including manual work or routine white-collar employment in factories, shops and offices. The parents of other participants, who were currently not in work, had usually held similar jobs in the past. Most participants – whether from families in work or not – had experienced deprivation as children, experiences reproduced in their own emerging adulthood. One example is Jasmine, a young woman who was 18 and living alone when we first met her in Decem-ber 2010. Jasmine had an intermittent series of boyfriends, a turbulent relationship with her mother and a number of volatile friendships; she was also a frequent cannabis user and prone to bouts of heavy drinking and other nihilistic behaviour. Jasmine believed she had bi-polar disorder and, generally, her personal life was full of drama. In January 2013, she became pregnant. In many ways, Jasmine's chaotic life seems to reflect underclass discourses – but it is worth considering her case more closely before passing judgement.

## Work, deprivation and exclusion

One of the benefits of ethnography is that it enables researchers to see beyond the immediate and to understand change over time, and whilst Jasmine was NEET during most of our fieldwork, at certain times she engaged in various kinds of formal and informal employment. Although Jasmine's periods of employment tended to be short-lived, this was partly due to her frequently changing goals and ambitions:

> Since January 2010 Jasmine has wanted to work in childcare, policing, youth work and catering. Morag [housing charity worker] tells me that she wanted to do dance at Middlebridge College but they would not accept her as she had already reached that level in performing arts. Jasmine is now interested in catering....
>
> (Field notes 08/10/10–24/06/11)

The nature of Jasmine's labour market experiences are also worth examining, as they may well have contributed to her shifting priorities and her intermittent pattern of engagement. Towards the end of 2011, Jasmine began work with H-Care, a company providing care to the elderly in their own homes.

> Jasmine left H-Care in January 2012 after questioning a pay packet – she felt she was underpaid and kept getting ill. She describes 'throwing up' in a client's house; the client phoned H-Care and asked for someone take Jasmine home. He was told that if Jasmine didn't do his care nobody would. She describes them as 'dodgy'. Jasmine shows me her final pay slip: her pay was docked by £60 for training. There is also a pen mark at the top of her pay slip which states that £5 was deducted for loss of a staff handbook. Jasmine visited eight or nine elderly people in their homes each working day. She was not paid for travelling time between clients' homes.
>
> (Field notes 29/02/12)

One of Jasmine's friends, Becky, was also employed by H-Care for a short time before leaving to take a job in a residential care home.

> Becky says she has learnt a lot of things in her new job, like how to handle people properly – and that she was taught this wrongly at H-Care. She says you shouldn't stand on Zimmer frames; you shouldn't drag or pull but should always use a hoist or belt if the old people cannot get up. Becky says it is dangerous for their back and for the person they are lifting. She says a lot of H-Care's activities were 'illegal' and that they would be shut down if it was brought to officials' attention. Becky said she left H-Care as she was underpaid and was being put with inexperienced girls when two people were needed for lifting.
>
> (Field notes 1/12/11)

Even for those in work, the great majority of participants remained perilously close to – or below – the levels of income and wider social engagement that might be regarded as dividing experiences of inclusion and exclusion. They all experienced various forms of deprivation during the research and, in some cases, their standard of living bordered on a state of absolute poverty. Many struggled to pay the rent, heating bills and other basic necessities. Affording sufficient food was a problem for some:

> ... what the fuck do you expect me to do? I'm spiralling downwards; I can't live; I can't even stay in my own flat because it is unliveable; no gas, no electric; no food. Jack shit!.
>
> (Interview with Jasmine 18/12/2012)

There was also widespread evidence of less extreme deprivation and, in a number of cases, these presented important barriers to getting work, accessing support services or finding decent accommodation. Whilst some would regard such items as a luxury, many participants did not have their own computer and found a lack of ready internet access a hindrance in looking for work. Jasmine experienced difficulties in getting somewhere decent to live:

> I had to bid to get this place but I got my friend to bid for me because I didn't have the internet and I was going from place to place. I couldn't live in Berrywell Flats – they're called the crack head flats, for God's sake – so I was living ... all over the place.
>
> (Interview 20/7/2012)

The increasing use of online systems to access benefit payments may also disadvantage young people without a computer. Of course, a lack of access to information technology at home does not necessarily prohibit individuals from applying for jobs, getting benefits, housing or using the internet for social or educational purposes – it may well be possible to use friends' computers or to access the internet in a public library. However, time limits normally apply to the use of computers in libraries and other shared facilities, which may not be accessible at short notice.

Travel constraints, difficulties accessing public services and patterns of consumption and social relations characterized by narrow and sometimes erratic forms of engagement might justify describing participants as being socially excluded, although the form and degree of exclusion differed between individuals and tended to vary over time. Physical and social isolation and a lack of daily structure were recurrent themes. Social exclusion was experienced in culturally specific ways and related to particular personal circumstances. Hailey, a young mother who gave birth shortly after we first met her, found the demands of childcare curtailed her opportunities for education and work, and her social circle became substantially reduced. As we have seen, Hailey felt that her status as a teenage mother meant that many people viewed her negatively, especially in her own neighbourhood – an area with a large Asian Muslim population. She was uncomfortable visiting the local park and children's centre, feeling that she was seen as a 'White trash teenage mum'.

Danny, another young person we will meet later in the book, experienced isolation in different ways. Danny had a history of youth offending and had been asked to leave the family home some time before we first met. He now lived alone in a high-rise local authority flat and, whilst he engaged intermittently and, frankly, quite half-heartedly with various training programmes, he spent most of his time NEET. The environment in which Danny lived lacked any feeling of community and his actions mirrored and reproduced the social behaviour within the flats: Danny seldom talked to anybody else he saw there, he would keep his head down, and avoid looking neighbours in the eye. As we will see later in the book, Danny also dabbled in various illicit activities which eventually led him to be the victim of a violent crime at his flat.

Danny looks out of the window as we chat, on edge and constantly looking who is about. He says he has a good view from there to see

who is about, he points to one of the people's houses he is avoiding ... he says it's right outside the bus stop so he uses other bus stops
or carefully watches the man leave before he does

(Field notes 24/05/2012)

Despite these instances of economic and social deprivation, social exclusion may not be the best lens – or set of lenses – through which to
understand the lives of the participants in our study. In fact, the term
we think most effective in describing their position is *marginality*, and
the remainder of this chapter will explain the ways in which we conceptualize marginalization and how we mobilize it in the rest of the
book. In one sense, it is quite easy to see how the young people featured
in this book could be described as marginalized. Although the circumstances of each participant varied according to their particular situation,
their lives were, in various ways, played out in places and practices on
the margins of society. As Shields (1991, p.3) points out, marginal places
are not necessarily on geographical peripheries; rather, they occupy liminal positions within hierarchically organized cultural systems which
have been shaped by decades of social and political change. Rather than
being permanently excluded from education, work and social activities,
their experience was largely one of circulation between these liminal
positions, comprising different but inter-related forms of marginality.
Each young person spent significant periods of time outside education
and work, and as we shall see, the jobs they were able to get were largely
insecure and poorly paid. In some cases, their employment experiences
were highly exploitative. Education and training were also often disconnected from real opportunities for advancement: as we will show, it
was not uncommon for training programmes which purported to make
young people more employable to provide them with little or no labour
market advantage. More generally, participants' social activities and personal relations were, over time, constrained in various ways by their
position on the fringes of the labour market, and social isolation was a
recurrent problem. How, though, do these experiences differ from social
exclusion?

## Conceptualizing marginality

Most economic models divide the labour market into three separate
categories: employed, unemployed and inactive. However, it has been
suggested that this classification is too broad to provide an adequate
understanding of contemporary labour market participation and, perhaps especially, the experiences of many young people (Geerdsen 2002).

Jones and Riddell (1998) propose a fourth category of labour market relations – the marginalized – who are not excluded but are nevertheless in 'outsider' positions within the economy. This category is diverse, including those in education who, although not actively seeking employment would nevertheless prefer to be in work, and people invisible to official statistics – for example, those working in the informal economy, recently arrived migrants, the homeless and those from other particularly 'hard to reach' groups. Whilst we agree that including marginalized people as a labour-market category is important in exploring the situation of both young and adult workers, our understanding of marginality is broader than this, encompassing certain vulnerable sections of the employed, unemployed and inactive groups. Indeed, as our discussion of in-work poverty has shown, many people holding insecure, low-quality jobs – both young and more mature – could, whilst not excluded from the labour market, be described as marginalized in this sense.

Van Berkel et al. (2002) identify a state of marginality which occupies the borderline between inclusion and exclusion and shares features of both. Marginalization is then 'conceived as a process whereby people voluntarily move or are pushed or pulled away into marginality and further into exclusion' (p.28). Marginalization may also occur in the opposite direction: whilst this may be thought of as a positive process in which people move nearer to an included state, the experience of marginality – whether in the labour market, in education or in social systems more generally – is not necessarily better than the experience of exclusion. Indeed, a constant theme in our research was the question of whether doing something was better than doing nothing. For some young people, being included in marginal ways – for example, in poor work or in what we increasingly saw as poor education – led to negative experiences or perceptions which actually reduced the prospects of moving further away from exclusion (see also Simmons et al. 2014). Fergusson (2004, p.291) explains that discourses of marginalization portray their subjects as shaped and constrained by social and economic structures that maintain and reproduce power relations. Difficult behaviours, or beliefs and attitudes lying outside dominant social norms, are dealt with by relegating people to powerless positions at the margins of the social world. In these positions, opportunities, resources and forms of participation are not withdrawn but are systematically limited, and discourses constructed which redefine such limitations as necessary to the reintegration of the marginalized.

As with social exclusion, the concepts of marginality and marginalization give rise to the question: who is responsible? Just as with exclusion, we can regard marginalization as arising from the failings of individuals, who withdraw voluntarily, or of an over-generous welfare system, which facilitates this withdrawal and also – through benefits such as working tax credits – encourages employers to offer low pay and/or create underemployment through strategies such as zero-hours contracts. Alternatively – and this is the view we favour – marginalization can be seen as a process which is integral to the alienated conditions produced by the relations of modern capitalist production, encompassing both individual behaviour and tendencies towards exploitation and increasing inequality. This type of explanation is analogous to the notion of advanced marginality proposed by Wacquant (1996; 2008), in which processes of marginalization are driven, not by economic decline, but by structural logics connected with neo-liberalism and globalization: the transfer of wealth from poorer to richer members of society; the degradation and fragmentation of wage labour; and an ideologically driven assault on welfare states. Wacquant (1996, p.123) means the qualifier 'advanced' to indicate that particular forms of marginality are not in the past, and being progressively cushioned by welfare states or left behind by the further commodification of social life through free-market expansion; they stand *ahead of us* because they are inherent in dominant economic and social policy.

Wacquant (1996) proposes an ideal-type characterization of advanced marginality containing six distinctive features. The first two concern the increased precariousness of wage labour under flexible employment policies and the fragmentation of work, leading to 'the erosion of the integrative capacity of the wage-labour relation' (p.124), and the disconnection of those in marginal positions from expansionary phases in economic cycles. Wacquant argues that, whilst the economically marginal are hardest-hit by recessions, they do not share in subsequent periods of prosperity, reducing the power of policies based on boosting the labour market to improve conditions at the bottom. Moving from the economic to the socio-spatial, Wacquant identifies both territorial stigmatization – the poor living conditions and reputation of 'bad neighbourhoods' – and the *loss* of a sense of place, as stemming from de-industrialization and global movements of capital. These trends are exacerbated by what Wacquant calls the 'loss of hinterland' – the diminution of social capital associated with high concentrations of unemployment, multigenerational worklessness and the erosion of local public facilities. Finally, Wacquant contrasts processes of advanced marginality from earlier forms because they appear to be taking place in a period of class decomposition rather than formation – the splintering of the working class under the pressure of deproletarianization. As will be seen in later chapters, whilst not all of these features apply to the context of our research, many of them do, and unify to a significant extent the disparate experiences and responses of marginalized young people.

Two further comments on our use of marginality are necessary. Firstly, marginality does not imply a deliberate rejection of what Germani (1980) calls 'the normative scheme', that is, 'the set of values and norms which define... the legitimate, expected, or tolerated areas of participation and the assignment mechanisms of individuals to each category' (p.51). Rather, marginalized people are unable to participate in social systems according to these norms because of a lack of objective resources, both material and cultural, such as education, employment, financial resources or decent housing, and a related lack of subjective resources including attitudes, motivations and cognitive abilities (ibid.). These deficits in subjective resources, we emphasize, are not inherent, but *are part of* processes of marginalization which are ongoing and cumulative. As will be seen later in this book, the young people in our research did not reject conventional social norms – indeed, their aspirations reflected those of many people from all backgrounds, and concerned jobs, family life and security. Marginality, for them, was an undesirable state at odds with their values rather than a deliberate rejection of dominant normative schemes. Secondly, although we will at times highlight situations in which certain forms of marginality appear to be the result of voluntary decisions and actions, we do not regard voluntary exclusion as necessarily different in nature to exclusion which is clearly involuntary. As Pierre Bourdieu points out in relation to cultural reproduction, exclusion 'has most symbolic force when it assumes the guise of self-exclusion' (Bourdieu and Passeron 1990, p.42); voluntary exclusion should therefore be seen simply as a particular aspect of overall processes of marginalization.

# 3
# Young People Not in Education, Employment or Training

## Social change and youth transitions

The last 50 years have seen profound changes in how young people experience early adulthood, reflecting more fundamental alterations in economy and society. For three decades after the end of World War II, the majority of young people left school and entered full-time work at the first opportunity, and youth transitions were perhaps at their most condensed and unitary in post-war Britain (Jones 1995, p.23). Most school-leavers were able to find the types of work they expected and, for the majority, leaving home, marriage and parenthood took place soon thereafter. A small minority of mainly middle-class young people went on to higher education, but lengthy periods of study at college or university were quite rare amongst working-class youth. Day-release at a technical college often formed part of the apprenticeship programmes which – especially in construction, engineering or manufacturing industry – were prized by many school-leavers, especially young working-class men. However, few young people in unskilled or semi-skilled work experienced post-compulsory education and there was often considerable pressure from family and friends to leave education and start earning as soon as possible (Goodwin and O'Connor 2005, p.214).

For young men especially, school-to-work transitions could be both speedy and collective and the mass transfer of boys from school into local industry, often to work alongside their fathers or other family members, was a significant feature of the post-war labour market. Industrial culture was predominantly masculine and certain occupations – for example, coal mining – were almost entirely male, but in many manufacturing industries women were an integral part of the workforce.

Millions of girls and women were employed, not only in secretarial and administrative roles but as manual workers and machine operatives on the production lines of Britain's factories. For both sexes, workplace relations were often associated with certain kinds of working-class camaraderie, and whilst trade unionism offered one form of class-based solidarity, football teams, social clubs and leisure activities were also connected with manufacturing industry. Employment alongside older, more experienced workers also provided a certain moral framework for many young people and helped reinforce shared attitudes, values and opinions. Work offered a degree of stability and continuity that, for most young people, has largely disappeared today and it is tempting to look back at the post-war era with a sense of loss. However, youth transitions in post-war Britain should not be romanticized, and factory life was a bleak and alienating experience for many workers (Beynon 1973). Although young people were often eager to leave school, not all settled easily into working life, and the ready availability of employment masked the way that some young people 'churned' chronically from job to job (Finn 1987).

Nowadays, for most young people, the journey into adulthood is more complex and extended than was the case for previous generations. Few gain full-time work immediately after leaving school, and secure employment has become difficult to obtain, especially for those with limited qualifications. Social structures appear less fixed and predictable and traditional patterns of social reproduction have been disturbed: for many young people, access to the traditional signifiers of adulthood has become disordered or suspended – in some cases, almost indefinitely (Ainley and Allen 2010). These changes have been driven, amongst other factors, by the collapse of much of the UK's industrial base, the demise of the traditional youth labour market, and greatly reduced opportunities for stable working-class employment. Mass de-industrialization has been accompanied by pain and suffering, especially in working-class communities, and the consequences for young people's identities, aspirations and material circumstances have been profound, particularly for young men (McDowell 2000; Nayak 2003; Nixon 2009). We will examine the impact of these changes later in this book, but it is important to understand the causes of de-industrialization as well as its effects.

According to some conceptions, the industrial collapse which took place in the UK from the 1970s onwards was largely unavoidable. New technologies, the disappearance of protected export markets following the end of Empire and growing international competition, especially from nations with significantly lower labour costs, meant that a degree of industrial contraction, certainly in terms of employment, was inevitable. There were, however, other forces at work – and militant trade unions, managerial incompetence and a culture of complacency are frequently cited as other causes of the UK's industrial decline. Undoubtedly, certain companies were poorly run and slow to innovate, and the motor industry is often cited as a prime example of the failure of British manufacturing (Sandbrook 2013).

Whatever the underlying reasons, manufacturing output as a proportion of gross domestic product has fallen substantially since the late 1970s, and the number of people working in manufacturing industry has shrunken dramatically. Today, 83 per cent of all employment in the UK is located in the service sector (ONS 2013c). This is related to the factors outlined above, but political change has also played an important part in the decline of the UK's traditional industries. Although Conservative and Labour governments had different emphases, the period 1945–1970 was largely characterized by consensus politics involving a partnership between government, industry and the trade unions. By the end of the 1960s, however, the UK's economic troubles were becoming increasingly apparent and this consensus began to collapse after the oil crisis of 1973. Margaret Thatcher's Conservatives swept to power following a series of high-profile strikes during the 'Winter of Discontent' of 1978–1979. Alongside curbing trade union power, cutting taxation and reducing welfare provision, Mrs Thatcher was committed to reducing the public sector and making industry stand on its own two feet. Social democracy and consensus politics were replaced with individualism, entrepreneurialism and economic monetarism. Neo-liberal philosophies came to dominate the political and economic landscape of the United Kingdom.

Economic liberalization and escalating interest rates in the early 1980s had serious consequences for British industry, and almost a quarter of all manufacturing jobs were lost during Mrs Thatcher's first term of office. Two million more disappeared between the mid-1980s and the mid-2000s. A further 400,000 manufacturing jobs were lost following the 2008–2009 recession, and employment in manufacturing has struggled to recover from its low point of under 2.6 million in 2011 (ONS 2013c). Profound shifts in the nature of work and the economy have been accompanied by other social changes, including increased expectations and rights for women. Dramatically increased levels of migration have made the UK more culturally diverse than was the case in the post-war era. Whilst compulsory schooling has lengthened and, in some ways, the experience of education has become more homogeneous for the majority of young people, the ideal of the common school has been largely abandoned and replaced with ideas of market forces and diversity (Fielding and Moss 2011). Meanwhile, the cultural and political significance of traditional working-class institutions, including trade unions, workingmen's clubs and the co-operative movement, has declined substantially. These changes, alongside increased levels of home ownership, developments in information technology and growing popular consumerism have led to claims that class-based analyses of young people's lives are now inappropriate (Jeffs and Smith 1998). However, whilst working-class consciousness has diminished, and young people today often interpret the social world in highly individualistic ways, this does not mean that their life chances are free from patterns of inequality relating to gender, ethnicity and especially social class (Furlong and Cartmel 2007).

Some indication of the degree of continuity and change in British life may be obtained by comparing data on social and educational outcomes from two large-scale longitudinal studies, the 1970 British Cohort Study (BCS70) and the Longitudinal Study of Young People in England (LSYPE).[1] Long-term unemployment was considerably more widespread in the later cohort, and the proportion of young people growing up in workless households increased threefold, to 13 per cent. Young people themselves were less likely to be employed in the later cohort, with only 40 per cent in full-time work at age 18 in 2009 compared with 69 per cent in 1988. Parental education had improved significantly: two-fifths of participants in BCS70 lived in families where neither parent had any educational qualifications, compared with only 12 per cent in LSYPE. The proportion of participants who grew up in low social class households showed little change, whilst the proportion living in social housing fell from a third to one-fifth. Living with lone parents increased substantially; however, contrary to moral panics about early pregnancy, the number of young people born to a teenage mother was virtually unchanged, and the proportion of female participants who were mothers at age 18 actually fell slightly (Duckworth and Schoon 2012).

## From youth unemployment to NEET

Whilst significant concerns about youth unemployment have existed for almost 40 years, the NEET category is a policy construct associated with structural and ideological shifts which have occurred in the UK and elsewhere since the 1980s. Although teenagers were traditionally an integral part of the workforce, by the mid-1980s over half of all 16–17-year-olds and a quarter of 18–19-year-olds were unemployed (Finn 1987, p.187), signalling a rapid decline in youth employment which lasted for nearly ten years (see Figure 3.1). This precipitated the introduction of a range of work-related training programmes, overseen by the Manpower Services Commission (MSC), which attempted to both manage and disguise youth unemployment (Finn 1987, p.49). Beginning in 1978, the Youth Opportunities Programme (YOP) was the first of these schemes, which became a familiar part of the youth labour market in the 1980s and 1990s. The New Training Initiative aimed to replace traditional forms of training, such as time-served apprenticeships, with work preparation more adapted to the contemporary labour market, and paved the way for the Youth Training Scheme (YTS) introduced in 1983. YOP and its successors were, however, often criticized for offering poor quality training under 'slave labour' conditions: as Bynner (2012) points out, YTS had little credibility with employers, young people or their families. Widely perceived as an inadequate substitute for 'proper jobs' and

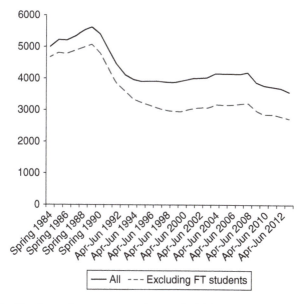

*Figure 3.1* Number of young people aged 16–24 in employment (UK, thousands), 1984–2013; FT, full-time
Source: Authors' analysis of data in ONS (2012, p.2).

paying only half the average youth wage, many participants rejected it at the first opportunity. However, not all young people had negative experiences on these programmes and some gained valuable work experience and personal development from MSC provision.

Whatever the experiences of individual young people may have been, participation in post-compulsory education and training became normalized during the 1980s – although many young people chose to stay on at school or enrol on full-time courses at FE colleges rather than go onto YOP or similar provision. At the same time, the availability of welfare benefits for 16–18-year-olds was progressively reduced. From 1983, benefit sanctions were applied to those who refused a YTS place, and access to other benefits was reduced for young people in education. In 1988, changes to the National Insurance system effectively disqualified all 16–17-year-olds from unemployment benefit, and the Social Security Act ended the entitlement to means-tested benefit payments for most young people under the age of 18. Such changes may have helped to reduce welfare expenditure and disguise the true level of worklessness, but they left policymakers searching for new ways of describing youth unemployment and labour market vulnerability (Furlong 2006). In the early 1990s, 'Status 0', a classification deriving from careers service records, was briefly used to describe 16–18-year-olds outside education, training and employment (Istance et al. 1994). Perhaps understandably, government departments disliked this terminology, which had obvious negative connotations as 'a metaphor for young people who, in policy terms, at that time counted for nothing and were going nowhere' (Williamson 2010). In 1996, a Home Office official proposed the acronym NEET (not in education, employment or training) as a more neutral alternative (ibid.), a definition which at the time encompassed around 175,000 16–18-year-olds in England, representing some 10 per cent of the age cohort and not greatly different from more recent NEET rates for this age group (DfE 2013a; see also Figure 3.2).

Although adopted under a Conservative government as a technical classification, the NEET category as an object of governance (Fergusson 2013) is particularly associated with New Labour. Building on a growing body of research evidence suggesting that early exclusion from employment and training significantly increased the chances of unemployment and ill-health in later life, the reports *Bridging the Gap* (SEU 1999) and *Learning to Succeed* (DfEE 1999) argued for significant interventions to reduce the NEET population, largely through targets for increased participation in full-time education or work-based learning. Initiatives such as

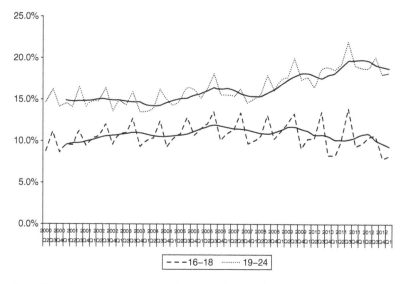

*Figure 3.2* Quarterly NEET rates for ages 16–18 and 19–24 in England, 2000–2013, together with their annual trends
Source: NEET Harmonized Supplementary Tables 16–24 taken from the Labour Force Survey (DfE 2013a).

Connexions, the integrated advice service for young people aged 13–19, and the Education Maintenance Allowance (EMA) both stem from this period.

Alongside other policy initiatives, such as the expansion of higher education and raising the age of compulsory participation in education or training, these measures were underpinned by the view that social problems such as unemployment, poverty and social inequality could be alleviated by transforming them into problems of educational access, achievement and quality (Keep and Mayhew 2010). Thus, skill supply came to be seen as *the* legitimate avenue for government intervention, further marginalizing those who leave education at the earliest opportunity. Employment, as such, was not given a high priority for 16–18-year-olds; indeed, jobs without training were regarded as undesirable outcomes for this age group and young people in such employment were problematized in similar ways to the NEET category (Lawy et al. 2009). Globalization and the demands of a knowledge economy, it was argued, had rendered traditional concepts such as a job for life and career progression through increasing experience outdated. Instead, the ability to continually transform oneself through participation in lifelong learning became a fundamental responsibility of the good citizen; those who rejected this responsibility – whether employed or unemployed – were portrayed as actual or potential burdens on society, afflicting themselves and their families with a lifetime risk of poverty and benefit dependency.

A significant weakness of NEET as a policy category is that – unlike unemployment, which has an internationally agreed definition (ILO 1982) – its usage varies from country to country, making cross-national comparisons difficult. Initially a term specific to the UK, but resonating with more widespread tendencies to individualize social problems, the use of NEET spread to other English-speaking countries, Scandinavia and Japan – although its precise definition varied (Eurofound 2012, p.20). More recently, increased youth unemployment since the onset of recession in 2008 has led to a systematic effort across the European Union to introduce statistical indicators of disengaged youth based on the NEET concept. Although there are wide disparities between member states, the EU average NEET rate in 2011 stood at 13 per cent of 15–24-year-olds, accounting for some 7.5 million young people (Eurofound 2012, p.1). Figure 3.3a shows changes in NEET rates in Europe since 2000; however, EU averages conceal the extent to which circumstances differ between

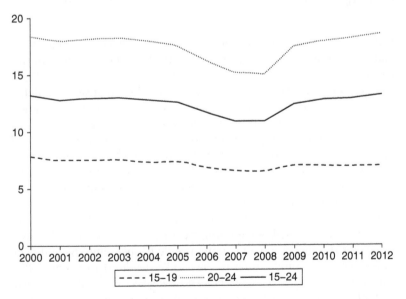

*Figure 3.3a*   NEET rates for ages 15–19, 20–24 and 15–24 in the European Union (EU27), 2000–2012

Source: Eurostat Data Explorer, *Young people not in employment and not in any education and training, by age and sex (NEET rates)*.

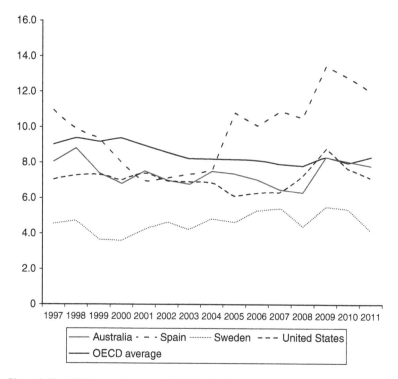

*Figure 3.3b* NEET rates for ages 15–19 in OECD countries, 1997–2011
*Source*: Table C5.4a Trends in the percentage of the youth population in education and not in education, employed or not, by five-year age group (1997–2011) (OECD 2013a).

countries, as can be seen from the very different trends for Spain and Sweden in Figure 3.3b.

As in the UK, the global adoption of the NEET category as a policy instrument has been prompted by the long-term decline of youth labour markets in many countries. In addition to secular trends prompted by globalization, de-industrialization and the impact of neo-liberal policies, or cyclical factors such as economic recessions, we may also enquire into more specific factors influencing unemployment rates amongst young people, which show considerable variation between countries. One obvious possibility is cohort size: if at certain times there are more young people in a particular age group, is it not natural to expect youth unemployment to be higher? However, evidence for cohort-size effects is inconclusive (Korenman and Neumark 2000; Gangl 2002). Bell and Blanchflower (2010) note that, whilst increasing cohort size between 2000 and 2008 may partly explain greater youth unemployment, there were still 700,000 fewer 16–24-year-olds than in 1981, and the size of this cohort began to decline again in 2009. Other possibilities might include the overall structure of the labour market, labour market regulation and the organization of education systems, as well as contextual features such as welfare systems and family structures. A number of authors have developed the concept of a 'transition system' to encompass these institutional and structural factors, which they argue shape youth transitions and can help to explain differences between countries (Raffe 2008). Considering Organisation for Economic Co-operation and Development (OECD) data from the late 1990s, Breen (2005) concludes that market forces interact with institutional factors to shape patterns of youth unemployment. In this respect, labour-market regulation, and the effectiveness of educational qualifications in signalling the suitability of a young person for specific forms of work have a particular impact. Although NEET is often used as a synonym for youth unemployment, the two are not identical. As Figure 3.4 illustrates, the size of the NEET population for a particular age group is the number of young people in that age group who are not in any form of education, employment or training; the NEET rate is obtained by dividing this number by the size of the cohort. The number of unemployed young people follows the International Labour Organization (ILO) definition, and comprises only those who are not in work, *and* are seeking and available

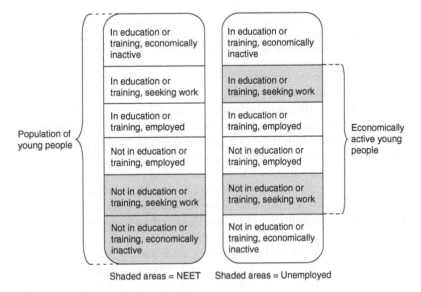

*Figure 3.4*   Definitions of NEET and unemployment

for employment. The NEET population, by definition, excludes those in education, but classified as unemployed because they are looking for work; however, it includes young people outside the ILO definition of unemployment: those not in education who are economically inactive (either not looking for work, or not available for work). Unemployment rates are calculated by dividing the number of unemployed young people by the number who are economically active (employed or unemployed) rather than the size of the whole age group. For this reason, NEET rates are typically lower than youth unemployment rates, even though the NEET population is larger than the population of unemployed young people (see Figure 3.5).

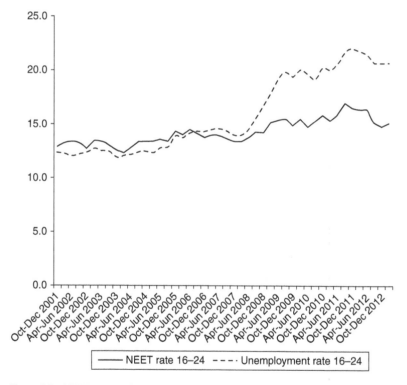

*Figure 3.5* NEET rate and unemployment rate for ages 16–24 in the UK, 2001–2013

*Source*: Young People not in Education, Employment or Training, May 2013, available online at http://www.ons.gov.uk/ons/publications/re-reference-tables.html?edition= tcm%3A77-306844 and A06: Educational status and labour market status for people aged from 16 to 24.

Whilst the need to create a technically accurate and at least ostensibly neutral terminology to capture labour market vulnerability led to the adoption of NEET as an official classification, its ideological basis has been extensively critiqued (Fergusson 2004; Thompson 2011). Traditional understandings of youth unemployment were rooted, at least to some extent, in a sense of collectivism and social responsibility. However, the designation of young people as outside education and work can be used to individualize non-participation and, at least in official discourse, tends to overlook social and economic inequalities and to create a spurious dichotomy between inclusion and exclusion (see Chapter 2). Strathdee (2013) argues that the NEET category is part of the state's response to a legitimation crisis (Habermas 1975), as its ability to guarantee living standards wanes under the impact of globalization and neo-liberal policies.

## Structure of the NEET population

One difficulty with the NEET category is that it comprises individuals from diverse backgrounds and circumstances, defining young people by what they are not, rather than who they are (Yates and Payne 2006; Spielhofer et al. 2009). This problem has been exacerbated by a shift in usage, and nowadays NEET is often used to describe young people up to the age of 24 who are outside education and employment. One consequence of this extended definition is that a greater number of individuals are drawn into the category than was the case hitherto, and the number of 16–24-year-olds classified as NEET has been around one million for a number of years. This presents a dilemma for policymakers. Broadening the NEET category allows the responsibility for unemployment to be shifted, at least tacitly, onto a wider range of individuals. However, this shift has led to headline-grabbing statistics, and consequently youth unemployment has become even more contentious. It also diminishes the conceptual clarity of the term NEET. The inclusion of young people under 25 increases the heterogeneity of the NEET population, bringing within its scope graduates seeking work and new mothers in their early 20s with partners in full-time employment, as well as teenagers with few qualifications and no experience of work.

Disaggregating NEET young people into more specific subcategories according to various objective or subjective conditions or circumstances helps us to understand the diversity of the NEET population, and such analyses have been used to inform a range of targeted interventions and initiatives (Scottish Executive 2006; Spielhofer et al. 2009). The

European Foundation for the Improvement of Living and Working Conditions identifies five main subcategories:

- the conventionally unemployed, the largest subgroup, which can be further subdivided into long-term and short-term unemployed;
- the unavailable, which includes young carers, young people with family responsibilities and young people who are sick or disabled;
- the disengaged: those young people who are not seeking jobs or education and are not constrained from doing so by other obligations or incapacities, and takes in discouraged workers as well as other young people who are pursuing dangerous and asocial lifestyles;
- the opportunity-seekers: young people who are actively seeking work or training, but are holding out for opportunities that they see as befitting their skills and status;
- the voluntary NEETs: those young people who are travelling and those constructively engaged in other activities such as art, music and self-directed learning. (Eurofound 2012, p.24)

These diverse categories illustrate the range of vulnerabilities encountered in the NEET population. Conditions such as unemployment and ill-health, which are largely involuntary and known to be more likely for those from deprived backgrounds, sit alongside activities which require considerable financial and cultural resources. Nevertheless, it can be argued that all NEET young people share certain risks, not least by missing the opportunity to acquire work experience or further qualifications (Eurofound 2012, p.25). Thus, while it is tempting to dismiss the last two categories outlined above as temporary diversions of more privileged young people 'finding themselves', they may potentially lead to longer-term exclusion. Although this type of analysis can be valuable in understanding the structure of the NEET category, Finlay et al. (2010) point out that individuals with certain common experiences or characteristics are not necessarily members of a homogeneous subgroup. Whilst, for example, young people with caring responsibilities share a particular circumstance, they are likely to experience and view their situation in diverse ways and to need different forms of support (Russell et al. 2011a). Moreover, some young people do not necessarily fall neatly into a particular category – it is quite possible, for example, that a young parent may also have a disability or be a youth offender. Being outside education or work may not be the most immediate or important challenge facing a young person. It is also important to remember that most NEET young people are outside education and work for fairly short periods of time – for the majority, non-participation is interspersed with periods of education, training or employment, even if engagement with such activities is short-lived (Furlong 2006).

## NEET rates over time by age and gender

The demographics of young people outside education and employment are the outcome of a complex interplay of economic, social, cultural and individual factors, and trends in NEET rates need to be understood from this perspective. As opportunities for youth employment have declined, particularly amongst 16–18-year-olds, participation in post-compulsory education has become increasingly the norm, not only as an alternative to unemployment but as a way of competing for higher-status jobs. Most young people now continue in education rather than leaving to seek employment. In England, participation rates in education and training for 16-year-olds are nearing saturation – a trend long pre-dating the raising of the compulsory participation age in 2013. As Figure 3.6 shows, engagement in full-time education at ages 16, 17 and 18 have all shown significant increases since 2001, particularly since the onset of recession in 2008. Young people aged 16–18 who do not participate in full-time education are therefore a relatively small proportion of the age group, and those who are neither employed nor undertaking other forms of education and training constitute an even smaller proportion. Nevertheless, as we saw in Figure 1.2, the NEET rate for 16–18-year-olds in England is by no means insignificant, and has fluctuated around 10 per cent for over ten years, with peaks and troughs corresponding to particular points in the educational calendar. This currently represents approximately 200,000 individuals (DfE 2013a).

Beyond the age of 18, educational participation is considerably lower; the higher education segment in Figure 3.6, which shows the participation rate for 17–20-year-olds domiciled in England, indicates that tertiary education is much less saturated than is upper secondary. This point should be borne in mind when interpreting the age-dependence of NEET rates. The stability, and even slight decline, for 16–18-year-olds seen in Figure 3.2 (and for age 15–19 in Figure 3.3) can in part be attributed to the relative ease with which many young people in this age group can remain in or re-enter education in difficult economic circumstances, whilst the rise since 2008 for older age groups can be related – again partly – to more restricted educational opportunities, particularly for those lacking in cultural and material capital. Indeed, Clark (2011) suggests that the state of youth labour markets has a significant impact on enrolments in post-compulsory education; see also Britton

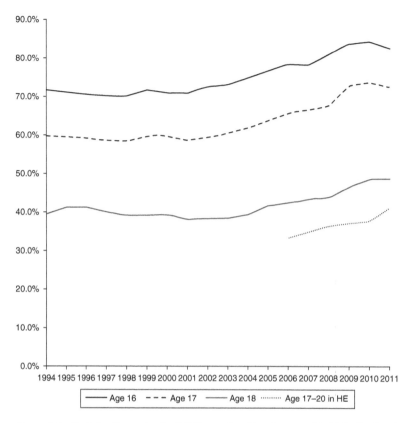

*Figure 3.6*   Participation rates in full-time education for ages 16–18 in England, 1994–2011; HE, higher education
*Source*: DfE (2013a); BIS (2013).

(2012, p.115) for a discussion of the effect on NEET rates of educational decisions made following the recession.

The existence of a structural, rather than cyclical, component of the NEET population is clear from these figures, and may be related to a number of more deeply embedded factors associated with individuals withdrawing from education and the labour market. Figure 3.7 shows this structural component in a striking way, differentiating between 'unemployed NEET' and 'inactive NEET' – young people who, for whatever reason, are outside education but not seeking work. As this graph shows, the inactive NEET rate in the UK has remained remarkably constant for over a decade, in spite of changing economic circumstances and a host of government initiatives to tackle the 'NEET problem'.

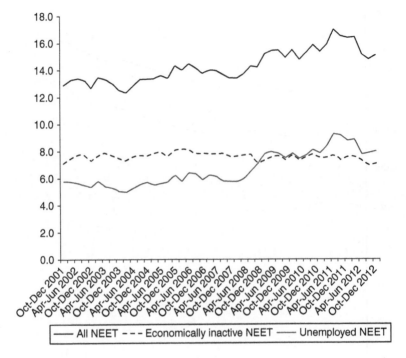

*Figure 3.7*   NEET rate in the UK as a percentage of the whole 16–24 age group by economic activity, 2001–2013

Source: Young People not in Education, Employment or Training, May 2013, available online at http://www.ons.gov.uk/ons/publications/re-reference-tables.html?edition=tcm%3A77-306844.

A similar picture obtains in the European Union (Eurofound 2012, p.33). Unlike in Europe, however, the rise in overall UK NEET rates for 16–24-year-olds in the UK predates the 2008 recession, and in Figure 3.7 a rising trend can be seen from the beginning of 2004 onwards, due largely to an increase in the unemployed NEET group.

The causes of this rise are unclear. Britton (2012) considers a number of possible factors influencing NEET rates in the UK, including migration from Eastern Europe, the extension of the National Minimum Wage to 16–17-year-olds in 2004, and sectoral shifts in the labour market. Britton concludes that, whilst migration may have had some effect on NEET rates, its actual impact is probably very low, particularly if London is excluded. Similarly, the minimum wage appears to have had little effect prior to 2010, although there is weak evidence that it may have had a small adverse impact thereafter (Crawford et al. 2011; Low Pay

Commission 2013). The idea that young people have priced themselves out of jobs is not sustainable, and in the UK the earnings of young people relative to other workers has fallen from above the OECD average in 1996 to below it in 2008 (Bell and Blanchflower 2010). Goujard et al. (2011) propose that changes in social policy, which diverted some attention and resources away from NEET as a specific issue, may also have been an important contributor. It appears likely that the demand for labour in the sectors employing large numbers of young people at greatest risk of unemployment – including retail, hotels and restaurants – is the most significant factor affecting NEET rates.

Figure 3.8 shows NEET rates for young men and women in the UK, and the way in which the gender-dependence of these rates reverses with increasing age. Thus, for 16–17-year-olds, young women are less likely to be NEET than their male peers, whilst the opposite applies for 18–24-year-olds. However, the gender disparity in NEET

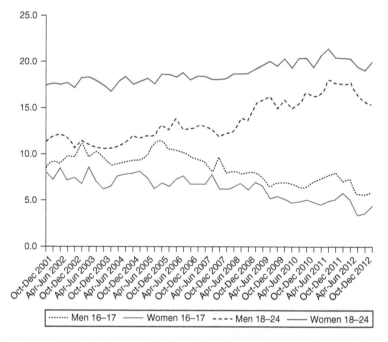

*Figure 3.8*   NEET rates for ages 16–17 and 18–24 by gender in the UK, 2001–2013
*Source: Data on 16–18-year-olds not in education, employment or training (NEET).*
Available online at http://www.education.gov.uk/childrenandyoungpeople/youngpeople/
participation/neet/a0064101/16-to-18-year-olds-not-in-education,-employment-or-training.

rates for 18–24-year-olds has narrowed since 2008 – the greater stability in rates for young women suggesting a larger structural component deriving from childbearing and homemaking, whilst unemployment rates for young men have increased. Across the European Union male youth unemployment, historically lower than for young women, rose above female youth unemployment from 2008 onwards (Eurofound 2012, p.7).

### Educational levels within the NEET population

Figure 3.9 analyses the composition of the NEET population in England by their level of educational achievement at age 16. Although the relatively high proportions of better qualified young people are perhaps surprising, the explanation is that, whilst young people with higher levels of qualification are less likely to become NEET, educational expansion over many years has dramatically increased the number of young people achieving benchmarks such as five GCSE grades A*–C. Whilst the proportion of these young people who become NEET is low, their absolute numbers are quite high, so that young people with such qualifications form a significant proportion of the NEET population.

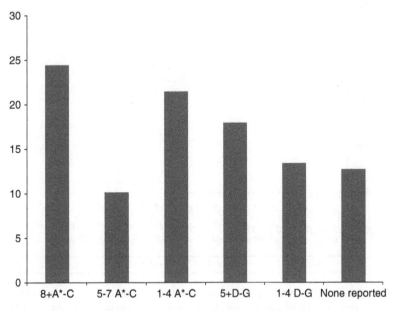

*Figure 3.9*  Composition of young people who were NEET aged 18 in 2009, by GCSE attainment in Year 11
*Source*: DfE/ONS (2010).

The extension of the NEET category to 16–24-year-olds has intensified the issue of well-qualified young people outside education and employment across Europe. Whilst in some countries – for example Denmark and Germany – the NEET population contains few young people with tertiary-level qualifications, in the UK, France and Belgium around 10–13 per cent of NEET young people aged 16–24 have achieved this level (Eurofound 2012, p.31). Nevertheless, in most countries, young people with low levels of education are significantly over-represented in the NEET population, even in the 16–24 age group.

## Activities and immediate prospects of NEET young people

We have already highlighted the composition of the NEET population in terms of various subgroups; some idea of the relative size of these subgroups may be obtained from survey research on the activities of young people, such as the Youth Cohort Study and the LSYPE. In Figure 3.10, the main reasons given by 17-year-olds for their NEET status are shown, broken down by gender. For young women, pregnancy or caring responsibilities bulk large as perceived barriers. For both males and females, lack of qualifications or work experience, health problems and disabilities, and age-related barriers to participation are all perceived as important – although the first of these is most significant for young men. Factors associated with poverty may also have some effect, and although as we have seen there is little evidence that cultures of worklessness are responsible for young people being NEET, relative levels of pay and benefits appear to have some influence.

Also using data from the Youth Cohort Study, Spielhofer et al. (2009) provide an analysis of the NEET population into three groups characterized by different levels of vulnerability in terms of their likelihood of resuming participation in the near future. Around 41 per cent were classified as 'open to learning', and likely to return to education or training in the short term; in general, this group were better qualified and had more positive attitudes to learning. Around 21 per cent were 'undecided NEET'; they were not greatly dissimilar to the 'open to learning' group and their NEET status seemed to arise mainly from dissatisfaction with the opportunities available to them rather than from more general disaffection. The remaining 38 per cent were 'sustained NEET' and unlikely to re-engage, even in the medium term; they tended to have lower school attainment and negative experiences of education, and were more likely to have truanted or been excluded from school. Thus, for nearly two-thirds of NEET young people aged 16–17, re-engagement was thought likely to occur with minimal intervention

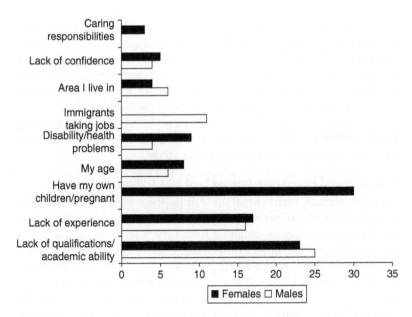

*Figure 3.10*  Main barriers to learning or employment cited by young people who are NEET at age 17 (%)
*Source*: DCSF/ONS (2009).

or by providing more attractive opportunities. However, the 'sustained NEET' group which constituted over one third of the sample appeared to require significant long-term support.

## Risk factors associated with being NEET

In spite of its shortcomings, the term NEET provides a reference point from which to critique social inequality and, for most young people, being outside education and employment for significant periods is not only a consequence of poverty and disadvantage, but increases the likelihood of long-term social exclusion (Simmons and Thompson 2011). Although its diverse composition makes generalizations about the NEET category difficult, young people from deprived backgrounds are significantly over-represented and sustained experience of being NEET is associated with a range of social problems, including an increased likelihood of involvement in crime, drug use and anti-social behaviour, as well as greater risk of long-term unemployment, poor health and other sustained disadvantages. In this section we focus, firstly, on the factors in childhood associated with an increased likelihood of becoming NEET after leaving school, and secondly, on the consequences in later life of spending significant periods outside education and employment in early adulthood.

From the earliest research with NEET young people up to the present day, disadvantaged family backgrounds and negative school experiences have been a constant theme, often exacerbated by depressed local labour markets and the stigma attached to deprived neighbourhoods. In the pioneering study of 'Status 0' in South Glamorgan (Rees et al. 1996), many young people had little expectation of sustained employment and were hostile towards training schemes: one is quoted as saying: 'If there was enough jobs going, then we'd be doing them. But jobs have become YT [Youth Training] and we're expected to be skivvies' (p.227). Low attainment and disaffection from school were common, often associated with sustained truancy. Research into the experiences of young people living on disadvantaged housing estates in Sunderland raised many of the same themes (Wilkinson 1995). The shortage of decent jobs was often implicated in poor self-esteem and low expectations. As in South Wales, a complex picture emerged of multiple disadvantages, problems at school, perceived lack of careers advice and negative perceptions of training. Similar findings were uncovered in Northern Ireland, although non-participation was somewhat lower than elsewhere (Armstrong et al. 1997). Other early research, including *Wasted Youth* (Pierce and Hillman 1998) highlighted similar themes.

Summarizing this body of research, *Bridging the Gap* (SEU 1999) identified three overlapping factors associated with a high risk of becoming NEET: having parents who are poor or unemployed; membership of some ethnic minority groups; and having personal circumstances likely to create barriers to participation. The latter group includes young people with a learning difficulty, disability or long-term illness, those in or leaving care, young offenders and those involved in drug or alcohol misuse, as well as teenage parents, carers and homeless young people (Coles et al. 2002). More recent studies tell similar stories (Spielhofer et al. 2009; Russell et al. 2011a; Duckworth and Schoon 2012). A striking feature of research into NEET young people is the degree of continuity, both with earlier studies and with research into the experiences of young people and adults on the margins of work and education (Russell et al. 2011b; Shildrick et al. 2012a). Such research demonstrates the importance of not distinguishing too sharply between being NEET and other forms of labour market marginality; concentrating on the boundary between participation and non-participation diverts attention from inequalities within the included majority (Thompson 2011). As will be seen later, the various interventions aimed at NEET young people have had limited success in compensating for the cumulative effects of disadvantage and structural changes in employment, implying that the concept of marginality in education and employment offers a more powerful way of understanding young people's experiences than exclusion alone.

Although educational and social disadvantage underpin many of the factors involved in becoming NEET, it is possible to identify a number of specific risk factors and, to some extent, quantify the degree of risk associated with them in terms of 'odds ratios': the chances of an event occurring for a particular group, compared with the chances for a comparison group. In an early but important analysis of longitudinal data from the 1970 British Cohort Study, Bynner and Parsons (2002) outlined some of the most significant factors associated with becoming NEET between the ages of 16 and 18. This study deployed a conceptual framework based on the notion of 'identity capital' (Coté 1996), which combines Bourdieu's social and cultural capitals with a range of psychological attributes, but also took into account aspects of material advantage and disadvantage. Summarizing their findings, Bynner and Parsons (2002) conclude that NEET young people were:

> likely to...have grown up in inner city public housing estates in homes marked by poverty (free school meals and state benefits) and lacking cultural capital (parents not reading to the children and lacking interest in their children's education). Although cognitive ability at age 10 did not appear to be involved, when highest qualification at age 16 was taken into account, a strong effect of educational achievement was evident. Young people with no qualifications were six times as likely to be in NEET status as those with 'O level' or above qualifications...For boys inner city housing had a large effect...whereas for girls family poverty appeared to matter more
>
> (pp.298–299)

Conversely, Coles et al. (2002) noted that young people least likely to be NEET were those living with two parents in owner-occupied housing with a father working full time. However, although its influence on the chances of becoming NEET is strong, social class and/or family poverty appear to operate indirectly in shaping early labour market outcomes, operating largely through levels of educational achievement (Bynner and Parsons 2002; Ianelli and Smyth 2008).

## Educational attainment

Although the relationship between educational attainment and post-16 participation is complex and mediated by gender and ethnicity, qualifications achieved at school are a major factor in whether young people join the NEET population (Eurofound 2012, p.56). As noted above, Bynner and Parsons (2002) found that young people with no qualifications at age 16 were six times as likely[2] to become NEET than those with 'O' level qualifications[3] or above; for boys taken separately this ratio was nine. Researchers in other countries also report an association with low educational attainment, for example in Australia (Hillman 2005) and Scotland (Furlong 2006). There are, however, two caveats to these findings. Firstly, Crawford et al. (2011, p.7) use LSYPE data to show that, whilst at age 18/19 young people who are NEET have significantly lower attainment at both KS2 and at GCSE than university students and those in work, those who are NEET have similar attainment levels to those in education but not following higher education programmes. It is, therefore, not necessarily the case that those who stay in education longer have higher prior achievement. Secondly, even those with higher levels of qualification at age 16 have an increasing chance of becoming NEET as they grow older (see Table 3.1). In England, 37 per cent of young people with no qualifications were NEET at age 17,[4] compared with only 2 per cent for those with eight or more GCSE grades A*–C (DCSF/ONS 2009, p.30). A year later, corresponding proportions for the same cohort were 51 per cent and 8 per cent. Nevertheless, the greatest increase in the chances of being NEET was for the least qualified.

*Table 3.1*  Qualification levels at age 16 and main activity at ages 17 and 18

|  | Age 17 | | | | Age 18 | | | |
|---|---|---|---|---|---|---|---|---|
|  | FTED | In work | GST | NEET | FTED | In work | GST | NEET |
| 8+ A*–C | 87 | 8 | 3 | 2 | 62 | 26 | 4 | 8 |
| 5–7 A*–C | 60 | 26 | 9 | 5 | 39 | 42 | 8 | 11 |
| 1–4 A*–C | 43 | * | 13 | 9 | 31 | 42 | 11 | 16 |
| 5+ D–G | 33 | * | 12 | 16 | 22 | 43 | 9 | 26 |
| 1–4 D–G | 32 | 28 | 9 | 31 | 18 | 34 | 6 | 42 |
| None reported | 33 | 24 | 6 | 37 | 23 | 21 | 5 | 51 |

*Note*: FTED: Full-time Education; GST: Government-Supported Training.
*Source*: DCSF/ONS (2009); DfE/ONS (2010) *incomplete data.

## Parental attainment, attitudes and aspirations in education

There is substantial evidence that parental attitudes towards education are an important factor in the transitions of young people (Payne 2003, pp.30–33; Crawford et al. 2011). Whilst most parents have high educational aspirations for their children, lack of parental interest and support have been related to early leaving and dropout (Crawford et al. 2011). Children whose parents have vocational training tend to opt for earlier labour market entry, as do those with parents who regard entering a trade as important. However, parental attitudes become statistically insignificant when the young person's qualifications at age 16 are taken into account (Bynner and Parsons 2002); this suggests that parental influences may operate largely through educational achievement rather than as an independent factor. Nevertheless, recent research on the secondary effects of social stratification – class-based differences in the educational choices of young people with similar attainment – may imply that parents can have a direct influence, certainly in terms of the type of post-16 education embarked upon (Jackson 2013). Low levels of parental achievement in education have also been associated specifically with increased likelihood of becoming NEET. Duckworth and Schoon (2012) find that low parental education was a factor both in the BCS70 cohort and in LSYPE, with a slight increase in this association for the later cohort. Hillman (2005), reporting on Australian data, finds a significant association between becoming NEET and parental education, but notes that this is largely driven by the protective effect of having both parents educated to degree or diploma level.

## Social disadvantage and social adversity

Aspects of material, social and cultural disadvantage are, of course, strongly linked to becoming NEET (Duckworth and Schoon 2012; Eurofound 2012), although there are many nuances to such findings. Bynner and Parsons (2002) found little independent effect from social class, but significant contributions from a small number of related factors which also showed gender differences relating to specific aspects of material disadvantage. Although, as we have seen, educational achievement showed the strongest effect for both males and females, living on a council estate or inner-city housing was next in importance for young men, whilst for women family poverty, indicated by eligibility for free school meals or particular state benefits, had a strong influence. This suggests that in some respects family circumstances add to educational achievement, rather than simply operating through it, in influencing post-16 participation. That is, for young people with similar levels of educational achievement, the likelihood of becoming NEET was further increased by factors such as living in social housing estates and poverty.

Duckworth and Schoon (2012) structure their analysis around the notion of socio-economic adversity, which comprises circumstances such as low social class background, coming from a workless family, living in social housing, living in a lone parent family and having been born to a teenage mother, all of which pose socio-economic challenges. This analysis parallels the analysis of deprivation by Peruzzi (2013), discussed earlier. Controlling for income, gender, ethnicity and geographical region, Duckworth and Schoon found that the majority of these factors were associated in both BCS70 and LSYPE with significantly increased risk of being NEET at 18, although having a lone parent was a significant risk only in LSYPE, whilst low social class was of marginal significance in BCS70. Living in a family with parents who have experienced long periods of unemployment remains a risk factor even when social class and parental education are controlled for. However, in general, parental worklessness *per se* does not appear to be responsible for this increased risk; the socio-economic risks faced by workless families are more significant (Barnes et al. 2012).

Having a combination of risk factors greatly increases the likelihood of becoming NEET, particularly when three or more such factors are present. Furthermore, later cohorts appear more sensitive to such risks. Duckworth and Schoon (2012) estimate that young people in BCS70 with three or more risk factors are between two and three times more likely to be NEET at 18 compared with those having no risk factors; in LSYPE, this increases to nearly four times. However, it is important to recognize that, even amongst young people having a number of risk factors associated with NEET status, many do not become NEET. Duckworth and Schoon (2012) find a number of protective factors, including prior achievement, educational aspirations and engagement at school, experience of part-time work and attending a school with a relatively low proportion of children from poorer backgrounds. For those at 'deep risk' – having three or more socioeconomic risks – aspirations, school engagement and school characteristics are particularly important.

## The long-term consequences of being NEET

There is considerable international evidence that unemployment and disengagement from education can have serious longer-term consequences, with a number of potentially 'scarring' effects being reported (Gregg and Tominey 2005; Bell and Blanchflower 2010; Scarpetta et al. 2010). These range from economic consequences, such as recurrent unemployment and reduced future income, to emotional impacts, including anxiety, feelings of shame and rejection, and an increased likelihood of drug dependency or criminality. For most young people, the effects of short periods of unemployment on subsequent labour market and social outcomes may be temporary. This is likely to be the case for young people taking a gap year between school and university or those suffering from a short-term illness, particularly when other socio-economic risks, such as those discussed in the previous section, are absent. However, this is not the case for more vulnerable NEET young people and a serious concern about the long-term consequences of non-participation in the years after leaving school has been a major factor in the intensive policy focus on this group in recent years.

Perhaps the most immediate consequence of NEET status is an increased chance of being NEET in the future. Bynner and Parsons (2002) found that those who are NEET at age 16 were considerably more likely to be NEET at 21, even when qualifications and family background were taken into account. Crawford et al. (2011)[5] highlight a number of adverse consequences associated with NEET status at 16, 17 or 18, including an increased risk of unemployment up to five years later – although they point out that the relationship is not necessarily causal. Those who are persistently NEET between 16 and 18 are more likely to remain unemployed in the longer term. Furthermore, young people who are initially NEET at age 16/17 and who later find work are more likely to end up in a job without training, whilst wages and other employment outcomes are also adversely affected (Crawford et al. 2011, p.8). These authors conclude that young people who are NEET at age 18/19 are at particular risk, either because of underlying characteristics or because an initial period of being NEET increases the likelihood of being NEET in the future. For young women, being NEET at age 16 has consequences extending beyond education and the labour market, including early motherhood and emotional problems (Bynner and Parsons 2002). There is also some evidence that young people who are NEET between 16 and 18 are more likely to suffer poor health and depression (Bynner and Parsons 2002; Coles et al. 2002). These effects tend to persist: Bell and Blanchflower (2010) report evidence from the National Child Development Study that spells of unemployment before the age of 23 lowered life satisfaction, heath status, job satisfaction and wages over 20 years later.

Differences between countries in their transition systems (Raffe 2008), particularly in relation to labour-market policy and welfare systems, appear to modify the long-term effects of earlier labour-market exclusion. Nor is it entirely clear whether NEET status in itself has an independent effect, or is simply mediating more fundamental differences between people such as educational attainment and degrees of socio-economic risk. However, even in Sweden, where during the 1990s comprehensive welfare benefits were combined with extensive labour-market intervention, long periods outside education and employment in young adulthood were associated with increased risk of inactivity seven years later (Franzen and Kassman 2005). By contrast, some North American research suggests that employment outcomes in later life are largely unrelated to early experiences (Coles et al. 2002).

Such exclusion is costly, both for the individuals concerned and for society more generally. The long-term social costs to society of a significant NEET population are substantial. Coles et al. (2010) estimate the cost to public finance over the lifetimes of young people who have been NEET for significant periods as between £12 billion and £32 billion, largely due to benefit payments and lost tax receipts. Moreover, they estimate the overall costs to the UK economy as between £21 billion and £76 billion, reflecting lost productivity and additional welfare payments to formerly NEET young people and their families. These authors conclude that 'It is salutary to learn that many of the costs, often far exceeding the intervention cost of attempting to prevent them, accrue before the young people reach 25 years of age. "Cost cutting" measures can, therefore, rebound, well within a single decade' (Coles et al. 2010, p.49).

# 4
# Researching the Lives of Marginalized Young People

This chapter examines some of the methodological issues connected with the research. It first locates our work within the ethnographic tradition, particularly in relation to questions raised by working across multiple sites using individual young people as the unit of analysis, and the need for a critical ethnography to fully illuminate the lives of young people outside education and employment. It introduces the research project on which this book is based, relating it to other work we have undertaken and outlining the data collection methods used. This chapter also discusses some of the epistemological and ethical questions raised by ethnography, illustrating the discussion with extracts from our data.

## Ethnography in social research

Ethnography is well-established as a research methodology, with a distinguished history which includes such classic sociological studies as William Foote Whyte's *Street Corner Society* (Whyte 1943/1981) and, in education, David Hargreaves' *Social Relations in a Secondary School* (Hargreaves 1967) and *Learning to Labour* by Paul Willis (1977). Originating in nineteenth-century anthropological research and achieving prominence in sociology through the work of the Chicago School in the 1920s and 1930s, ethnography has come to inform a range of social science disciplines. Consequently, ethnographic research is diverse, and in some ways ethnography is contested territory (Walford 2009). However, for many researchers – and certainly in our understanding of the term – ethnography retains its distinctive feature: the attempt to explore social phenomena by the close and prolonged involvement of the researcher with the people and places where it occurs. Ethnography entails:

> the study of people in naturally occurring settings or 'fields' by means of methods which capture their social meanings and ordinary activities, involving the researcher participating directly in the setting, if not also the activities, in order to collect data in a systematic manner but without meaning being imposed on them externally.
>
> (Brewer 2000, p.10)

Participant observation is invariably central to ethnographic research, and the success of an ethnography depends on the researcher developing and maintaining a sustained engagement with participants (Denscombe 1995, p.178). A range of methods may be used in conjunction with participant observation, including loosely structured interviews, textual analysis and visual records such as photographs or video. As well as enabling the researcher to uncover similarities and discrepancies between different forms of data – a process known as triangulation – this allows a richly descriptive body of data to emerge which, unlike methods based on questionnaires and structured interviews, is not overly burdened by predefined issues. It is usual to take a flexible, inductive approach to data collection and interpretation, moving through successive iterations from a relatively open research design which is refined as data emerges (see Hammersley and Atkinson 2007).

Ethnographies do not exist in a social vacuum, and the settings in which fieldwork takes place cannot be isolated from their wider social context; ethnographers cannot escape concerns about social inequality and the need for social change, concerns which recognize ethnography's potential for illuminating the nature of social structure, power, culture and human agency (Carspecken 1996, p.3). Ethnography should, in our view, have a distinctively *critical* function, producing not merely descriptions of facts and immediate appearances, but capturing and contextualizing lived experience within the social location and significance of the field (Denzin 1994, p.83). Considerations of power, social structure and theory are central to interpreting the data at our disposal. Whilst the research aims to give voice to marginalized young people, by exploring their views, understandings and aspirations, it is not confined to voice alone, and the experiences of participants are located within broader considerations of inequality and power. In terms of the triadic conceptualization associated with the philosopher Henri Lefebvre, the practices in which young people engage and the meanings they construct cannot be viewed in isolation from the broader discourses and practices which produce these cultural hierarchies – they must be interpreted in relation to discourses constructed by policymakers, researchers and the media, and also to the ways in which such discourses are recirculated or contested by practitioners working with these young people (Thompson et al. 2014).

Ethnographers work on the premise that important knowledge can be gained by 'hanging around' in the field and 'picking things up' – and that some of this knowledge can be acquired in no other way. Of course, such expressions are somewhat understated, as the work of building relationships, getting to know what is going on in the field and participating in its culture is not achieved without a great deal of experience and application. Understanding the (often contradictory) perspectives of participants and their relationships to both local and global contexts requires sustained involvement in people's lives, studying their activities and discourses in everyday settings over a significant period of time. Although physically just 'hanging around', the researcher's mind is engaged with the discourses and practices of the field. Whilst timescales vary considerably, classic ethnographies have typically involved a year or more of fieldwork, a commitment increasingly difficult given the working lives of academics and constraints on research funding (Jeffrey and Troman 2004). Although for these reasons, short-term and intermittent ethnographies (Jeffrey and Troman 2004; Pink and Morgan 2013) are increasing in popularity, they are inevitably limited in terms of what can be achieved, particularly in relation to research with marginalized participants where trust in the researcher–participant relationship is crucial (Russell 2005). The opportunity to conduct fieldwork over a period approaching two years with young people on the margins of education and employment was an important feature of our research project, and it was clear from the outset that maintaining the interest and co-operation of participants with often volatile lives over such a lengthy period would require much more than occasional contact. From an epistemological point of view, we saw a distinct difference between the accounts of participants several months after an event, and direct observation or near-contemporaneous reports and discussions. As Howard Becker points out, qualitative research based on careful, first-hand observation encompassing a wide variety of matters relevant to the investigation is better than work which relies on inference and more remote kinds of observation (Becker 1996, p.69). Whilst no researcher can be with participants all the time, and the nature of ethnographic time is determined as much by the quality of the research process as by its duration, we regard the traditional timescales of ethnography as best suited to investigating the questions with which we are concerned in this book.

Ethnography is traditionally associated with an intensive focus on tightly specified places and cultures, usually involving just one or a very small number of sites. It is therefore possible to describe the researcher as entering or leaving 'the field' at defined and relatively stable spatial and temporal locations, and to encounter people, discourses and practices that do not change drastically between visits. However, this traditional picture has increasingly been extended by the notion of multi-site ethnography, in which the focus of research:

> moves out from the single sites and local situations of conventional ethnographic research designs to examine the circulation of cultural meanings, objects, and identities in diffuse time-space ... This mobile ethnography takes unexpected trajectories in tracing a cultural formation across and within multiple sites of activity that destabilize the distinction, for example, between lifeworld and system ... Just as this mode investigates and ethnographically constructs the lifeworlds of variously situated subjects, it also constructs aspects of the system itself through the associations and connections it suggests among sites.
>
> (Marcus 1995 p.96)

The ethnography described in this book faced precisely these opportunities and challenges in attempting to follow the trajectories of more than 20 young people who, whilst sharing certain characteristics – notably, their precarious engagement with work and education – differ markedly in others, such as their gender, ethnicity, age, the spaces they frequent, their social networks and their social and cultural capital. We considered each young person as an ethnographic case, and throughout the fieldwork the sites, actors and institutions to be investigated were determined by the changing experiences and practices of the young people themselves. The research was led by participants, in the sense that the frequency and location of meetings, interviews and observations were dependent upon their preferences, circumstances and the unfolding events of their lives.

An approach in which individual young people are the units of analysis raises both ontological and epistemological questions. To take the ontological question first, what exactly is the object of our study: what reality is being constructed or reconstructed by the ethnography? If we are to claim that our research has a significance beyond describing individual lives, then – as Marcus notes above – it must enable us to identify a 'cultural formation' which unites and gives meaning to individual cases. This formation cannot simply be equated with a banal notion of 'the NEET experience'; the diversity of the NEET category and the range of situations and experiences of the young people encompassed by it are well-attested by our own research and the wider literature. Nevertheless, by focusing on what Marcus calls 'the circulation of cultural meanings, objects, and identities' within and between individual lives, we will draw attention to certain common themes underlying the experiences of our young participants. As will become evident from the case studies presented in this book, in some ways young people on the margins become caught up in a distinctive world, of places and practices not entirely disconnected from more mainstream experience, but intertwined with and existing alongside it. Nevertheless, the ways in which they interpret, respond to and act within this liminal world are characterized by diversity, contextual variability and contingency rather than uniformity. One of the aims of this book is to construct, through our ethnographic data, the world with which NEET young people interact, the differing practices by which they negotiate its challenges, and its relationship with social change.

The second question is epistemological: to what extent can we rely upon ethnographic data in constructing our picture of the world as it is faced by marginalized young people? In some ways, ethnography has always been contested and controversial, and has been subjected to searching epistemological scrutiny (see, for example, Hammersley 1992). Ethnographers have often reversed this scrutiny in a critique of more positivistic social research, particularly where large-scale surveys or controlled experiments lay claim to the authority of natural science. Ethnography challenges such claims on a number of grounds, arguing that quantitative research overlooks threats to validity, such as the difficulty of transferring from controlled to natural settings, and that some forms of qualitative research rely too much on participants' accounts of their actions rather than on direct observation. By contrast, ethnography claims to capture social processes and the meanings underlying them, through 'thick descriptions' (Geertz 1973) in which theoretical analysis is interwoven with rich description of the case. Perhaps the central claim of ethnography is that it achieves *greater* validity in answering the type of questions in which ethnographers are typically interested than other approaches, whilst recognizing that judgement must be exercised in how data are used. For Becker (1996), the epistemological superiority of ethnography is not compromised by specific cases – relatively straightforward to anticipate – in which participants may modify their behaviour in response to the research process:

> Social scientists who study schools and social agencies regularly find that [their] personnel... think of research as some version of the institutional evaluations they are constantly subject to, and take measures to manipulate what will be discovered... But... ethnographers typically make this a major epistemological point: when they talk about what people do they are talking about what they saw them do under the conditions in which they usually do it... They are seeing the 'real world' of everyday life, not some version of it created at their urging and for their benefit...
>
> Becker (1996, pp.62–63)

The following extract from Lisa Russell's field notes illustrates some of these points in the context of our research. It recounts the first meeting with two young mothers: Jess, who later agreed to participate in the research, and Jodi. Describing a session in a parenting course at a Sure Start centre in Middlebridge, the extract introduces several points which became recurring themes in the research – the recirculation of young people within training providers and charities with which we were already familiar from our earlier research, perceptions of poor-quality education for marginalized young people and experiences of domestic conflict. It also – in our view – provides support for the claim that people tend to behave more naturally in the world of everyday life than might be the case in interviews and other settings.

*Wednesday 2 February 2011*

**12.00** I arrive at the Sure Start centre. Two young mums are already present with their children. One [name not recorded] is White (mum of Leo, 9 months) and one an Asian mum (Jodi), she has two girls, today she is with her youngest Aisha who is around one year old.

Anna, the session leader (she is fairly new to the post) and two volunteer students (from Middlebridge University) are also present. One student, Lianne (on a youth work course – wants to specialize in sexual health, has two children) is doing part of her 15 hour work experience here and the other girl (health course, has no children) is about to finish her third year and is trying to get some work experience before completing. All are dressed fairly informally in leggings or jeans.

Lunch is available on the table as I arrive, sandwiches with tuna mayonnaise or egg mayonnaise fillings, grapes, fromage frais and crisps. Lianne offers to make me a cup of tea as I enter. The babies are in high chairs waiting to be fed.

Later Jess arrives with her baby daughter and her friend Veronica. Jess has bleached blonde hair. All the mums are dressed fairly casually in tracksuit bottoms and tops, Jodi wears flip flops and Lianne later comments that she has more make-up on than normal as she has a bruised eye. The other girls wear minimal make-up.

I sit and eat with them, make an effort to play with the children on the mat on the floor and take some time to sit with the mums to introduce myself and the research.

A woman who works for the housing association arrives; Anna says she tries to come once a month. There is a notice on the door informing people when she comes to visit. She has information concerning changes to housing benefit for those who are private tenants – basically they will have to pay more money if they want to stay in that house and could be moved if they have no family ties, or work reasons to stay. Also empty rooms will be looked down on. Jodi is under a private tenancy agreement, as is Veronica, both take the documents. Jodi sits there trying to work out her outgoings and incomings on a sheet of paper.

After lunch the girls are asked to paint a piggy bank in preparation for their budgeting session next week – a session on how to manage your finances. The three mums seem happy to do this while the two volunteers and Veronica play with the children on the blankets. While they do this they chat to each other – they obviously know one another.

Jodi became pregnant in year 10 at school. When she was 28 weeks she went to 'pregnant school' [a Pupil Referral Unit] – her own school said she could no longer stay there for health and safety reasons. Jess says she went to a 'pregnant school' too – the two talk about how the teachers there are not properly qualified and complain about them teaching content below their ability. Jodi says she did leave with some GCSEs but she can't remember what in. Jodi has two children by different dads, she was living with Joe, Aisha's dad but they broke up over the weekend. 'The social' are involved – the eldest was kicked and Jodi says she banged her eye on a door as he left. Anna says that she has to inform social services if she hears anything concerning a child protection issue – on this occasion she thinks they are already aware and so just needs to check this.

Jess and Leo's mum know each other from MGC Training [a private training provider] (OC – Observer Comment – You get the impression that these people are shifted round from one destination to the next, all experiencing the same thing). Jess says she finished the training, Leo's mum says she didn't as she had morning sickness and found the staff unsympathetic.

All three mums come most weeks; they don't attend anything else as they don't feel comfortable in other groups. Jess is awaiting a phone call about a job at a care home – she worked there before she had her baby, she says they stopped her when she broke her foot and got pregnant, they told her they had no more shifts, Jess suspects they just wanted to get rid of her. She says she knows the job inside out and wants a few hours as she does not want to be known as a benefits scrounger, she wants a job and is dubious about her other half getting work.

A further question raised by ethnography's claim to reveal social processes and meanings is whether the idea of a single reality, to be captured by ethnographic methods, is defensible. Is ethnography – literally 'writing culture' (Clifford and Marcus 1986) – inescapably constructive, creating rather than describing its social worlds? Ethnography has moved on considerably from its nineteenth-century origins, in which the researcher was seen as external (and, by implication, superior) to the culture being studied – often a faraway and 'primitive' tribe. Today, ethnographers recognize that the values and interests of the researcher cannot be separated from the research process, highlighting the need for reflexivity in considering how the researcher's standpoint may influence how research is conducted and reported. We cannot assume that ethnographers, as socially situated individuals, can reproduce social reality. However, whilst ethnographies are socially constructed and liable to error and bias, this does not imply a capitulation to relativism, in which one account is as good as any other. Hammersley (1992) and Denzin and Lincoln (1998) propose alternative forms of realism, which propose that, although knowledge is socially produced, it more or less accurately describes phenomena which exist independently of our claims about them. They propose that reasonably objective criteria exist for establishing the credibility of competing knowledge claims, such as compatibility with other well-established knowledge, and the nature and robustness of the evidence. Although social inquiry cannot reproduce reality, it can represent it with some degree of completeness.

## Young people and the research process

Gaining and maintaining access to NEET young people is not straightforward and, in many cases, their non-participation in education and work means they are sometimes described as 'hard to reach'. Our participants were therefore selected as much by serendipity as by theoretical design – although constructing our sample was still a rather convoluted process. Initial contact was made through young people's services, through training providers and by means of 'snowballing', whereby existing participants put us in touch with others. Many avenues were explored, and considerable persistence was needed to gain knowledge of the field, including who worked where and what provision was on offer. In fact, 18 meetings with practitioners and over 40 telephone conversations and email exchanges were conducted before we met a single young person (Russell 2013, p.50). The following field note extract gives some flavour of the process:

### 18 November 2010 – meeting at Connexions

I spend the day at Connexions in Middlebridge. I meet Heather [from the leaving care team] at 9.30am…Heather has asked young people by letter to come here today, I will then introduce myself and the research and arrange a follow up meeting. She has emailed her contacts and has been given some names; others she knows personally and feels they will engage; some are starting her 'employability' programme in January.

Cayden is aged 19. His mum died round about a year ago…Heather says he has a learning disorder and will probably never work. He went to a school for young people with learning difficulties: he liked it there, but when he went to college things started to break down as he was thinking about his mum. He has lived with his foster carers and uncle – they have had joint care, but have since left to live in Scotland – a dream they had, Cayden says he decided to stay here. He currently lives alone in Eastville. Cayden just wants a happy life, he sometimes wants to work but sometimes doesn't. He has been in nothing since college and doesn't feel ready to go into anything just yet.

We start a life history record and agree a follow-up meeting date – Thursday 2nd December, which was cancelled due to snow – Cayden rings Lisa to cancel as he gave her an incorrect phone number.

*17 November 2010 – meeting at Cayden's flat*

9.00–10.00am I ring the bell, Cayden runs down the stairs to meet me; he lives in an end flat at the top level. It is fairly quiet around here, he has a good view. He describes his flat as 'fairly big' – he has a bedroom, bathroom, kitchen and living room. He offers me a drink, I take a water...

I ask about interviewing him on our next meeting and he jokes about meeting me at 1am – at least I think he is joking (OC he seems very lonely). I arrange to meet him on Thursday 13th Jan at 9am.

Although we would not claim that the young people in our study constitute a representative sample of all NEET young people, we aimed to include participants from the major subgroups discussed in Chapter 3, such as care leavers, young people with learning disabilities, young parents, early school-leavers and young offenders. Practitioners working for voluntary sector training providers, Jobcentres, local authority teams supporting care leavers or young offenders and the Connexions service were particularly helpful, both in locating young people willing to participate and by providing us with data through interviews, supplying documents and inviting us to meetings. Table A.1 indicates how we established contact with each young person, and the length of their participation in the research. To some extent, the practicalities of gaining access and the 'gatekeeping' role of practitioners – who, after all, have a legitimate interest in safeguarding those for whom they are responsible – limited the diversity of our participants. It could, of course, be argued that the most vulnerable young people are precisely those *not* accessed by researchers because they stay out of the reach of support agencies, whilst the 'ordinary' young people whose NEET status is short-lived and who form a large proportion of the NEET population (see Chapter 3) may also evade the interest of research designs which focus specifically on the NEET category. Nevertheless, we found that the range of circumstances represented in our sample reflected most of the categories suggesting high vulnerability, and care leavers in particular tended to have multiple barriers to engagement.

In addition to young people and practitioners, we also sought to involve employers and parents. As we found in our E2E research, the perspectives of parents were particularly difficult to obtain, for various reasons. Perhaps most importantly, participants were often reluctant to allow us to contact their parents, or had lost touch with them. In other cases, the parent was either too busy or simply did not wish to take part in the research. In the end, after a number of false starts, only one parent was interviewed, although there were sometimes other forms of contact with parents. Employers – or, more accurately, local managers and supervisors – were easier to access, although in most cases the young people concerned were undertaking voluntary work rather than paid employment. Nevertheless, the perspectives of these managers were valuable in extending our knowledge of young people's working lives and in providing points of comparison with our other data. They also provided insights into local labour markets and the challenges facing young people attempting to find employment.

Approaches to qualitative research which engage marginalized groups have attracted increasing attention in recent years (Curtis et al. 2004; Finlay et al. 2010; Russell et al. 2011a). Such studies discuss the difficulties encountered by researchers working with 'hard-to-reach' young people and the need to move beyond formalized interviews and focus groups in which participants may feel pressured by external agendas. The extended timescale of our research, and the prolonged involvement with young people it made possible, highlighted these difficulties but also enabled us to develop the trust and familiarity so important in ethnographic research (Russell 2005). Participant observation formed the bedrock of our methodology – 'hanging around' with young people in their homes and other places where they spent significant amounts of time, such as benefit offices and Connexions centres, the premises of work placement and training providers, and those of other support services. Although we decided at an early stage not to offer financial incentives to young people, meetings often took place in cafés or fast-food restaurants where a meal or drink could be provided. We needed young people to participate because they wanted to, but in many cases they struggled financially and were thankful for a paid lunch; but we also needed to create 'meeting' spaces as participants were often outside education, training or employment. Ethnographic research with vulnerable young people involves spending time alone with participants, raising concerns about the researcher's safety; only after a significant period of time can reliable judgements be made about entering young people's homes and other social spheres (Russell 2013, p.58). A range of other approaches were used to engage participants and to elicit information. Most young people were interviewed at least once, and some several times. A particularly helpful instrument in the early stages of the research was a life-history record, in which researcher and participant worked together to complete a tabular or pictorial representation of key events and interests in the young person's life. Whilst initial reactions often included suspicion that Lisa was an agent of Connexions, many young people welcomed the opportunity of regular contact with an adult, and a few saw engaging with the research as a positive addition to their CV.

Whilst our approach attempted to enable young people to influence the processes and outcomes of the research, and to allow their voices to be heard outside the research team, we recognize that the notion of participant voice is problematic. Adults, including the research team, may respond to and understand this voice differently depending upon how it is framed; what is said, by whom and where can influence discursive practices between researched and researcher, as well as between young people and adult practitioners (Cremin et al. 2011). Some young people appeared surprised at our interest in their stories, and a number of them questioned and challenged aspects of the research – why were we asking that question, the purpose of the research and so on. In some circumstances with tight timescales, such as structured interviews or focus groups, researchers may regard these challenges as problematic. In our view, however, they are a legitimate part of ethnographic research and promote a dialogue between the researcher and participant which enriches the data, facilitates trust between the ethnographer and participants and increases responsiveness to the concerns of young people. Nevertheless, we had to accept that some young people did not wish to stay with the project; the following field note extracts show the concerns which led Sara, a young mother, to end her involvement after 18 months:

> Sara is about to go out so I try not to keep her. I ask if she is ok for us to meet again, she says we can but questions why I want to come and what I do with all the data I collect. I say I am a researcher who is interested in looking at what she does now and in the future education and work-wise. I say I'm interested in her because she is a new mum and I'm keen to learn how this might affect things, how she feels and what she is able to do. She says this is fine but says she doesn't want to be interviewed any more – I agree that we won't do any more interviews.
>
> (Field notes 26/10/11)

She asks again what it is I do, she apologizes for asking me again. I say I am a researcher looking at NEET young people's lives and telling their side of the story with their words. I say I use participant observation, so I listen and spend time with young people rather than sitting in a corner scribbling notes – she says she understands, she asks what happens to the interview transcript, I say her name is changed and some of it may be used for analysis and writing up, I offer to show her a methodology paper I have written next time. She says she would like to see it. She says again that she doesn't want me to interview her again (OC I think she has become distrustful and more guarded since having her child).

(Field notes 18/01/12)

I ring Sara after another failed appointment – she wants to leave the research – she is still at home with her daughter who is about to turn one. She wants to look into nursing, but hasn't spoken to anybody about this yet – she has just looked on the internet. She will wait another year or so until her daughter is older and she can sort out childcare. She is also looking after her elderly grandmother, which takes up a lot of her time. I tell her she can ring me if she ever wants to but we agree to part.

(Field notes 21/09/12)

As a research project unfolds and participants become less guarded in their responses and the actions they are willing to have witnessed, ethnographers may be confronted by ethical problems which go beyond initial concerns about gaining access and obtaining informed consent (Russell 2013). In our case, becoming privy to information which may need to be passed on to official bodies such as Connexions, local authority services or even the police was always possible. Domestic violence, drug use and possible involvement in crime or benefit fraud were all encountered during the research, and what course of action would be in a young person's best interest was a frequent topic of discussion in research team meetings. This led sometimes to difficult decisions that required us to strike a balance between breaking a participant's confidence and broader issues of safeguarding. Such considerations also posed problems for the degree of completeness used in reporting the research and whether to change minor details in order to protect confidentiality. Underpinning these debates was a conviction that the best way of advocating young people's perspectives and rights was to report as much of their experiences as possible, provided this was consistent with their well-being. However, the extent to which vulnerable young adults can form judgements about the impact anonymized publication may have is not self-evident; whether consent to take part in research can be regarded as informed when given by a young person with little awareness of the academic world is open to question. As Russell (2013) argues, the answer to this question is a matter of judgement in individual cases and the ethnographer must be prepared to take responsibility for it.

Relationships between participants sometimes presented ethical challenges. Some of the young people knew each other from attending training courses or through other contacts, and it was impossible to prevent them from knowing that they were both participants. Nevertheless, confidentiality was maintained as far as possible, which sometimes created difficult situations:

Jasmine talks about how someone has tried to break in to her flat. She shows me her back door, the white PVC has clearly been knocked out near the lock and upper area, bits of it are smashed on the floor outside. The flat has green open space at the back. She says she has informed the council who have agreed to get her a new door.

Jasmine had friends round last night, she complains that one of them had a takeaway and then didn't clean up after himself, she chucked him out, he said 'come on lets bounce' and the others followed him. Jasmine seems angry and frustrated at the fact that they all followed him out, she often comments on how she can't abide childish behaviour. She says she prefers adult company.

Jasmine shows me her bedroom window, some orange food has been thrown at it – this happened last night, she said, 'I shit myself, well not literally'. She rang the police...Jasmine says she thinks it was Kelsey and two others who did this – I don't quite get to grips with her reasons. I ask if it is Kelsey Formby. Jasmine says yes, looking at me confused, I say Kelsey is part of the project (OC I'm in a real predicament here – I don't want to divulge any more information but I was curious to know if it was Kelsey as she lives nearby). Jasmine says a friend described them 'to a tee' – she rang Kelsey's flats to see if they were in and they said she was [Kelsey lived in a supervised housing scheme] (OC I know Kelsey was out all last night as I saw her this morning at her employability course – I say nothing). Jasmine suspects the housing scheme staff of lying to her or failing to record details correctly.

(Field notes 03/02/11)

As with all ethnographic research, careful thought was needed about the ramifications of data collection and the layers of consent needed when working with different people across multiple sites (Russell 2013). Whilst in succeeding chapters we will be largely concerned with developing our findings from the research, the underlying questions of whether an ethnographer can form a relationship unaffected by power and truly gain informed consent, alongside practical considerations about managing sensitive information, were constantly with us.

## Locating the research – Middlebridge and Greenford

As might be expected from the discussion of the social and economic factors influencing NEET rates over several decades, these rates show considerable regional variation within many European countries. In England, differences in proportions of young people outside education and employment tend to follow familiar fault lines – between poor urban areas within major cities and de-industrialized coastal and former mining towns on the one hand, and more affluent areas with greater proportions of middle-class employment. However, such divisions are not rigid, and high NEET rates may be encountered in places which have not experienced de-industrialization – for example in Brighton. Figure 4.1 shows NEET rates by region in England for 2011 and 2012, using data from the Client Caseload Information System database, which is collected by local authorities as part of their statutory responsibility to monitor and support vulnerable young people. Whilst a broad 'north–south divide' is evident, the figure shows that, with the exception of the North East, differences are relatively small – around one or two percentage points.

The Client Caseload Information System data suffer from two major disadvantages; firstly, the proportion of young people for whom data is missing or incomplete can be as great as – or even greater than – the local NEET rate itself. Secondly, it relates to 16–18-year-olds only. Using a different approach based on data from the Annual Population Survey, Lee and Wright (2011) map the geography of 16–24-year-olds outside education and employment for a sample of 53 towns and cities across Great Britain, including London subregions. This mapping highlights the NEET category as a post-industrial legacy, all of the ten cities with the highest NEET rates being located in northern England or South Wales. In London, although neighbouring boroughs can have very different NEET rates, the worst-affected places include Haringey, Hackney and Tower Hamlets.

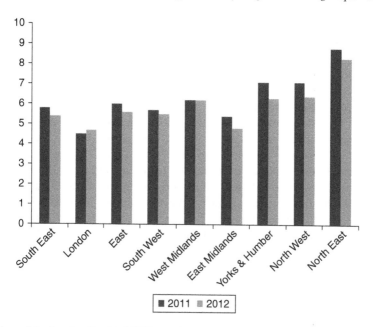

*Figure 4.1*   Local authority NEET rates for age 16–18 in England, 2011–2012
*Source*: *Data on 16- to 18-year-olds not in education, employment or training (NEET).* Available online at http://www.education.gov.uk/childrenandyoungpeople/youngpeople/ participation/neet/a0064101/16-to-18-year-olds-not-in-education,-employment-or-training.

In Yorkshire and Humberside, the region where our research was located, NEET rates vary considerably. The city of York has one of the lowest rates in the sample considered by Lee and Wright (2011), whilst Grimsby, Doncaster and Barnsley are amongst the highest. Our own research was conducted in two neighbouring local authorities in this region, Fernside and Northdale, a district in which – whilst not amongst the highest in the country – 16–24 NEET rates are in excess of 18 per cent. In order to locate the research in the social and economic circumstances of this district, we briefly outline some of the main characteristics of the two authorities.

Middlebridge has a population of 133,293 and is the biggest town in Fernside, a local authority which also includes a number of smaller towns and villages and for which Middlebridge acts as the administrative centre. Although it has a rich industrial heritage and its popular image is stereotypically northern and working class, nowadays Middlebridge is a university town and ethnically quite diverse: it has a long history of Irish migration and there have been significant

African-Caribbean and South Asian populations in Middlebridge since the 1960s. More recently, migrants from Eastern Europe, the Middle East and elsewhere have arrived in Middlebridge and other parts of Fernside. Today, just over two-thirds of the town's population is classified as White British. There are also substantial numbers of ethnic minorities elsewhere in Fernside, with established Pakistani communities in the nearby towns of Eastville and Gadley. In contrast, some parts of Fernside are almost exclusively white, especially the relatively affluent southern suburbs of Middlebridge and the semi-rural villages beyond.

Middlebridge experienced tremendous growth during and after the Industrial Revolution, based mainly on the textiles industry and the demand for labour associated with the areas many factories and mills. However, Middlebridge has never been a one-industry town: mining, engineering and other forms of manufacturing and commerce also have a long history in the area. Its diverse range of industries and the ready availability of work meant that, for much of its history, Middlebridge was regarded as a relatively affluent town, especially in comparison to Eastville, Gadley and other nearby places; and, despite the demise of much of its traditional industrial base, Middlebridge remains more prosperous than many of its neighbours.

Although its population of around 83,000 is significantly smaller, Greenford shares a number of characteristics with Middlebridge. Like its neighbour, Greenford is located in the Pennine hills of northern England, and the textiles industry has played a key role in its history. Wool has been manufactured in the town since the fifteenth century and textiles were central to Greenford's transformation into an industrial town during the nineteenth century. Nowadays though, like Middlebridge, Greenford acts as the commercial, cultural and administrative centre for Northdale, a local authority which contains a number of other settlements, some of which are quite small and geographically remote. In total, Northdale, has a population of around 204,000, around 90 per cent of which is White, and some of the more affluent and rural settlements in Northdale are almost entirely White. Most of Northdale's ethnic minority population is located in central Greenford, and is concentrated in the town's most deprived wards. Pakistanis constitute by far the largest minority group with around 70 per cent of the non-White population being of Pakistani descent. However, like Middlebridge and many other British towns and cities, a significant number of East Europeans and other migrants have come to live in Greenford over the last decade or so.

Although there has always been an element of rivalry between Middlebridge and Greenford – their rugby league teams are traditional rivals – they also have common bonds. Whilst the industrial revolution played a central role in the history of both towns, the factory system was not established without opposition in either Middlebridge or Greenford. Both were centres of political unrest and radical activity in the first few decades of the nineteenth century, and there was a strong Luddite presence in both towns. The two towns continue to have much in common today: health care in both places is delivered by a combined Fernside and Northdale NHS Trust; there is a single Fernside and Northdale Careers Service; and both local authorities are covered by common police, fire and ambulance services. Many voluntary and charitable organizations operate across the two authorities in a unified way, formally or otherwise. Similarly, a number of sporting leagues operate across the two areas and, generally, there is a degree of social and cultural similarity between Middlebridge and Greenford. The nature of the local labour market means that many people commute to work across the Fernside–Northdale border and the University of Middlebridge recruits many of its students from across both authorities.

Middlebridge and Greenford exemplify the changing nature of youth transitions within contemporary British society, and over the last 40 years, both places have been greatly affected by globalization, de-industrialization and other aspects of economic, social and political change. As manufacturing has declined, the nature of employment has fragmented and is increasingly located in the service sector. Although, historically, both towns were relatively prosperous, nowadays unemployment rates are above the UK average; around one-third of employment is part-time, and many jobs are insecure and low paid. Young people often experience difficulty in gaining employment – a phenomenon recognized by practitioners working in local support services:

> There aren't the jobs … 60 per cent of the employers in Fernside don't employ anybody under the age of 25. We're working on that with the local authority and the regeneration department, and our engagement team and our recruitment advisors are working with employers to try and get them to give a young person a chance. And that's why the Future Job Fund was so successful for these young people. So it is difficult because, of course, that's finished now.
>
> (Jobcentre manager, 04/02/11)

In both Fernside and Northdale, 18–24-year-olds have considerably higher claimant rates than other age groups (see Table 4.1). In both authorities the number of people claiming Jobseeker's Allowance

*Table 4.1*   Job Seeker's Allowance claimants by age and duration in Fernside and Northdale (% of resident population, January 2013)

|  | Fernside | Northdale | Great Britain |
|---|---|---|---|
| **Aged 18–24** |  |  |  |
| Total | 9.6 | 10.9 | 6.7 |
| Up to 6 months | 6.6 | 6.2 | 4.5 |
| Over 6 and up to 12 months | 1.4 | 2.6 | 0.9 |
| over 12 months | 1.6 | 2.0 | 1.3 |
| **Aged 25–49** |  |  |  |
| Total | 4.8 | 2.9 | 3.9 |
| Up to 6 months | 2.6 | 5.1 | 2.1 |
| Over 6 and up to 12 months | 0.8 | 1.2 | 0.6 |
| over 12 months | 1.4 | 1.7 | 1.2 |
| **Aged 50–64** |  |  |  |
| Total | 2.4 | 2.6 | 2.2 |
| Up to 6 months | 1.2 | 1.1 | 1.0 |
| Over 6 and up to 12 months | 0.4 | 0.5 | 0.3 |
| over 12 months | 0.9 | 1.0 | 0.8 |

exceeds the national average across all age ranges, although claimant rates are generally somewhat higher in Fernside than in Northdale. At the end of 2012, 6.5 per cent of 16–18-year-olds in Fernside and 5.9 per cent of 16–18-year-olds in Northdale were classified as NEET.

Fernside and Northdale are both characterized by lower than average educational attainment, although qualification levels are a little higher in Northdale than in Fernside. Nevertheless, both local authorities have fewer residents with advanced and intermediate level qualifications than the national average, although Fernside has slightly fewer people without any qualifications at all than is the case across Great Britain in general. Whilst patterns of employment in Fernside and Northdale reflect the national shift from manufacturing to service sector work, manufacturing continues to play a significant part in the local economy, and the proportion of jobs in manufacturing is greater than the national average in both authorities (see Table 4.2). Some of Middlebridge's largest employers include plastics, chemicals and engineering companies and across Fernside manufacturers of greetings cards, biscuits, paints and pharmaceuticals all have relatively large workforces. Nevertheless, the majority of jobs are in service industries, particularly in the public sector. Despite recent cutbacks, Fernside Council still employs over 19,000 people, and other large employers include the NHS and Middlebridge University. The local authority is also the

*Table 4.2* Employee jobs in Fernside and Northdale (% of jobs, in 2008)

|  | Fernside | Northdale | Great Britain |
|---|---|---|---|
| **Mode of employment** |  |  |  |
| Full-time | 65.7 | 67.1 | 68.8 |
| Part-time | 34.3 | 32.9 | 31.2 |
| **Employee jobs by industry** |  |  |  |
| Manufacturing | 20.2 | 18.7 | 10.2 |
| Construction | 5.1 | 4.7 | 4.8 |
| Services | 73.9 | 76.2 | 83.5 |
| *Distribution, hotels & restaurants* | 24.1 | 21.8 | 23.4 |
| *Transport & communications* | 4.2 | 4.0 | 5.8 |
| *Finance, IT, other business activities* | 13.6 | 25.1 | 22.0 |
| *Public admin, education & health* | 27.8 | 21.4 | 27.0 |
| *Other services* | 4.2 | 3.8 | 5.3 |
| Tourism-related | 6.8 | 7.0 | 8.2 |
| Total employee jobs | 150,200 | 100,000 |  |

largest employer in Northdale and provides work for almost 10,000 people. As in Middlebridge, the NHS is also an important source of jobs. Although Northdale does not have a university, banking, insurance and finance are substantial employers. Although Northdale has a slightly lower proportion of manufacturing jobs than Fernside, two industrial plants in Greenford employ over 1,000 people – one producing white goods, the other concrete products; another manufacturer, which produces confectionery, provides around 600 jobs.

# 5
# Education, Training and Youth Employment

## Education, society and economy

Education in advanced Western economies such as the UK can be conceived in various ways. Some focus on education's emancipatory possibilities and its power to transform the lives of individuals and groups. For John Dewey (1966), the main functions of schooling can be summarized as providing social stability and integration; promoting moral and personal fulfilment; and offering individuals the opportunity to rise above the social circumstances into which they were born. However, whilst according to Émile Durkheim (1903/1956, p.123) education is a systematic process of socialization which aims, up to a point, to produce a common social and cultural heritage, it also aims to differentiate and select according to the social division of labour. This functionalist critique has been taken much further, especially from Marxist, feminist and critical race theory perspectives, which see education in terms of conflict and domination rather than social consensus. Pierre Bourdieu has argued that 'It is probably cultural inertia which still makes us see education in terms of the ideology of the school as a liberating force' (Bourdieu 1974, p.32). More recently, critical race theorists have focused on how education is implicated in the production and reproduction of racial inequality (Gillborn 2008). According to such critiques, the structure and content of education reflects the power and dominance of certain groups. The value society places on certain forms of knowledge reflects prevailing forms of inequality, and the way that education systems are structured and organized plays a significant role in perpetuating patterns of advantage and disadvantage.

A significant debate within the sociology of education centres upon the connection between education and the economy. For proponents of human capital theory, the bond between education and the economy is based upon two interrelated assumptions. The first is a belief that the demand for skilled, educated workers is increasing due to rapid technological change, and that the proportion of low-skill, routine employment is shrinking as mass production shifts to poorer parts of the world. The way forward for nations such as the UK, it is argued, is to transform themselves into 'knowledge economies' focused on technological and creative industries and value-added labour processes. Flowing from this, the role of the education system is therefore to provide an increased supply of flexible and creative workers able to function in a rapidly changing environment (Avis 2007). Such discourses have led to the notion of lifelong learning, or – in terms of Basil Bernstein's trenchant critique of 'trainability' – to attempts by policymakers to normalize the assumption that people of working age will engage in 'continuous pedagogic re-formations and so cope with the new requirements of "work" and "life" ' (Bernstein 2000, p.59). The second assumption is that increased investment in education and training will lead to social and economic advancement, both for the individual and for society. Human capital theory is thus related to liberal meritocratic ideals whereby it is assumed that the most hard-working and talented rise to the top, and that an improved education system is the key to overcoming social and economic inequalities (see, for example, Becker 1994).

Such notions have been popular for decades and, to a certain extent, they complemented the social democratic ideals which underpinned the creation of the welfare state and the expansion of all forms of education in post-war Britain. However, education was not the highest priority at this time and policymakers were often more concerned with economic and industrial policy, the Cold War and loss of Empire. This situation changed radically from the end of the 1970s, and since then successive governments have placed an increasing emphasis on the economic role of education and training and have attempted to reform the education system accordingly. Whilst different governments have had different emphases, education and other supply-side factors have increasingly been presented as the solution to the escalating demands of globalization and growing levels of economic competition which accompany it (Hyland and Winch 2007, p.98). Consequently, successive governments have concentrated on skills and creating a flexible workforce rather than on using employment regulation or job creation to stimulate the demand for labour. In some ways this is logical: under neo-liberalism skill-supply initiatives are one of the few legitimate areas for state activity (Keep 2006). Consequently, whilst particularly in more deprived areas of the UK New Labour used investment in the public sector to bolster employment, a range of possible interventions have been largely excluded from the policy agenda. The introduction of licence to practice requirements for workers, statutory rights to collective bargaining on skills or, indeed, the reintroduction of training levies, such as those which existed in Britain in the 1960s and 1970s have, for example, all been consistently overlooked. At the same time, attempts to raise the status of vocational education have largely foundered, with many forms of vocational education in England continuing to be regarded as spaces for the containment of low-ability or disaffected young people (Hodgson and Spours 2010; Fuller and Unwin 2011; Simmons and Thompson 2011).

Phil Brown (2013) argues that the failure of the labour market to meet the growing demand for professional employment is particularly acute in developed economies with large middle classes, mass higher education and wide income inequalities, such as the UK; and that the experiences of many young people, especially those from working-class backgrounds, are defined by social congestion rather than social mobility. Education plays a crucial role in this process as young people seek to gain positional advantage by using educational attainment to 'stand out from the crowd'. The irony is that if only a few use these tactics they may stand a chance of success, but no one gets any further ahead if everyone tries to do the same thing. Under present labour market conditions, educational expansion only contributes to the very congestion people are trying to escape.

Although the interactions between education, the labour market and the social class system are complex, certain patterns are discernible. Whilst in post-war Britain redistributive policies connected with the creation of the welfare state enabled many children from the old industrial working-class to be upwardly mobile, large-scale social mobility effectively stalled thereafter (Goldthorpe and Mills 2008). Although a combination of globalization, de-industrialization and neo-liberal policies underpins such processes, continuing social class inequalities in education, the failure of high-status job opportunities to keep pace with educational expansion and high levels of income inequality, provide severe obstacles to individual mobility. Without stimulating the demand for higher-level employment opportunities, increasing the supply of highly qualified young people only extends the 'social distance' between what is needed to do a job and what is required to get it, particularly for young working-class people. Meanwhile, as increasing numbers of students from middle-class backgrounds enter higher education, it becomes more difficult for them to reach a higher social status than their parents (Boudon 1974, p.6). Gendered patterns of educational performance have intensified social congestion as young women, often with higher academic credentials, compete for a livelihood with young men (Francis and Skelton 2005; Penny 2010). Nevertheless, those with more extensive reserves of social, economic and cultural capital are better positioned to meet the increasingly selective demands of employers, whether they are male or female.

## Employment in the UK

The notion that the UK is transforming itself into a knowledge economy contains a number of flaws, one of which is the conflation of its dwindling industrial base with a reduction in low-skilled, low-paid work. Whilst the number of manufacturing jobs has declined since the 1960s and 1970s, it does not necessarily follow that there is less unskilled work (Avis 2004, p.203). Although many people nowadays are engaged in so-called knowledge work, millions operate supermarket checkouts, work in call centres, clean offices and wait on tables in the expanded service sector (Resolution Foundation 2013). The UK's biggest private sector employer is the supermarket chain Tesco. While there has been some change in emphasis since the Coalition came to power – for example, George Osborne's (2011) call to 'get Britain making things again' – manufacturing jobs continue to head overseas.[1] In Figure 5.1, we see the changing pattern of employment in the UK at three key points: the election years of 1979, 1997 and 2010. The decline in manufacturing jobs and the corresponding shift to health, education and administration is evident, but the relative stability of employment in construction and in retail operations is also noteworthy. Although the contribution of the financial services sector has been lauded as part of the shift towards a knowledge economy, the number of people actually employed in this sector has changed little over the years, and its direct contribution to job creation has been slight. Figure 5.2 shows the nature of jobs across all sectors, using the Standard Occupational Classification (SOC 2000). Less dramatic than the decline in manufacturing seen in Figure 5.1, but still notable, is the decline of skilled trades, machine operatives and secretarial work, whilst the increase in personal services and professional or technical employment lends some support to the thesis that knowledge work is increasingly important. Nevertheless, routine forms of

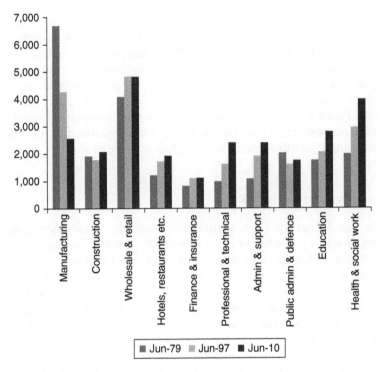

*Figure 5.1*   UK jobs by employment sector (thousands), 1979–2010

employment – sales, machine operatives and elementary occupations[2] – provided around 7.2 million jobs in 2013 compared with 7.9 million in 2001.

The location of jobs in particular sectors or occupational categories is only part of the story, and as Holmes and Mayhew (2012) point out, it is necessary to analyse the occupational structure at finer levels to reveal the variations in pay and conditions involved. In recent years, this type of analysis has led to the proposal that a significant degree of polarization has occurred within the labour market, with the distribution of jobs assuming an hourglass shape as it becomes increasingly concentrated at the high-paid and low-paid ends. The creation of this 'hour-glass economy' has been attributed to the decline in routine jobs – for example, process operatives in manufacturing and certain forms of administrative work – which tended to be concentrated in the middle of the wage distribution. Goos and Manning (2007) report that, over recent years, the UK has experienced one of the largest declines

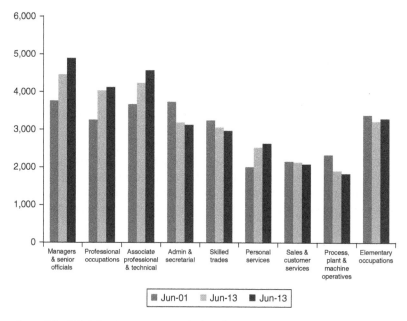

*Figure 5.2* UK jobs by occupational classification (SOC 2000, in thousands), March 2013

in mid-range occupations amongst comparable nations, although some modest growth in lower and higher skilled work has continued. However, polarization of the wage distribution is less than might be expected (Holmes and Mayhew 2012). Although the reasons for this are complex, an important factor is that job categories generally considered to be well-paid contain an increasing number of lower-paid jobs. As Boudon (1974, p.157) argues, changes in the distribution of occupations lead to changes in their sociological meaning. Despite high-status titles – such as 'manager' – many such jobs offer mediocre pay and underutilize the skills and abilities of an increasingly well-qualified workforce. It is also likely that the continued presence of substantial amounts of middle-paid work is partly due to displacement of formerly high-paid workers as their skills command less of a premium. The increased supply of people qualified for knowledge work, alongside the growth of 'digital Taylorism' in which such work is increasingly codified and subjected to industrial processes, has led to increased downward pressure on certain forms of professional and managerial employment (Brown et al. 2011).

Further down the earnings distribution, Holmes and Mayhew (2012) find an increase in low-wage work (see also Lloyd et al. 2008), partly because of a decline in mid-range routine work but also because of decreasing unionization in many sectors. For the lowest earners, pay levels have increasingly fallen behind: Figure 5.3 shows the widening gaps between the hourly pay of the lowest 10 per cent and lowest 25 per cent of earners on the one hand, and their counterparts at the opposite end of the pay distribution. These changes in occupational and earnings structures have affected the prospects of young people, as experienced adult workers have been displaced from mid-range employment, intensifying competition at the bottom of the labour market. Moreover, it is becoming increasingly difficult to progress from low-level work into better quality jobs; the notion that so-called entry-level employment

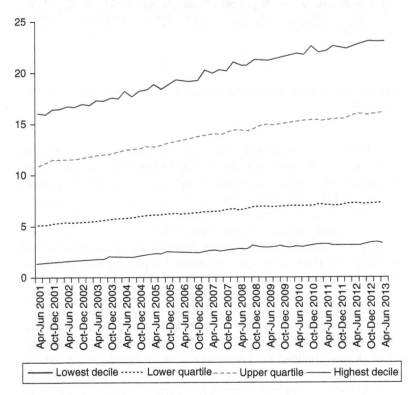

*Figure 5.3* Distribution of gross hourly earnings (£/hour), of all employees earning less than £100/hr in UK, 2001–2013

provides a stepping-stone to better things is increasingly untenable (Bell and Blanchflower 2010).

It is increasingly understood that work does not necessarily offer a way out of poverty: low pay rates, often combined with long-term underemployment associated with part-time, temporary and casual work have led to benefit claimants in work outnumbering the unemployed. Indeed, in-work benefits now subsidize wages to the degree that David Byrne has written about the recreation of the Speenhamland system in twenty-first-century Britain (Byrne 2005, p.111). Although the salaries of high earners continue to rise, average real wages have been declining since 2009 (ONS 2013d) and increasing numbers of people have dipped below the level of the living wage (£8.80 per hour in London; £7.65 per hour outside the capital in November 2013). Whilst, in 2009, 3.4 million people in the UK were paid below the living wage, by late 2013, this figure had risen to 4.8 million, or 20 per cent of the workforce. More than three-quarters of employees under the age of 20 earn less than the living wage (Resolution Foundation 2013). Indeed, in recent years, single young people under 35 have been the hardest hit in terms of living standards and job prospects: in this group, the number with incomes below half what they need for an adequate living standard rose from 100,000 in 2008–2009 to nearly 200,000 in 2010–2011 (Padley and Hirsch 2013).

The employment relations involved in work are also important. In the case of traditional conceptions of professional or managerial work, employment is on the basis of a service contract relationship, in which levels of service to the employer rather than discrete parcels of time are exchanged for a salary. By contrast, more routine, lower-skilled employment operates according to more closely defined and surveilled labour processes. Since the work of John Goldthorpe and his colleagues during the 1970s and 1980s (see, for example, Goldthorpe 1980), the nature of employment relations has formed the basis of socio-economic classifications in the UK, most recently exemplified in the NS-SEC[3] system used by the Office of National Statistics. Using this system, Figure 5.4 shows changes in the socio-economic status of jobs in the UK since 2001. The growth in professional and managerial employment over this period reflects the pattern in Figure 5.2.

High skills are not the only route to competitive advantage. An economy can be successfully run on a low-skill basis as long as it maintains good growth and low unemployment, even if productivity is unimpressive (Coleman and Keep 2001). In fact, the UK economy relies substantially on low-cost, low-specification and often low-quality goods

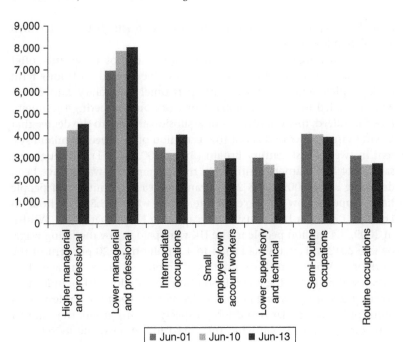

*Figure 5.4*  UK jobs by socio-economic classification (NS-SEC, in thousands), 2001–2013
*Source*: Sissons and Jones (2012, p.20)

and services which are affordable for those on low incomes, either at home or abroad. It is still largely trapped in what Finegold and Soskice (1988) famously described as a 'low-skill equilibrium'. Moreover, the post-colonial assumption that developing economies will be content with a global division of labour which allows Western nations like the UK to cream off more profitable and highly-skilled production processes is increasingly untenable. There is substantial evidence that such economies are able to compete with Western nations on the basis of both cost and quality (Diamond 2008, p.1), and recent skills panics concerning the UK's lowly position in global league tables[4] suggest that this is now understood, particularly in relation to the huge numbers of graduates produced by countries such as India and China.

Whilst government and employer groups call for more flexible labour markets in the pursuit of economic growth, it is easy to lose sight of what this means for ordinary people. The factors determining labour market flexibility fall into three main groups. Functional flexibility refers to an employer's ability to transfer workers between different tasks; a functional workforce tends to be multi-skilled and trained for a range of work roles. Supply-side flexibility includes factors such as the nature and effectiveness of a country's education and training system, but also refers to numerical flexibility: an employer's ability to adjust the size and composition of its workforce according to market conditions or adjust their working hours. Increasing numerical flexibility therefore entails weakening employment protection legislation. Finally, labour-cost flexibility includes not only micro-level arrangements such as incentives and bonuses, but also national minimum wage policies and legislation affecting the operation of collective pay bargaining. In 2013, the UK was ranked tenth out of 144 world economies in terms of labour-market flexibility (WEF 2013), and many economists agree that this has to some extent protected the UK against job losses. Although some aspects of flexible labour markets could support high-skills strategies and improved working conditions, in practice it has been achieved by emasculation of the trade unions, structural unemployment, weaker employment protection than in many other European countries and low minimum wage levels.

The contrast between these aspects of flexible labour markets and social democratic models of industrial citizenship is identified by Standing (2011, p.10) as one of the defining features of precarious labour market engagement. Standing suggests that growing numbers of people work under conditions in which few, if any, forms of labour market security are available. Functional, labour-cost and numerical flexibility lead to reduced security in terms of job role, income and tenure, whilst other forms of security – including the opportunity to develop and deploy skills, to be represented effectively by trade unions and to enjoy reasonable working conditions – are threatened by decreased protection and regulation of employment. For example, in a relatively recent development, zero hours contracts – where staff are required to work whenever an employer requires them to do so but are not actually guaranteed any work at all – are becoming the norm in some sectors of employment. Whilst official estimates from the Labour Force Survey put the number of workers on zero-hours contracts at around 250,000, this is likely to be an underestimate (Pyper and McGuiness 2013). According to the Chartered Institute of Personnel and Development, in mid-2013 over a million people in the UK were employed in this way. The retailer Sports Direct employs 20,000 of its 23,000 workforce under zero-hours arrangements, and around 90 per cent of those working for the fast-food giant McDonald's are employed on zero-hours contracts (BBC

2013). Although young workers and those aged over 50 are most likely to be employed in this way, women returning to work after having children and migrant workers are also particularly vulnerable to insecure forms of employment, and poor terms and conditions. Nowadays, underemployment is arguably as significant as unemployment.

Some of these trends may be understood in terms of segmented labour market theory (Tomlinson and Walker 2010). This proposes that labour markets are not unitary, but segmented in various ways within and between industries. In some versions of the theory, terms such as primary and secondary labour markets are used, the emphasis being on distinctions between industries or the quality of employment offered at different levels within an industry. In other versions, the terms core and periphery are used to recognize that different kinds of labour market may exist within a single company. Either way, markets for more advantaged workers are contrasted with those less fortunate. Primary or core labour markets are characterized by more stable employment, progressive career ladders and higher wage returns to education. Secondary or peripheral labour markets offer little security, poorer working conditions, few qualification requirements, and little opportunity for career progression.

The objective conditions of labour markets in the UK and many other countries make it difficult to avoid mobilizing the Marxist concept of the reserve army of labour (Marx 1867/1976, p.781) to conceptualize the working lives of many ordinary people – although as Bourdieu (1998, p.98) points out, 'army' is not the most apposite term to describe the contemporary landscape of mass unemployment and underemployment, which effectively isolates, individualizes and demobilizes large sections of the population. Either way, the creation of an expendable pool of surplus labour serves two main functions. Firstly, employers are able to maintain or expand production whilst driving down labour costs; and secondly, a pool of unemployed workers provides capital with a powerful disciplinary tool as replacements can be drafted in if existing workers are not sufficiently cheap or obedient. Whilst such processes are less potent in times of high employment or where individuals possess scarce skills, they are particularly effective in post-industrial capitalist societies where workers are often relatively easy to replace, particularly in low-skill areas of the service sector (Byrne 2005, p.42). Byrne (2005, pp.106–107) sees the UK labour market as becoming split into three identifiable parts. This, he argues, comprises a small elite of privileged workers who have benefited from post-industrial change and whose terms and conditions have improved substantially in absolute and relative terms; an intermediate category of workers who, despite being better qualified than their parents and grandparents, are often less well paid and have more insecure jobs; and a large pool of disposable labour engaged in various forms of poorly paid, precarious employment. Those located in this latter category effectively consti-tute the reserve army of labour, shifting in and out of work as they are required.

## Young people and the labour market

Young people are particularly disadvantaged within the labour market and, although this disadvantage decreases with age and qualification levels, it remains significant. Furthermore, whilst it is generally agreed that since 2008 job opportunities for young people have been hard hit by recession, structural changes in the UK economy over several decades have driven a secular decline in youth employment. The great majority of employers in the UK do not recruit any young people direct from education, and those that do so are more likely to recruit those leaving higher education (see Table 5.1). Sectors which recruit school or col-lege leavers – notably retail, community and personal services, and the catering industry – tend to offer low-skilled employment unlikely to pro-vide secure work. Young people are more often employed on a part-time and/or temporary basis, and much of their employment is concentrated in the sectors just mentioned, although health and social work, con-struction, and manufacturing are also significant employers of young people (UKCES 2011). In Figures 5.5 and 5.6, we see the distribution of working young people across industry sectors and occupational groups; whilst service sector employment has always been important for young people, these distributions parallel the decline in manufacturing and other traditional industries.

In some ways, the reasons why young people find it difficult to gain a foothold in the labour market are obvious: 16-year-old school-leavers in particular are likely to have lower levels of qualification and to lack experience of the world of work, and may lack the qualities which older workers are likely to bring. As competition for employment intensifies, many young people encounter a 'Catch 22': without experience they cannot find work; without work they cannot accumulate experience. Nevertheless, skills panics over young people's supposed lack of 'work-readiness' are exaggerated. In a large-scale survey of employers across the UK, 59 per cent of companies in England, Northern Ireland and Wales recruiting 16-year-old school-leavers found them to be well-prepared for

Table 5.1  Recruitment of education leavers by sector (in England, Northern Ireland and Wales)

| | Any education leavers | 16-year-olds from school | 17–18-year-olds from school | 17–18-year-olds from further education | From higher education |
|---|---|---|---|---|---|
| Overall | 24 | 7 | 9 | 8 | 10 |
| *By sector* | | | | | |
| Agriculture | 18 | 7 | 6 | 5 | 3 |
| Mining and quarrying | 18 | 9 | 11 | 3 | 9 |
| Manufacturing | 23 | 8 | 9 | 7 | 7 |
| Electricity, gas, water | 21 | 6 | 7 | 8 | 8 |
| Construction | 21 | 10 | 6 | 7 | 3 |
| Wholesale and retail | 26 | 11 | 12 | 11 | 9 |
| Hotels and restaurants | 33 | 12 | 17 | 15 | 13 |
| Transport and communications | 18 | 4 | 5 | 5 | 9 |
| Financial services | 25 | 4 | 8 | 7 | 15 |
| Business services | 19 | 3 | 5 | 5 | 11 |
| Public administration | 24 | 4 | 9 | 9 | 17 |
| Education | 45 | 6 | 10 | 12 | 34 |
| Health and social work | 29 | 5 | 10 | 12 | 14 |
| Community, social and personal services | 28 | 11 | 10 | 10 | 10 |

*Source:* UKCES (2012).

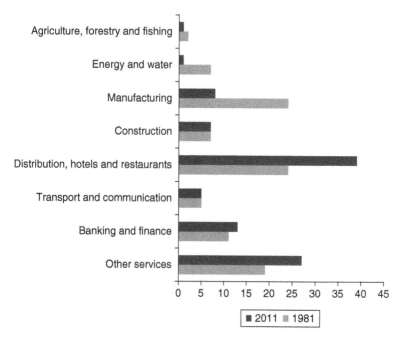

*Figure 5.5* Employment of young people age 16–24 by industry sector (%), 1981 and 2011
*Source*: Sissons and Jones (2012, p.20)

*Figure 5.6* Employment of young people age 16–24 no longer in full-time education, by occupational group, Oct–Dec 2011
*Source*: Young People in Work 2012 (ONS 2012).

work, rising to 82 per cent of those recruiting from institutions of higher education (UKCES 2012). For older school-leavers and those leaving further education, satisfaction was 64 per cent and 72 per cent, respectively. For the majority of young people, their work-readiness is therefore less of an issue than competition for employment affecting all age groups; that is, their suitability for employment is an issue of *relative* rather than *absolute* employability:

> For some employers the sheer volume and calibre of candidates available allowed them to raise their recruitment standards. This has the effect of further disadvantaging low skill candidates and bars candidates who would have been acceptable in the past... [However,] while tackling employability issues is important, there is a risk that employability skills become over-stated as an issue in tackling youth unemployment.
>
> (UKCES 2011 p.19)

The most vulnerable young people are the most affected. Research in a range of OECD countries shows that obtaining work with poor terms and conditions, job insecurity and a lack of progression opportunities is even more likely for NEET young people than for others (Scarpetta et al. 2010).

The importance accorded to 'soft' skills, particularly by service sector employers, is well documented (UKCES 2011; 2012; Sissons and Jones 2012). Whilst this term is not particularly well defined, it is generally understood as including self-motivation, time management, a sense of responsibility and the ability to relate to others. Many employers who do not recruit recent school-leavers report deficiencies in these skills (and more diffuse qualities such as 'common sense') as key reasons for rejecting young applicants (UKCES 2011, p.18). A particular issue raised by employers is that young people often lack understanding of competence-based recruitment processes, and fail to recognize the importance of responding to interview questions in ways appropriate to the company's needs (p.19). For young people lacking work experience and specific job-related skills, being rich in the forms of identity capital (Coté 1996) discussed in Chapter 3 therefore places them at a significant advantage relative to their peers; conversely, vulnerable young people in the NEET category, who are often reported as lacking confidence, self-esteem and self-presentation skills, are likely to be further marginalized.

Young people often draw on family, friends and other social networks for advice and information on finding work. However, particularly amongst those from working-class backgrounds, this often leads to traditional – and now arguably ineffective – job-search strategies (Shildrick et al. 2012a). Whilst formal application procedures based on web-based advertising, online applications and employment agencies are increasingly preferred by large employers – in theory at least – we found that the young people in our research often relied upon localized networks and communication with family, friends and other personal contacts. Unsolicited applications, sometimes by email or post but often involving dropping off a CV at an employer's premises were also used. In some cases, this appeared to have a partly symbolic function, demonstrating that the young person was doing something to find work. As a new mother, Hailey was anxious that her partner should find permanent employment to increase their income and also demonstrate commitment as a breadwinner; however, her preferred strategy involved footwork rather than more formal methods:

> I'm hoping that he gets some work. He just needs a job that is steady instead of not knowing when he's going to be working. And he needs to know how much he is being paid every week or every month because he just doesn't know...

> I said to Peter print some of your CVs out and go round and you can hand them out but he said he weren't going to do it because he didn't like doing that. So I said 'do you expect them to walk up to you and go "hello"?' It don't work like that because there are about 2 million people that are unemployed so you've got to fight for it.
> (Hailey interview 18.11.2011)

Sometimes informal strategies worked: as we will see, Sean found work as a trainee chef by responding to an advertisement placed in the employer's window, and Jasmine was able to obtain work with a private care provider through her friend Jess, who already worked for the company. For Sara, a participant who we met through a course for young expectant mothers, the opportunities for immediate financial and social rewards, but also the insecurity and social immobility, offered by work obtained through social networks were evident. On leaving school after a troubled education in which she truanted throughout Year 11, Sara obtained work with her father:

> We worked for a bit on the construction site and sometimes we'd be in the van all day driving to Hull emptying the van, and if he were there now I'd be there if I weren't pregnant because I want to get back

into work... I loved that work... I was the only female there but I got along with them because I get along with boys more than girls. [It was long hours] but, at that time, it was a lot of money. And I like having a routine. [But after] about six months... there wasn't the work for me so my dad carried on and then it got to, like, two days a week and then eventually there was no work at all.

[I was upset when I lost my job] because when you come straight from school and you're earning £120 a week and I could go out and buy me own clothes and then that just stopped... After I finished with my dad I got depressed and then went to work with my mum... at the dye factory... packing the dye and putting dye into pots and making big tins of paint... from seven in the morning to half four [and I was getting about £230 a week there.

                                                                (Interview 24/03/2011)

Tendencies towards social reproduction may be intensified by the potential of early low-skilled employment to divert young people's attention from the longer-term benefits of staying in education or training, particularly when courses experienced in the past have seemed of little value. The kind of 'hyper-conventional' work ethic described by MacDonald et al. (2005), and also uncovered in our own research, may cause young people to prioritize work – any work – over learning, particularly when their experience shows the limited labour-market returns of any qualifications they are likely to obtain in the foreseeable future. In Jasmine's words, 'I don't need to be in college, I need to be in a job' (Russell et al. 2011a).

Although most jobs available to young people in contemporary Britain are of poor quality, for many people they are still preferable to unemployment. Shildrick et al. (2012a) discuss a range of evidence that even low-skilled, low-paid work can be preferable to being out of work, and this was evident in some of the data from our research. For Steph, who obtained a position as an assistant in the café of a large supermarket in January 2012, this was certainly the case:

Steph says she is working really hard, she has signed a contract for 10 hours a week but usually works between 40–50 hours. She is working 6 days a week at present with Tuesdays off. She was in at 6.15am this morning, preparing and cooking food for breakfast, now she is 18 years old she has cooking responsibilities. She is on £4.95 an hour; this will not increase until she is 21. She says she isn't bothered as she has enough money. She is talking about moving out of her dad's and getting a one-bedroomed flat in Northdale, she says her dad … drove her into work this morning on the way to his cleaning work.

(Field notes 26.04.12)

When I arrive at [the supermarket] I see Steph sitting with her manager at a table doing paperwork, she comes over and explains that her boss is busy, I order a hot chocolate and ask Steph how she is; she replies that she is well. She is dressed in black and maroon uniform, apron and hat with her hair tied back. She seems to look at ease and knows how to talk to customers and manage food orders and the till with confidence.

(Field notes 26.09.12)

Sean, the subject of one of the detailed case studies in this book, had similar experiences working for a multinational restaurant chain. However, the degree to which low-paid, low-skilled work can promote well-being, appears to depend strongly on the working conditions involved; as we will see in other cases, poor work can have detrimental consequences.

## Half our future? Educating the 'missing middle' and below

In the UK and many other countries, the policy response to young people being unable to find work is that they should remain in or return to education in order to increase their attractiveness to employers. Increasing educational opportunities promises to bring benefits to the whole of society, and educational achievement is a central factor in individual social mobility. However, as Bernstein (1971, p.47) points out, how a society distributes educational knowledge reflects broader distributions of power and principles of social control. Measures such as raising the age of compulsory education or training cannot be seen in isolation from the curriculum problem: what will be learned by those who may not otherwise have continued in education, and to what ends? Since the debates over the 1944 Education Act, and the subsequent introduction of a tripartite system of secondary education, this has been a fiercely contested political issue (Simon 1999). Solved initially by limiting grammar school places and excluding secondary modern pupils from public examinations, restricted opportunities for up to 80 per cent of schoolchildren became increasingly untenable. Particular concern was expressed about institutional and curriculum arrangements for pupils of average ability and below, leading to the Newsom Report (CACE 1963), whose title *Half Our Futures* spoke eloquently for an educational system which would provide opportunities for the many young people poorly served by the post-war reforms. More recently, Hodgson and Spours (2013) argue that a 'missing middle' – those below the top 30 per cent of attainers but not NEET – constitute an important group of young people who were supported only in limited ways by New Labour because of incompleteness and contradictions in its 14–19 reforms, and are now largely overlooked by Coalition policy.

Debates over curriculum are bound up with the question of *educability*: whether a process that could legitimately be called education can be extended to all without submerging the best minds and thereby ensuring long-term economic decline. The counter-argument, that every country contains a limited pool of talent, has been a recurring theme as the educational system has expanded, and was explicitly addressed in the Robbins Report on higher education in the 1960s. In its contemporary form, the pool of talent thesis is expressed in doubts over the wisdom of mass higher education, and the fierce defence of the A-level 'gold standard' against calls for an integrated system of academic and vocational education. For students variously deemed as disaffected, of low ability or disengaged from education, these debates have been effectively concluded: the explanation for their failure, according to the dominant discourse, is that they are unsuited to academic learning and must therefore be re-engaged by more practical activities.

Whilst bridging the academic–vocational divide is a constant theme of policy discussion, and various forms of broadened post-16 study have emerged – for example, the now-defunct 14–19 Diplomas (Hodgson and Spours 2010) – all have tended to fall by the wayside. The alternative approach, employed by both the Coalition Government and its Labour predecessors, has been a discourse of vocationalism which, whilst seeking to valorize work-based learning as an alternative to academic study, nevertheless positions it as a second-best pathway aimed largely at lower-attaining young people. This entails the promotion of hands-on learning as a more attractive alternative to academic work, at least for certain sections of the population. These are the young people deemed to be 'good with their hands, not their heads', for whom learning activities involving writing or calculation must be kept to the barest minimum (Thomson and Russell 2009). However, as Fuller and Unwin (2011) observe, 'The way knowledge is conceptualized and integrated in vocational curricula is a critical indicator of the character of provision, including the extent to which it provides a platform for progression and supports the development of "vocational practice"' (p.197). Whilst the idea that work-based learning can offer *all* young people an alternative route to success is attractive, the exclusionary potential of a system which separates the practical from the academic is obvious. The association between such pedagogies and the social control of disaffection has been critiqued by Bernstein, who points out that substituting the practical for the academic 'occurs usually with the less "able" children whom we have given up educating' (Bernstein 1971, p.58). Indeed, the Wolf Review (2011) highlighted research findings that many low-level vocational training programmes provide participants with little or no advantage when seeking employment and, in some cases, may have *negative* labour market returns. Whilst the reasons for this are unclear, one possible explanation is that the low quality of such programmes may stigmatize participants and deter potential employers from offering them work. In spite of such evidence, the reconstitution of a tripartite system within post-compulsory education, based on academic education for the most advantaged, apprenticeships or general vocational qualifications for the next tier, and for the rest various forms of applied or work-based learning, appears to be now entrenched in policy discourse (Hodgson and Spours 2011, p.211).

## Apprenticeships

Since the 1990s, there have been various attempts to revive an apprenticeship system laid waste by de-industrialization. Since the relaunch of Modern Apprenticeships in the Cassels Report (DfES 2001), this mode of training has increasingly been seen, both as a central component of the tripartite post-16 system discussed above, and as a means of addressing youth unemployment and rebalancing the workforce towards manufacturing. However, the number of apprentices is still relatively low compared with many other countries; in 2010 there were 11 apprentices for every 1,000 employees in England, compared with 39 in Australia, 40 in Germany and 43 in Switzerland. In Germany, almost all firms with over 500 employees take on apprentices, while in England less than one-third of very large firms do so (IPPR 2011, p.9). The status of apprenticeships also differs between England and many other countries, where apprenticeships are offered at Level 3 or above; in England, whilst Advanced Level and Higher Apprenticeships are at Level 3 and Level 4, respectively, Level 2 Apprenticeships are also offered. Table 5.2

Table 5.2 Apprenticeships in England, 2011–2012

| | Apprenticeships | | | | |
| | Intermediate Level Apprenticeship | Advanced Level Apprenticeship | Higher Apprenticeship | Total Apprenticeships | % |
|---|---|---|---|---|---|
| **Total learners** | 506,200 | 317,000 | 5,700 | 806,500 | 100.0% |
| **Age** | | | | | |
| Under 19 | 144,200 | 53,300 | 500 | 189,600 | 23.5% |
| 19–24 | 159,100 | 118,900 | 2,900 | 272,100 | 33.7% |
| 25–49 | 166,800 | 127,500 | 2,100 | 291,500 | 36.1% |
| 50+ | 36,200 | 17,300 | 200 | 53,200 | 6.6% |
| Female | 256,400 | 172,500 | 3,400 | 420,200 | 52.1% |
| Male | 249,800 | 144,500 | 2,300 | 386,300 | 47.9% |

*Source:* Data Service (2013).

shows the distribution of apprenticeships across these levels. The minimum hourly pay rate for apprentices aged under 19, or those in the first year of their apprenticeship, was £2.68 in October 2013, compared with the National Minimum Wage rates of £3.67 for 16–17-year-olds, £5.03 for those aged 18–20 and £6.31 for adults. From 2010, employers meeting certain criteria were eligible for the Apprenticeship Grant for Employers, which initially[5] involved a payment of up to £2,500 for apprentices aged 16–17 who had previously been NEET (Wiseman et al. 2011).

Fuller et al. (2013) suggest that, whilst apprenticeship is a resilient model of vocational training, its traditional functions have always included at least two further dimensions in addition to skill formation: firstly, to provide a framework of social control directed towards constructing the young worker as good citizen; and secondly, to bridge the space between education and work, communities and employment, as well as between generations. In recent years, successive governments have championed apprenticeships, and their take-up has increased greatly since 2010. However, Fuller et al. (2013, p.64) argue that, since 2001, UK government policy has increasingly seen the apprenticeship system as a vehicle for the pursuit of social inclusion and, under the Coalition Government, as part of a strategy aimed at rebalancing skill supply as a means of achieving economic growth. The resulting tensions are difficult to overcome.

The term apprenticeship has long been associated with notions of craft, skill and job-security, and the notion of 'earning and learning' has an enduring appeal, especially to young working-class people and their parents. However, the attractiveness of apprenticeships to young people and their families has not been matched by their availability, and demand greatly exceeds the available places. The Wolf Review (2011) suggested an average figure of 15 applicants for each apprenticeship place, and for some high-profile schemes, such as those offered by BT and Rolls-Royce, competition is even more intense. Furthermore, whilst apprenticeships can play a positive role in helping young people into employment, in many instances, the training involved is very different from traditional conceptions of vocational education, and certain apprenticeship programmes stretch the meaning of the term. Fuller and Unwin (2012) draw attention to the short duration of many apprenticeship schemes – for example, apprenticeships for supermarket work and the like are often shorter than six months, and provide low-level qualifications with little labour market value. The practice of conversions, whereby existing employees are reclassified as apprentices, and the high proportion of apprentices who are over 25 – some as old as 60 – have also been highlighted as weaknesses of the present system. More than 40 per cent of apprenticeships in 2011–2012 were held by people over the age of 25 (see Table 5.2). There is also a significant under-representation of males in Higher Apprenticeship programmes, nearly 60 per cent of which are held by women.

In our research, holding or aspiring to an apprenticeship was not uncommon, with seven participants offered places or beginning programmes. However, apprenticeships were often not a happy experience, and none of these young people completed their programmes. Long hours, ill-health and the difficulty of combining work with study were the reasons given for this, although in some cases one wonders whether employers understood the nature of apprenticeships and entered too lightly into arrangements. This appears to have been the case for Johnny, who moved from Middlebridge to Birmingham and found work in a kennels business:

> Normally, I work Monday, Tuesday morning, all day Thursday, Friday and Saturday, and Sunday afternoon. Morning shifts are five hours and we get there for seven and we're out with the dogs till nearly eight... After we've done we'll walk them again for an hour and a half... we'll do more cleaning kennels and then, at eleven, we'll start walking the boarders again. After we've done that we'll do anything else that wants doing and then we're finished [the shift]...
>
> (Interview 30.3.2011)

Andrea, the owner, had agreed to provide an apprenticeship in Animal Management – Johnny was particularly insistent on his status as an apprentice, even though he had not yet started attending college:

> Johnny: I've been back at the kennels for a month [My first wage packet] comes on Friday... I'm getting the apprenticeship wage.
> Lisa: So do you have a day release at college or something like that? Yeah, but it doesn't start until September.
> Lisa: So at the minute you're just working and that will turn into the apprenticeship? It is the apprenticeship. Apart from my day release the college will come and see me every four weeks.
> Lisa: And that's going to be starting in September.
> At the college but the apprenticeship has already started.
>
> (Interview 30.3.2011)

Contact with Johnny was intermittent during this period because of the distance involved; at his next interview, in November, it transpired that the apprenticeship had ended after a few weeks at college in September:

> It was a joint agreement between me and Andrea ... to see if it worked and I was doing too many hours at the kennels ... I was working seven days a week and nearly seven or eight hours a day ... [I was coping] but it was still a struggle because I've got injuries to both knees and it was demanding to keep walking so it was just better that I leave. But it was a joint agreement ... the college course finished ... [because] when you don't have an apprenticeship you can't continue in college.
>
> (Interview 11.11.2011)

As we will see later, ill-health and the difficulty of combining college with work also led to apprenticeships being terminated in the cases of Sean and Isla. It is clear that, for the most vulnerable young people, obtaining an apprenticeship is by no means the end of the story; the degree of understanding and support provided is a significant factor in whether the programme is completed.

## Interventions for NEET young people: Policy and practice

Youth unemployment – particularly where vulnerable young people are concerned – is a complex problem requiring both supply-side and demand-side interventions. Consequently, policies in this area have always involved a range of government departments; co-ordinated strategies have been difficult to construct, and one initiative has followed another with little sustained effect. As we saw in Chapter 3, during the 1980s and 1990s youth training schemes became discredited because of low-quality provision, inadequate supply of training places and the expansion of full-time general education as an alternative to work-based learning. The Cassels Report (DfES 2001) acknowledged the continuing need for provision aimed at vulnerable young people, and in 2002 a new pathway was introduced. Entry to Employment (E2E) was conceived initially as pre-apprenticeship provision for young people having 'low levels of prior attainment, social or behavioural problems which stand in the way of sustained participation, or limitations on their innate ability' (DfES 2001, p.27). Whilst E2E had some strengths, and was often delivered by dedicated and highly motivated practitioners, it suffered from a number of deficiencies. Often, the young people referred to it by Connexions had needs too complex to be addressed by a relatively short-term programme; progression to further study or employment was not well-supported by its curriculum content; and the quality of provision, especially the work placements offered, was variable (Simmons and Thompson 2011). In Fernside and Northdale, the majority of young people completing E2E became NEET shortly afterwards.

Amongst these deficiencies, the lack of a qualifications-led approach was a particular government concern, and E2E was replaced by Foundation Learning in 2010. However, criticisms of many low-level qualifications in the Wolf Review (2011) largely overshadowed this programme, which in any case was found to be less effective in supporting vulnerable young people than E2E had been (Ofsted 2013). Indeed, critical issues such as the quality of work placements, support for progression – particularly the development of literacy and numeracy skills – and programme completion rates were largely carried over from E2E. Foundation Learning also highlighted the tension between attempting to provide vulnerable learners with the opportunity to achieve meaningful qualifications and their immediate needs, which often focus on creating the conditions under which they can re-engage with learning of any form. Practitioners frequently warned about this tension during our research.

> [The] biggest response we get here, when we bring up the question of training, is 'I'm not going back; I'm bored!' I mean sometimes the young people are bored because the training isn't stimulating and it isn't meeting their needs because it is classroom based and it's pen and paper and that isn't engaging some young people at all...The harder to help young people don't really see the value of qualifications...I would say [low-level qualifications] have no particular significance for employers [either]. But it can be seen as an achievement for young people to help them see that they are getting somewhere and that they have got something to write on their CV because if they come with nothing then they have no chance.
>
> (Careers practitioner)

From August 2013, young people with similar needs came within the remit of yet another initiative, the 16–19 Study Programmes. In our research, the lack of stability represented by these frequently changing initiatives caused some frustration amongst practitioners. Another careers practitioner summed up more than a decade of change:

> Every time something has been suggested and gets under way then the whole thing is completely removed and something else comes along and it starts all over again. So we've had – in my memory over the last 16 or so years – the Learning Gateway; then E2E which [was] a much more pre-apprenticeship programme and that was not appropriate for a lot of young people...and now we've got Foundation Learning which is very much focused on qualifications. And the funding regime is [also] focused on qualifications so training providers...cannot give as much time and attention...because they can't afford to. So funding regimes repeatedly have actually worked to produce uninspiring courses for young people because...they've always gone the wrong way and then, after a couple of years, they change and then a couple more years and everything is up in the air again.

Perhaps unsurprisingly, many of the young people participating in our study did not have particularly positive attitudes towards the employability programmes to which they were often directed. Jed, a care leaver with frequently changing job aspirations, felt particularly under pressure and beset by conflicting advice. At the time of this interview, he had recently taken up a place with a training provider offering Foundation Learning programmes, after having his benefits reduced as an 'incentive':

> [One] minute they're telling me one thing and the next minute they are telling me something completely different and that really annoys me. Basically, Heather gives me advice on jobs and training downstairs but she and everyone else is just saying to me 'why can't you go and find your own jobs and be like everyone else?' But they are there to help me and when I do go and try to find my own jobs they always put me down. They've asked me to do certain things but I don't want to do them...Like training and stuff...I don't want to go to them. I just said to Heather 'I don't want to go there'. And then she says 'Oh, we'll find you something else' but it somehow always comes back to one of these training places...I'd rather do some work.
>
> (Interview 17.11.2011)

Young people's perceptions of training were not wholly negative. In general, they spoke highly of practitioners, and some participants identified specific features of value in the courses they attended. However, their attitude towards such programmes tended to deteriorate with time, and they often spoke of repetition and lack of progression as particularly frustrating. In general, we found that training programmes aimed at 'disengaged' young people were ineffective in supporting progression, and by far the most common destination for those participants who completed them was back to being NEET. The exceptions were those few programmes which provided young people with skills for which there was a labour-market demand. For example, Jackson, a young man who closely resembled 'the lads' of Paul Willis (1977) in his working-class hyper-masculinity and resistance to schooling, had wanted to be a PE teacher but abandoned this (somewhat tenuous) ambition after acquiring a criminal record. Eventually, he was directed to a training provider which ran courses in motor-vehicle maintenance, and had the staff and facilities necessary to train young people in welding. Jackson responded well, motivated by the fact that his brother-in-law knew the owner of a firm which required welders. Although he became unemployed after completing his course, Jackson eventually found employment as a welder, working 45 hours a week for an hourly pay of £11.82, and receiving a three-year contract with this firm:

> I went to the Jobcentre and I found a job through them. I'd been unemployed for about 18 weeks before I got this job. I had a good personal adviser at the Jobcentre. She was the best one because she had loads of contacts and her husband works at a firm... She's my mum's friend and that's why I asked for her... it's good pay. And I get bonuses for doing a good job. I get a 250 quid Christmas bonus.
>
> (Interview 23/11/2012)

Jackson said that he found the skills acquired at his training provider helpful, and his working life seemed a reflection of the youth transitions of earlier generations. Speaking of his workmates, he outlined an experience of work unlike that of any other participant:

> They're all old; they're all like in their fifties and stuff. There are a couple of young ones as well who are my mates and we go out for a few bevvies and stuff after work [on] Friday nights. But I only have a couple and then I go home to bed.
>
> (Interview 23/11/2012)

We do not wish to romanticize Jackson's experience, and this outcome was a result of several contingent factors involving social networks. Not everyone can be a welder, and not everyone who completed courses at this provider found work. But it does illustrate what is possible when skill supply coincides with the demand for labour, suggesting that engagement activities which relate to the local labour market may have more chance of success than those focusing solely on personal and inter-personal skills.

E2E and Foundation Learning were delivered by public, private and voluntary sector organizations, which were expected to work in partnership with Connexions, other local agencies and employers, and to provide expertise in working with young people having complex needs. However, this kind of co-ordinated provision has become increasingly difficult to achieve in a period during which far-reaching changes have occurred in information, advice and guidance (IAG) services for young people. Published under Gordon Brown's Labour government, the report *Unleashing Aspirations* (HM Government 2010) recommended a fundamental overhaul of IAG in England. Although Ofsted had found good IAG provision in 12 out of 16 areas visited, satisfaction levels amongst young people were reported to be low, and the report considered that Connexions had 'focussed on the disadvantaged minority to the detriment of the aspirational majority' (p.6).

Since 2010, IAG services have been reshaped and significantly reduced. In many local authorities, Connexions was effectively dismantled and replaced by the new all-age National Careers Service (NCS), although local authorities retained a statutory duty to support vulnerable young people up to the age of 19 (24 in the case of those with learning difficulties and disabilities). However, the NCS receives less funding than Connexions and, most notably, operates mainly via telephone helplines and online material rather than through personal advisers. Whilst NEET young people under the age of 25 are entitled to three face-to-face guidance sessions with a NCS adviser each year, it has been argued that the new arrangements limit access to support, particularly for the most vulnerable (Institute of Careers Guidance 2011; Sissons and Jones 2012). Evaluations of programmes for NEET young people have consistently indicated that the quality of the relationship with IAG staff is a significant factor in the effectiveness of interventions (Spielhofer et al. 2009), and research on the Connexions service highlighted the importance of personal advisers responding to the needs and interests of young people (Hoggarth and Smith 2004, p.14). Establishing a relationship based on trust and respect between personal advisers and young people was also highlighted as a key factor in evaluations of Activity Agreements[6] (Hillage et al. 2008, p.32). Evaluation of more recent programmes has reinforced this point (McCrone et al. 2013, pp.60–61); however, as we will see in Chapter 9, the young people in our research often felt that they were not listened to and that practitioners were pursuing their own agendas.

Other research findings include the importance of flexible learning programmes, in terms of start dates, attendance patterns and course content as well as the use of experiential learning approaches involving team working, peer mentoring and project work. Induction arrangements and on-going communication between providers, young people and employers are also important (Spielhofer et al. 2009). There is some evidence to indicate that relatively modest financial incentives can also help to re-engage young people in learning, although such incentives do not necessarily reach those most in need (Hillage et al. 2008, p.32; Spielhofer et al. 2009, p.7). A major challenge faced by provision of this nature is the need to compensate for previous negative labour market experiences. In an evaluation of one initiative for NEET young people aged 19–24, approximately half of those interviewed by researchers described having had many different types of jobs, and many participants suffered from lack of confidence and low self-esteem (McCrone et al. 2013).

Perhaps the most notable policy initiative for the period of research described in this book has been the Coalition Government's attempt to develop a more holistic strategy on youth unemployment. The 16–24 *Participation Strategy* (HM Government 2011), issued jointly by the Department for Education, the Department for Business, Innovation and Skills, and the Department for Work and Pensions, sets out initiatives on a broad front, including reforms to schools, vocational education, skills and welfare policy. These included reforms spanning all phases of education, but focusing particularly on early interventions with 'at risk' young people and implementing legislation introduced by the previous Labour administration on raising the participation age in England, which would require all young people to continue in some form of education or training (including employment with training) until the age of 18 by 2015. Other educational reforms included increasing the availability of apprenticeships and implementing the key recommendations of the Wolf Review (2011), such as removing the 'perverse incentives' said to have promoted low-quality vocational qualifications, and ensuring that young people obtained credible qualifications in English and mathematics. Although these proposals contained some significant enhancements to education and training provision, they also signalled that cuts in welfare and increased conditionality of benefits would extend to even the most vulnerable young people.

As with New Labour, the Coalition Government's youth unemployment strategy focused upon providing incentivizing employers to take on young people, rather than changing the structure of demand by regulation: wage subsidies, for example, are available to organizations taking on a young person aged 18–24 through Jobcentres or the Work Programme. Under the Participation Strategy, these measures, alongside other subsidies such as the Apprenticeship Grant for Employers, were brought within an overarching Youth Contract, which aimed to 'help get young people learning or earning before long-term damage is done' (HM Government 2011, p.5). The Youth Contract included tailored support for getting the most vulnerable 16–17-year-old NEET young people into education, apprenticeships or employment with training. As with earlier re-engagement programmes, public, private and voluntary organizations compete to provide services to eligible young people on a payment-by-results basis. Although such competition was intended to give organizations the freedom to design innovative and personalized support, early assessments of the Work Programme – a similar scheme for adults – indicated that contractors tended to focus their efforts on individuals who were easier to support than those classified as 'harder-to-help' (NAO 2012).

# 6
# Danny's Story

During the 1970s, authors such as Paul Willis (1977) in *Learning to Labour* and Bowles and Gintis (1976) in *Schooling in Capitalist America* problematized in different ways the role of educational processes in maintaining class differences and preparing young working-class people for a future of blue collar jobs. Whilst Bowles and Gintis developed a 'correspondence principle' between the class division of labour and the workings of differentiated education systems, Willis proposed that one of the central factors in social reproduction was the resistance of young working-class men to their schooling. One of his key arguments was that the behaviour of the young people he observed was, in many ways, a rehearsal for a future of long-term manual employment. The anti-school culture they created sprang from a partial recognition of the determining conditions of the working-class (Willis 1977, p.3), and the limitations of their own future. However, as Willis puts it, 'the tragedy' of this recognition is that it is 'limited, distorted and turned back on themselves', through oppositional behaviour which is ultimately self-defeating. Although the material and social circumstances in which youth transitions now take place are substantially different to those existing in the 1970s, it is still possible to discern elements of both of these accounts in the stories of some of our participants. For Danny, disruptive behaviour had effectively ended his schooling at an early age, and although he later returned to education he found the forms of learning in which he engaged deeply unsatisfying. However, unlike Willis's 'lads', Danny had not been part of an oppositional peer-group within school. Indeed, his resistance had separated him from his friends and closed off opportunities to take part even in working-class labour.

Danny was 17 when he began taking part in our research at the beginning of 2011, and in some ways his background was quite conventional. He was born and brought up in Middlebridge by his mother, who works with adults with special needs, and his long-term stepfather, a mechanic, who he calls 'dad'. Danny had a part-time Saturday job, washing pots in a local restaurant when he was at school; he had a girlfriend for a number of years, although this relationship seemed to have ended before we met him. Danny said that most of his friends were at college or in work, and his stated ambitions were quite conventional, at least at the beginning of the study.

> Lisa: Where would you like to be in five years' time?
> Danny: That would make me 22. Well... I'd like to have my own place; I'd like to have some mode of transport and a female partner. I'd like to be where every 22 year old wants to be.
>
> (Interview 04/03/2011)

Despite this, Danny was not particularly optimistic about either his current situation or his future prospects. To some extent, this was understandable: Danny has a history of youth offending and our first contact with him was through the Fernside Youth Offending Team. Although he was enrolled on an employability programme at the time, Danny had been identified as 'at risk' of becoming NEET. Danny had a history of disrupted schooling and, although he had officially remained on the roll at Traint Hill, a local comprehensive, until the age of 16, Danny was effectively excluded for the last two years of school. He did not attend school after Year 9, although he did receive some on-line tutoring until the end of Year 11 and achieved three GCSE passes: two D grades in English and a G in mathematics.

> Lisa: You were permanently excluded from Traint Hill. What was that for?
> Danny: ... I don't really remember but it would probably have involved violence or not complying with teachers. I was just a nuisance in general.
> Lisa: You had full attendance though.
> Danny: I was always there – causing trouble.
> Lisa: And you had some on-line tutors for a while [in GCSE science and English].
> Danny: Yeah, which I don't recommend.
> Lisa: Was that the last two years of school?
> Danny: Well, in Year 9 I think they got fed up of me and in Year 10 they just decided, well, in their own words, they said that I was too much of a risk to be let back in.

## Engagement and disengagement in education and training

Although Danny participated in a succession of training programmes during the course of the fieldwork none of these matched his interests or goals, or resulted in progression into employment or higher level study. Danny's perceptions of education and training were amongst the most negative of all the participants in our study, and he was often critical of the programmes he had experienced. Commenting on an employability course he was sent on by the Youth Offending Team in early 2011, Danny said:

> I thought we'd come in and have a structured lesson and we'd get work and do functional skills but, in reality, it's just come in and look at possible job applications; do a couple... and then they'd send them off. It's just a doss about... I think basically the tutors don't realize our potential and they just treat us like the people in this block – mentally challenged... It's not fulfilling any potential really and I'm not learning anything. I feel like I'm wasting my time...
>
> (Interview 04/03/2011)

He was equally scathing about the value of the qualifications associated with such programmes:

> Danny: They're pointless. Level 1 in IT – all that is, is turning on a computer.
> Lisa: Have you told prospective employers when you've been into shops that you've got a Level 1?
> Danny: No.
> Lisa: Has anybody ever asked you about those qualifications? Do people in shops know what a Level 1 is?
> Danny: I don't think so... That's the problem with these sort of courses: the teachers are not proper teachers; they're just there to get their money and I don't think they really care for the students.
>
> (Interview 04/03/2011)

Danny's experience of post-16 education was largely one of churning repeatedly between various low-level pre-vocational programmes, and when Lisa interviewed him a year later Danny was enrolled on another Level 1 programme in IT – although he had completed a virtually identical course two years earlier. Perhaps understandably, Danny seemed frustrated with his lack of progress.

Lisa: Last time... you were finishing the course at Middlebridge College. That came to an end in about September?

Danny: September, October.

Lisa: And you wanted to apply for a Level 2 in IT at Middlebridge College?

Danny: Yeah. So I sent in the application form; apparently they sent me a letter saying I could attend an interview. I never received this letter so I missed the interview. I ended up going for the open interview and they told me that I couldn't apply for the Level 2 now because of blah, blah, blah so I've got to go on to a Level 1 course... I've already done this course when I left school...

Lisa: So what sort of stuff are you doing?

Danny: It's like IT software. Sat on a computer near enough all day; Wednesday and Thursday I'm on the computer all day and Friday I'm doing maths and English, and a bit more IT.

Lisa: But you're not really going in – why?

Danny: I'm not into the routine here. No one questions anything.

Lisa: Have you got one tutor?

Danny: I've got one main tutor and I've got a maths tutor.

Lisa: And he doesn't say...

Danny: Yeah, he rings me up but he's pretty cool and he knows that the whole class are repeating the course.

Lisa: So the whole class is repeating it?

Danny: Well, there's four of us that have done this course...

Lisa: So how has that made you feel?

Danny: I felt screwed over.

Lisa: Do you think you'll pass [your exams] even if you don't go to college much?

Danny: I'm going to pass them! I don't know anyone my age who can't pass a Level 1 Functional Skills exam... It makes me agitated! I wake up early for nothing. I've done this course. I've done maths and English for two years and not got any qualifications.

(Interview 10/02/2012)

Danny was not alone in his negative views about these courses:

One girl talks about how she had hairdressing experience and has not got onto a L2 course; others in the class say they too are unsure about their destination after here. I ask Danny if anyone gets to where they want to be, and he says, 'No, it doesn't look like it, does it'. The girl says she feels 'thick' for not getting on something she is over-qualified for.

(Field notes 21/07/2011)

Sometimes Danny's boredom and frustration manifested itself in behaviour which seemed to fit some of the more negative stereotypes about young people on the margins of education and employment. During the course of the fieldwork, he was often late or absent from the courses on which he was enrolled and, when present, his conduct in class was sometimes inappropriate. On one occasion Danny announced 'Oh, I can go do a line then,' as the class were told it was time for a break; and, on another, he returned from break smelling of cannabis. Meanwhile, Danny continued to get into trouble with the police.

On Tuesday he was caught stealing DVDs and in possession of a firearm and an offensive weapon (a ball bearing gun and a lock knife). He said he just wanted to watch some DVDs – he dismisses this as petty crime... He has a court appearance on Tuesday – this could disrupt his college placement if he gets put away. The tutor tells me that she feels that the fact that Danny has a place at college will work in his favour.

As I leave the tutor asks if I am aware of his situation – I tell her I know about the court appearance. She tells me that his attendance on the programme has dropped to around 80 per cent but that she has made sure that Danny still receives his EMA as she was worried about the repercussions if he is left without money – the tutor worries about him stealing and getting into more trouble. She says she feels sorry for him as he was covering for two friends who were also stealing.

(Field notes 01/07/2011)

Yesterday Danny was in court, he got an £85 fine, 20 hours youth offending and 40 hours unpaid work. He says they would have given him 60 hours if he hadn't pleaded guilty. Danny describes getting annoyed as he had to wait around for two hours; he says he nearly got arrested again for disrupting proceedings.

(Field notes 01/07/2011)

When Lisa interviewed Danny some time later, he seemed yet again to be beginning a very similar programme of study to those he had completed before.

Lisa: So you're doing IT...

Danny: IT, yeah.

Lisa: Level 2.

Danny: Nope! Level 1. But I'm doing my Level 2 in maths and English.

Lisa: So you've got your Level 1 in maths and English. So you're really only there to improve your maths and English.

Danny: Again! Whilst looking for an apprenticeship.

Lisa: Are you on an apprenticeship or working towards one?

Danny: Working towards one.

Lisa: What is the IT in then?

Danny: Oh, that IT – that's just basic IT again...We don't do anything. We just have to turn up for three hours...We don't do anything. We play games and they don't bother us.

(Interview 20/06/2012)

Although Danny appeared thoroughly demotivated by the repetitive and unchallenging nature of the provision he experienced, he was not without ambition to study or work. However, he realized that his lack of qualifications and experience made getting a job far from easy, and that he was unlikely to be able to study the subject that most interested him, English literature, in the foreseeable future.

Lisa: Have you tried looking for work?

Danny: Yeah. I applied for a caravan-washing job last week. It was 40 hours a week but it was only for six months so it would mean quitting college for six months which would put me back. [I found it] on the internet but most jobs you need to be either 18 or have a driving licence. With not so many qualifications I'm always the last guy.

Lisa: Do you look on the net a lot?

Danny: Not really. I look maybe once a week. I look on [job websites] and they're probably the only two.

Lisa: And do you look in newspapers or in shop windows?

Danny: I'll look round but most jobs are basically all online now.

Lisa: So have you handed your CV in to places?

Danny: Yeah, I go around town maybe once a month... I've been in catering; I've been in sales places; IT places; just anywhere.

Lisa: So finding a job is tough?

Danny: Tough for some people.

## Living on the margins

The objective circumstances facing Danny – a labour market with few job opportunities for young people, especially those with low qualifications, and training provision offering little in terms of advancement, either in terms of entry to employment or higher level study – presented him with significant barriers to progression. There is, however, no doubt that Danny's involvement in various illicit activities also contributed to his marginalization.

After leaving his parental home Danny went to live with his aunt in another part of Middlebridge, where he was living when we first met him. This arrangement did not last long though, and Danny was asked to leave his aunt's house after he was arrested for possessing an offensive weapon. Danny then moved into bed-and-breakfast accommodation for a few weeks, before taking up the tenancy of a local authority flat in a high-rise tower block in a part of Middlebridge with a reputation for high levels of crime and violence. Danny also has a history of drug use and was a habitual cannabis user throughout the course of the fieldwork. He had been asked to leave one course because of drink and drug issues and it was clear, at certain times, that Danny used cannabis at college.

> People think I'm a bit addicted...My mum, tutors, Youth Offending, drug counsellors; the people that are close to me. I mean I am; I know I am but I don't like to think that. I mean I don't crave it and if I don't have it then I don't need it but I do want it.
>
> (Interview 04/03/2011)

Danny also became involved in drug dealing after he moved into the flat – an activity which led to him being the victim of a violent crime. Danny's flat was broken into twice in a few days; on the first occasion Danny was out when the break-in took place, although he was at the flat the second time the perpetrators struck:

> I'd just finished one business and I was going to another one and my mate was here for about 15 minutes and someone knocked on the door and he's opened the door...and someone bashed through and beat the crap out of him...The guys came in...I've run upstairs but I dropped the knife and went into shock and they grabbed me up against the wall and put his knife to me and the rest of them just searched. It lasted about a minute...I think it's the guy downstairs but I can't be certain.
>
> (Interview 10/02/2012)

Lisa's field notes provide some flavour of these events, and of Danny's account of what happened.

Danny lets me in. The flat appears somewhat empty. I notice his bedding has been tidied away, his cover has been taken off, and his duvet and pillow case are stacked at the top end. Nobody has slept in the bed.

Danny opens the window and has a cigarette while I sit down; he tells me that he hasn't been in the flat for around a month. He was broken into twice in five days, he thinks someone downstairs was responsible. Danny admits to dealing weed, he refers to it as 'business'. He tells me that someone broke in and stole all of his electrical gear, I say 'Do you mean weed?' – he looks at me, smiles and says yes, a guy came in while he was out and threatened his friend, beat him up and took the weed, then came back a few days later and stole some more. Danny is now £1000 in debt to his supplier. He has managed to scrape together around £600 from friends but has no way of paying back the rest. He says his friends won't expect the money back but he needs to find the rest to pay his man. He says he is avoiding his flat and certain places, although he doesn't think the man will kill him as he just wants his money.

Danny had to inform the police about the burglary as he needed to get his door fixed and didn't want to foot the bill. He told the police they just took some cigarettes and some cash; he says they knew what it was about but he wasn't about to admit dealing weed. Danny says he is no longer dealing as it isn't worth it – he describes having sleepless nights. He doesn't want to be in the flat but has to stay here another 12 months or so as he is under an introductory tenancy agreement. The only way he can get out of it is if the police decide that his life is under threat.

Danny explains that he just bought weed from this dealer, made general chit-chat about wanting to work for him, and he later gave him some bags to sell. Danny would go out to deal, a few people came to the flat – he thinks someone got to know his routine and decided to cash in. He is convinced it is a chap downstairs and talks about wanting to blow his house up. Danny talks about morals, he will only do harm to people who 'deserve it'. I ask him if he will go out stealing to try and find the money – he says he refuses to do that. He wants to be left alone and have a quiet life. I talk to him about my phone being stolen ... I joke about him doing it and he says he would never steal people's property. I say he has done before, and he says these people had wronged him in some way.

Danny is spending most of his time at his mother's house at the moment. He told her about the burglary but not the weed – he says she is smart and just knows not to ask. He says she is worried about his safety.

(Field notes 10/02/2012)

Danny claimed he had become accustomed to living in rough areas but described feeling most at home at his mother's house – although he also said that he enjoyed the freedom of living on his own, and liked having a place where he could avoid family conflict and socialize with friends. Danny's mother did not visit the flat; he saw her at her own house, which he still regarded as his home. There was a history of tension between Danny and his stepfather, connected with Danny's record of youth offending, and his desire to come and go as he pleased. When asked why he did not live with his mother and stepfather, Danny replied that:

I can't be trusted ... [my Mum] wants me but I don't want to be there. My stepdad is a bit edgy about me ... he's been there since I was about four but it's just that I've done some stuff in my time, and he's just on edge with me.

(Interview 10/02/2012)

For a time, Danny's flat was a place where his living, work and leisure spaces overlapped: he used his flat to socialize with friends and 'do business', dealing cannabis. But the break-ins proved to be critical incidents for him and transformed the flat into a place he feared and tried to avoid. Three months after the break-ins, Danny had gone back to living in the flat, although it was evident that he was becoming more socially isolated, and it seemed that he was facing real danger:

I ring the flat door bell and Danny buzzes me in. I go to the wrong floor again despite trying to read the signs. He lets me in. The flat is tidy and appears lived in, he has his X-Box back; he says he sold it to a neighbour but bought it back as it is the only thing he now does. He has lost contact with his friends as they lent him money which he has been unable to pay back. He describes them as ex-friends.

Danny has been attending college very rarely and is due to finish next week, although he has nothing in place. He says he doesn't know what he wants to do as he has done business and done IT. He says he really is in the shit. He says he started going back to the flat when 'I got over it'... his mum wants him to move back home but he doesn't want to bring the trouble home and so stays here.

He has told the housing people that his life is in danger and they have told him that he signed a tenancy agreement and so has to stay until September to honour his 12-month contract.

Danny still sees his mum every week or so. He says she is worried about him since he was abducted. He was standing at the bus stop and the drug dealer, who he owes the money to, pulled up in a car and asked him to get in. Danny got in thinking he needed to face him. The drug dealer drove him along the motorway, held a knife to his throat, and said he had two weeks to pay him back. Danny has no way of paying and says he will just have to stay one step ahead and avoid him.

(Field notes 24/05/2012)

Danny's interviews revealed other spatialized aspects of marginalization (Thompson et al. 2014). He did not really *know* any of his neighbours: although he knew some by sight, and others by their behaviour, most residents kept themselves to themselves. For Danny, movement and location came to represent his fellow residents in lieu of social interaction:

The guy over there is pretty old but I don't know his name. Come out of the elevator and turn to the left there's a piss head. I know that guy but I don't know his name. And there's a guy downstairs called Carl, and he's 21.

(Interview 10/02/2012)

Danny's behaviour mirrored and reproduced social behaviours within the flats. He would keep his head down and avoid eye contact with neighbours – he understood that this was the normal (and safe) way to behave in this environment.

As noted earlier, most participants had spent much of their lives in areas of significant deprivation. Although this was partly an issue of affordability, young people living alone are usually allocated a place to live; inevitably, these are in low-demand locations. Those living independently – either as care leavers or because of overcrowding or a history of family conflict or abuse – appeared to have little say in where they were housed. Like Danny, other participants often viewed the area in which they lived as rough or dangerous; although, conversely, they also often regarded more distant places as hostile and avoided going there. Some participants talked about needing to avoid particular areas at certain times, whilst perceiving other situations as 'unavoidable' – situations which must be confronted in order to survive. This knowledge of specific places and territories from the inside, their risks and affordances, can be regarded as a particular form of cultural capital (France et al. 2012), enabling participants to deploy appropriately spatialized practices, as Danny did in his dealings with other residents. Other participants demonstrated similar forms of knowledge and also developed strategies to cope with perceived risks.

> I ask if Danny if he feels safe living here and he tells me he has become used to it, he has been 'jumped' ... not at his home but in the local area. He said he panicked and ran, he doesn't know who the man was and questions whether it was a dream as he had just woken up. He says he is 'used to it around here' and talks about getting anesthetized to the area. He says there is no point panicking about what might happen, and that you can't show panic if it does happen – you have to just appear calm and get on with it.
>
> (Field notes 16/12/2011)

Although many participants spent large amounts of time at their place of residence, they did not necessarily regard it as their home. In this sense, home is a space consisting of physical places, social practices and mental meanings (Lahelma and Gordon 2003) and creating a 'home' requires resources not necessarily available to our participants, such as material and cultural capital, physical and psychological security, and some degree of continuity. For those in contact with parents, the parental home is often where young people feel 'at home' – a lived space in which they feel comfortable and familiar. However, this varies between individuals and can shift with time or circumstances, precipitated particularly by critical incidents such as Danny's violent break-in.

## Re-engagement to where?

Towards the end of 2012, Danny enrolled on a Level 2 Business course at Middlebridge College, but it was apparent that he was disenchanted with his life and lack of progress.

Danny describes himself as a 'punk' – a bum doing nothing useful with his life – he says he wants to change. He sees his friends doing 'adult stuff' like getting 'proper jobs and going to uni' and he feels he should be doing the same.

He makes a distinction between a career – something you want to do and have a set path to progress within and a job – something you do for money. He says he can't ever see himself gaining a career, he doesn't feel he has what it takes. He says he would take any job going. He talks about wanting to set up his own business and be an entrepreneur – he says he is not sure what in though – and this is why he is doing the business course.

Danny had talked about setting up a car-washing business with his friend, but he is still not speaking to his old friends – one of them beat him up a fortnight ago because Danny owed him money – he says the score has been settled now.

He is watching *Come Dine With Me* on TV. He says he doesn't like being in his flat as it is boring on his own. Danny goes to see his mum about twice a week, he sees a couple of people now who live in the flats – he calls them 'associates' rather than friends. When I ask if he has any friends he says 'yeah' but reminisces about his old friends who he no longer talks to.

Danny says he is just about coping financially. He has stopped smoking tobacco and weed as he says he never really enjoyed it and wants to save money and get his life back on the up. He describes his situation at the minute as 'on the up'. He says if he had an X-Box he would sit in all day and play on this, but he had to pawn it. The flat looks tidy but empty; he uses an old speaker as a table.

(Field notes 27/09/2012)

Danny stopped answering his phone in November 2012, and we lost contact with him thereafter. In many ways, it was hard to feel sympathy for Danny. His disruptive behaviour in school and involvement with illegal drugs contributed significantly to his own marginalization, and it is difficult not to see him as a juvenile delinquent. But individual choices are shaped, at least to some extent, by opportunity structures, and this is perhaps especially the case with young people. Danny's access to meaningful opportunity structures was limited, and he evidently felt frustrated at his lack of control over his educational career. Indeed, lack of control was a recurring theme in our research, with young people often caught up in what Lefebvre (1987) refers to as organized passivity.

Coercion appeared largely ineffective in supporting progression, particularly for older participants, many of whom believed they would never reach the level of education needed to move on and felt demotivated by the prospect of gaining another meaningless certificate. It does not seem unreasonable to apply the concept of alienation to the relationship between some participants and post-compulsory education and training; if alienation in a classical sense is about the disconnection between the labour process and people's humanity and autonomy, the feeling of doing education for someone else's purposes which was strongly suggested by much of our data might deserve the description of *alienated learning*.

It is worth revisiting our earlier discussion about marginalization and marginality in order to understand the nature of participation experienced by many young people like Danny. As Van Berkel et al. (2002) remind us, for certain individuals and groups, being in education or employment does not necessarily mean an end to social exclusion; and, in some circumstances, particular forms of participation may actually serve to perpetuate and reinforce disadvantage and inequality. John Smyth asks a searching question about so-called alternative education programmes which aim to reconnect 'disengaged' young people with learning: re-engagement to where? (Smyth et al. 2013). The nature of such programmes has been extensively critiqued, and their effectiveness is undermined by poor resources, low status and the marginalization of knowledge within their curricula (Simmons and Thompson 2013). Lacking more positive attributes, it is easy for them to be seen by participants and practitioners as having little purpose other than containment and social control; indeed, the term 'warehousing' has been used to describe these courses. Although, in Danny's case, his low level of educational attainment was compounded by his history of offending and continuing illicit activities, it appears that both the nature of the training available to him and a lack of meaningful labour market opportunities served to reinforce his marginalization.

# 7
# Hailey's Story

Angela McRobbie (2004) suggests that the increasing feminization of the workforce, the weakening of traditional family roles and greater opportunities for the construction of individualized female identities have initiated new forms of class distinction and differentiation, so that the representation and inscription of social divisions has itself become increasingly feminized. Both McRobbie (2004) and Skeggs (2004) see in the positioning of young working-class mothers as 'the abject of the nation' (Skeggs 2004, p.23) a particularly powerful element in the process of marking class and value. This transference of class antagonism and conflict from male to female bearers of working-class physicality is recirculated in media and political discourse, giving rise to persistent stereotypes of incontinence, wastefulness and bad parenting, creating 'tensions and impossibilities' in the lives of young mothers (Vincent et al. 2010). One manifestation of political discourses of this nature is the proliferation of courses aimed at working-class teenage parents, and as we have seen, we met some of our participants through such provision. In this chapter, we discuss the experiences of Hailey, who was 16 years old and seven months pregnant when she began to take part in our research in March 2011. In a later chapter, we will also trace Isla's story; both young women, in different ways, were required to confront moral evaluations of their behaviours, and their differing experiences of education illustrate the challenges facing teenage mothers from working-class backgrounds.

Hailey was born in the south of England and lived in a city on the south coast for the first seven years of her life before moving to Middlebridge, her mother's home town, when her parents split up. Hailey lives in the family home with her younger brother and her mother, who works as a support assistant in a local secondary school.

Hailey's elder brother went to university in another part of the country in September 2011. After completing primary school in Middlebridge, Hailey went on to finish her education at a local comprehensive school, gaining a number of GCSE passes.

> [I got] A* and an A in ICT; a B in art; a B in science and another C in science; a C in English Lit.; a C in English; a C in history; a C in graphics; a C in maths; and a D in Spanish. I think I could have done better with my maths because I was on for a B but it was more my teacher's lack of teaching skills... Because my brother always used to be, like, the star with all A* and A [grades] my dad said that mine were average. But my mum was happy.
>
> (Interview 24/03/2011)

Despite her achievements, Hailey said she 'didn't really like school', that 'the teachers weren't very good', and that, in some respects, she lacked self-confidence.

> I feel like I have low confidence really. I'm a bit, like, cautious... I feel I don't want to be judged by other people and I think about what people might think about me and the way I dress so I try not to stand out.
>
> (Interview 24/03/2011)

After school, Hailey went to a local sixth-form college to study A-Levels in accountancy, psychology, graphics and ICT. However, shortly afterwards, Hailey discovered she was pregnant and left in November 2010, although she says she was told that a place would be kept open for her until 2013. Hailey had a fairly conventional adolescence, avoiding alcohol and drugs 'because I don't like anything that takes control of my body' and having no involvement with crime. However, she described 'getting in with the wrong people' and being assaulted by the sister of a younger boy she had been teasing with a friend. Hailey also seemed to feel rejected by her father, who was 'having a baby with his new girlfriend', leading to 'a massive fall out on Christmas Eve' a year or so earlier.

Hailey had been in a relationship with Peter, the father of her child, for some time before we met her. The pregnancy was planned, following an earlier pregnancy by a different young man, which ended in an abortion after the relationship broke down.

I didn't get on with his dad and he wasn't a stable kind of guy to have a baby with ... So it was just a decision I had to make although it was not one I wanted to do but he wanted to get rid of it as well ... And then I got with Peter and he found it really hard, and he said to me if I were pregnant it would be alright ... we talked about having a baby and he said that he wanted one so we decided to just go for it.

(Interview 24/03/2011)

Although Peter knew about the abortion, Hailey said she had never informed her parents, nor had she told them that the current pregnancy was planned. In other respects, Hailey, like most of our participants, had conventional goals and ambitions, including getting a job, owning her own home and leading an ordinary family life. She did, however, realize that this would not be possible for some time and planned for the time being to continue living with her mother. In a number of ways, Hailey was untypical of the stereotypes of teenage mothers encountered in the media and in policy discourse; a Connexions personal adviser responsible for supporting young parents describes the tensions between these stereotypes and the more diverse reality:

I think to society it is deemed that these young people get pregnant by accident but that is not always the case; that they have low ability, which is also not always the case, and have come from extremely vulnerable families ... So all this cycle of benefit claiming and lack of a work ethic but, again, that is not always true. Some pregnancies are planned and some aren't. So they are a completely mixed bag.

(Interview 08/10/2010)

## Motherhood, learning and marginalization

After leaving college, Hailey was directed by Connexions to a ten-week programme aimed at providing basic information on pregnancy to young mothers-to-be, run by a voluntary organization. After this, she joined 'Springboard', an employability programme run by the same organization, which she completed a few weeks before giving birth. The mismatch between Hailey's educational background and the nature of this course highlights a particular issue about the nature of provision available for young women in Hailey's position. To some extent, this may be because higher-status providers feel less well-equipped to support pregnant students, although the demands of more academic study must also be acknowledged. The practitioner quoted above expressed the view that some post-16 institutions were more flexible than others, but that this could apply to employers and training providers as well as schools and colleges. However, Hailey felt that the Springboard programme was of some worth in that it helped her to explore future career options, particularly her ambition to become an accountant and the possibility of an apprenticeship in finance.

> Lisa: So what sort of stuff have you been doing with Springboard?
> Hailey: Well, finding out what your chosen career is, and then choosing different paths to get there. So instead of going to college you can do an apprenticeship. And they tell us that [you need] good English to get a job and we do, like, four units: healthy living; cultural diversity; community action and another one which I can't remember.
> Lisa: Do you think that is going to be useful?
> Hailey: Yes, I think it's better than doing nothing. It's just an extra tool to boost you up instead of having nothing.

Whilst Hailey already had GCSE passes at grade C in English and mathematics, most of those on the course needed support with literacy and numeracy, and a substantial part of the programme was orientated towards improving participants' basic skills. The awards Hailey gained – Level 1 qualifications in Employability and in Personal and Social Development – were at a lower level than those she had obtained at school.

Although teenage mothers are often depicted as benefit scroungers, Hailey was not content with living on welfare and her interest in finding an apprenticeship was partly motivated by a desire for financial independence. She assessed her options in the months after giving birth to her daughter, Leah, in May 2011:

> Hailey: I really want to do an apprenticeship because it's experience which you need for a job and they are more likely to take you on after, and you get money – because I don't want to be on benefits for the rest of my life ... I'm on Income Support and Child Benefit – but Child Benefit I'll have anyway ... it's the Income Support that I want to get rid of because that's what you get from Job Seekers.
> Lisa: And you're getting Income Support because you're a ...
> Hailey: Lone parent. I just want to get rid of that and be independent really because I don't want to be taking money off people because a lot of people criticize you for that ... people just think that I've got a

kid but I've got no money to support her and so I'm just dependent
on the state

(Interview 04/05/2012)

Hailey's attempts to find an apprenticeship were unsuccessful, although
it is not entirely clear her intentions were serious. On one level, the
vicissitudes of information technology proved to be a barrier when
Hailey tried to apply for an apprenticeship – a phenomenon which
we found can present various problems for marginalized young people trying to access work or benefits. However, Hailey seemed easily
discouraged by contingent factors such as a temporary interruption to
her internet access which prevented a last-minute application to an
apprenticeship in business administration. Perhaps more importantly,
financial barriers, especially those related to childcare costs, as well as
her educational priorities, made an apprenticeship less appealing. An
apprenticeship would not have been eligible for the financial support for
young mothers returning to education available under the Care to Learn
scheme,[1] and Hailey worried that childcare and travel costs would leave
her unable to manage. Her mother no longer received Child Benefit as
Hailey was receiving benefits in her own right; consequently, Hailey paid
her mother £200 per month in rent as her contribution to the somewhat
stretched family income.

> Me and my mum always talk about money because we have so little
> and it's always a struggle at the end of the day. She's been getting
> money for me but I'm no longer a dependent child so she's just got a
> letter saying she owes them about 700 quid because there was a mix
> up. So she has to owe that back and the boiler keeps going wrong so
> she has to keep paying more on that. So she keeps saying it's going
> to be, like, no Christmas.
>
> (Interview 18/11/2011)

Hailey was also attracted to the idea of a more broadly based course at
her sixth-form college, which would enable her to study Art alongside
business-related subjects, although she still would have liked to find an
apprenticeship in finance or accounting if this were possible. However,
Hailey's return to college was not as smooth as she expected and had
it not been for her mother's intervention it seems that she would not
have been able to return to her original course of study, despite previous
assurances to the contrary. During the time Hailey was out of education the college raised its entry requirements for the A-levels Hailey

was previously studying, and initially she was refused re-entry. The force of character displayed by Hailey's mother appeared was decisive in reversing this decision.

> Hailey talks about how her mum went into college to tell the principal she was promised a place and this is how she got in...she says her mum is like that. She says her mum works in a nearby school and so they can share lifts.
>
> (Field notes 23/05/2012)

Returning to college marked an upturn in Hailey's fortunes. She was now able to access the Care to Learn fund and generally seemed to adapt well to resuming study.

> Hailey looks really well...she seems to have lost weight. She has make-up on and is dressed quite smartly in a top and leggings. She is full of smiles...Hailey has started college now. Leah goes to a nursery that she can walk to from home.
>
> (Field notes 12/10/12)

## Caring, coping and conflict

Hailey's return to college came at the end of what was, in many ways, a difficult period after she became a mother and, to a great extent, two inter-related problems contributed substantially to her marginalization in the year after she gave birth: social isolation and difficulties in her relationship with Leah's father. Peter worked intermittently during the period of our fieldwork, but his pay was too irregular for them to have a realistic prospect of setting up home together. Although, at least initially, Hailey hoped to move in with Peter before too long, she remained living with her mother and younger brother in the family home throughout the research.

> Hailey answers the door to her mum's house in her nightie holding baby Leah – she is now seven weeks old...Hailey spends most of the time talking about how cute Leah is...She says as she gets older she sees her personality coming out more and more.
>
> Peter is looking for work but has found nothing yet. Hailey hopes to move out of her mum's place by this time next year. She shares a small room with Leah at the moment; she says her mum is happy for her to be here, she likes looking after them both. She says she

feels this is fair as it is easier and cheaper than trying to survive on her own.

(Field notes 01/07/2011)

It soon became evident that all was not well. Hailey's relationship with Peter was increasingly problematic, and her mental health appeared to be suffering.

Hailey answers the door with Leah in her arms. The TV is on; her mum is at work... Hailey says she thinks she was depressed when Leah was first born and suspects she might be getting that way again. She complains that she and Peter are not getting on, Hailey says she can't really talk to her mum about it as she doesn't think that women need men.

Hailey says that Peter was really good when Leah was first born but isn't doing enough to help now. She says it takes him half an hour to change a nappy when it would take her five minutes. Peter comes round for half an hour at a time. He goes to snooker twice a week and plays football too. She has had to give up her netball on Thursdays as it is his snooker league. Hailey seems upset by this and describes it as 'her time'. She says Peter doesn't appreciate what she does and it's got to a stage where he does very little...

Hailey also began to feel increasingly alienated from others in her locality, and that the neighbourhood was unsuitable for a young family.

I ask Hailey if she has gone out to any baby groups, she says no. Hailey says she wants to find out about a 'bumps and babies' session – she would go there as she knows the people who run it. She doesn't want to go anywhere more local as there are a lot of Pakistani women in the area and she feels that they look down on teenage mums... Hailey spends most days just inside, she says she doesn't even go to the park... it is all too much effort. She says her mum thinks she is going stir crazy.

(Field notes 21/10/2011)

Over time, Hailey's relationship with Peter continued to deteriorate.

I go to see Hailey and she is dressed, as always, in her pyjamas. She is still feeling lonely... and questions her relationship with Peter. Hailey seems fed up with his work situation. When I ask if she would consider going out to work Hailey says she doesn't see why she should have to do it all, look after baby and go out to work. She sees herself going to work in the long run but not right now. Hailey says Peter's mum is the only one who could look after Leah if she went out to work but is not happy leaving her with Peter's mother – their relationship is difficult... Hailey says she hasn't been to visit Peter's mother for a fortnight as she can't handle the stress.

Hailey says her dad would give Peter a job if they moved south, but she can't see Peter leaving his family, and she doesn't want to leave her mum on her own.

Ideally, Hailey would still like her own place with Peter and Leah – she thinks this may resolve some of the issues they're having, but she... can't see how they would manage financially without Peter... bringing in a secure wage. She says he needs a stable job.

(Field notes 18/11/2011)

Peter's own situation was itself quite complex. His health was poor, and he suffered from a congenital chest defect – although this did not prevent him from playing football. Whilst he attended employability courses at training providers and worked irregularly in the informal economy, Hailey did not appear to regard his engagement as serious, and viewed the job search activities he undertook at his training provider as something that could easily be done at home. Either way, it appears that his behaviour reinforced and perpetuated Hailey's marginalization in various ways, and that her criticisms of his labour market activities were born largely out of frustration. Peter spent less time with Hailey than previously, accused her of being unfaithful, and sometimes called her 'spiteful' and 'a bitch'. Hailey saw very little of anyone other than her mother and Peter; her feelings of isolation did not improve, and she complained of being bored 'every day and every night' and not sleeping. Lack of money, being alone all day with Leah while her mother was at work, and the relationship with Peter all contributed to this:

I said to my mum the other day 'Do you want to go out for a meal or some place?' but I can't really go out because I don't have the money. I can go out for a walk because that doesn't cost money but by the time my mum gets home at half four it's dark so I can't go for a walk with me mum...

I can't sleep at all. I've got too much going on in my head; my brain will not stop thinking. I'll lay in bed and me brain is just so active thinking about everything in so much detail that I can't sleep... [thinking about] Peter... and how the relationship is going and stuff like that... we used to see each other every day and now we don't and he don't talk to me hardly, so it's just making me think. And he's always on his bloody computer as well... Friday is his only night that he don't do owt... And this week he were working so there was not time for me so I had to make him drop football...

He said [being a father] were superb and brilliant at first, but now he can't be bothered.

(Interview 18/11/2011)

Unfortunately Hailey's relationship with Peter became increasingly volatile and degenerated into violence on occasion. Perhaps unsurprisingly, the couple split up on several occasions during the course of the research. Initially, these separations were for short periods, but their relationship seemed to have come to an end by the time our fieldwork was completed. Whilst the enactment of highly gendered childcare roles is of course endemic within society, it is clear that Peter could not be described as a 'hands-on father' and that, in some ways, his behaviour added to Hailey's domestic pressures.

Hailey: He's like a little baby! It's like caring for two babies. I've got to worry about him with his chest infections and stuff... I have to ring him up in the morning to get him down here to see his daughter... It's not the fact that I'm nagging him for me but it's for Leah because I know that if I hadn't had a dad around that often I would have felt awful...

Lisa: So do you see a future with Peter or are you thinking that you might be better on your own?

Hailey: I do wish there is a future for us because he says that he always wants to be with me forever – blah, blah, blah. But, in fact, I know I'm doing it all by myself already. I'm here 24/7 doing the bottles; doing the washing up; doing the, you know, not happy side to being a mum and then he'll come round and play with her and that's it...

And during the night he's awful... If I wake him up saying 'Leah's awake' he goes 'And why aren't you up?' Seriously, I want just one night's sleep; just one night of good sleep and I can't get it anyway because the last time I let him do it he... just stuck her back in her cot with some toys to play with... I know he does love her to bits but...

At one stage Hailey was offered part-time employment in a fish-and-chip shop, although she was unable to take the job following disputes with

Peter over childcare. Hailey's social isolation was intensified by poverty, a situation exacerbated by Peter's reliance on Hailey as a source of income.

> The money [Peter] gave me the other day was [just] what he owed me. I gave him money to go gaming... and that cost me £80. I had to pay for his computer to get fixed and that cost me £75... He just thinks that money grows on trees. I bought him a £55 hoody because he wouldn't stop nagging me... and I said to him 'Look, Peter I'm not going to spend money on that' and he said I were tight but I did buy it for him. And I took him to the cinema that week as well.

> I'm hoping he gets some work. He just needs a job that is steady instead of not knowing when he's going to be working. And he needs to know how much he is being paid every week or every month because he just doesn't know. And like this week he says 'Oh I might be home by about six or half six' and that's no good to me.

Material factors – both related to income and expenditure, and to her relationship with Peter – were significant causes of Hailey's frustration and isolation in the months after she became a mother. But social expectations and the attitudes and values of those around her also contributed to Hailey's marginalization. We have already described how Hailey felt uncomfortable in her neighbourhood and how this deterred her from using public services and leisure facilities in her locality, but Hailey often talked more generally about 'people' thinking negatively of her as a young mother on benefits.

> When I'm on the bus they will make comments and they think you just do nothing and smoke and drink but, on my behalf, I went to college, I dropped out of college and I took a year out but I'm going to go back to college. If I don't say that I have a kid they think 'oh that's cool' but as soon as I say I have a kid they sort of freak out.
>
> (Interview 23/05/2012)

## Making a future?

As we have explained earlier in the book, returning to education is often represented uncritically by political and media discourses as a way to make good young people's deficits. A popular notion is that engaging in education is a way of 'turning young people's lives around' and, in Hailey's case, restarting sixth-form college marked an upturn in her fortunes. Changes were evident only a month after she went back to college. Although the oldest in her class, Hailey felt that she fitted in well and had made new friends. Perhaps understandably, she was somewhat diffident about disclosing her status as a young mother.

> Hailey: I started college in September...I'm doing an extended diploma in business which is all BTEC, and it's the equivalent of three A-levels in business basically...The business course itself is sort of three assignments because there is finance and the environment of business, and then the marketing part of it...it's really good at the moment...I'm the oldest in the class. [Most of them are] 16, going up to 17. There's one person who is 17 because he did a year at Greyhand College before he came here.
>
> LR: Is the social aspect of college good as well?
>
> Hailey: Yeah, I've got my little group and we all stick together. Every Tuesday we have, like, an early lesson but then we have, like, two hours free and so we will go for something to eat on that Tuesday and that is like a little ritual now. It's quite nice...I've only spoken to my own circle and they know now that I've got Leah and everything and they haven't judged or owt...[I wasn't really nervous about telling them] because I knew I shouldn't be ashamed of it and I'm doing something with my life. I think some of [my tutors know].
>
> (Interview 12/10/2012)

Although in the event she had not been able to continue with the subjects she had previously studied – there were insufficient students to make the course viable – Hailey was enjoying her college work and talked about going to university to study accounts and finance, although this would have to be in Middlebridge because of her responsibilities to Leah. However, she retained some ambivalence towards higher education, and was still attracted to the idea of going directly into paid employment if possible:

> I sometimes think I'd rather have a job when I think that, like, two years ahead I'm still in education because, in education, if you are ill, there is a lot to catch up on whereas if you are out working you don't really miss the educational side of it you just have to catch up on the work and you get paid for it. I don't know if I might not just try and find a job straight into finance and stuff like that and work my way

up in a business because if you think about it I know you get more pay if you've got a degree and that but if you've spent the four years you would spend in education getting established in a business you'd be earning about over 20 [thousand] anyway.

(Interview 12/10/2012)

Hailey's fear of how ill-health may impact on her studies was perhaps prompted by her early experiences on returning to college. Hailey had dropped economics after falling behind in her work, thinking that she needed to focus on her main subjects. The sheer pace of sixth-form studies seemed to have been a factor in this and posed a significant challenge to a young mother:

I fell ill a few weeks ago and missed, like, four and a half hours of economics, because if you miss a day that's like four hours or something and they managed to cover a whole unit and I were already a unit behind and... also behind on my business because it was our first assignment and nobody knew how to do it... I [thought] I couldn't catch up on both. I spoke to one of my friends and they said that all you need really is three A-levels at a good standard. So I thought I'm better off concentrating on getting distinctions in my business which is what I want to do [at] university... I talked to my mum and she said as long as nobody at college had told me I wasn't good enough to do it, because she didn't want me thinking that I wasn't good enough or capable of doing it, but if I felt like it was going to be a better option for me then I should do it.

(Interview 12/10/2012)

In her research on learning identities amongst previously NEET young people in New Zealand, Higgins (2013) writes of the importance of 'identity work' in reconstructing the learning careers of those who have experienced lengthy periods of marginalization. Rediscovering an educational sense of self, related to an appreciation of one's own learning capacities and aspirations, is a central part of this identity work. Higgins notes that, in this respect, young mothers returning to study were in general strongly motivated, driven like Hailey to avoid being seen by their children as benefit-dependent. Nevertheless, identity work can be difficult as young returners struggle to balance the demands of study with its rewards, often against a backdrop of earlier failure. In Hailey's case, a certain degree of confidence in her capacity to learn, alongside her mother's support, appeared to be winning out against other factors – although the role of financial support from the state in enabling Hailey to attend college should not be forgotten. Identities are not forged in isolation from social and institutional structures, and the learning identities projected by the state can shape experiences of education and training in particular ways (Bernstein 2000). Nor should it be forgotten that identities are not unitary or monolithic; Hailey negotiated a complex web of identity, in which learning was required to compete with motherhood, sexuality and family. Furthermore, Hailey's return to college was at times precarious; one of the deficiencies of discourses about 'turning young people's lives around' is that they promote a myth of watershed moments dividing former from present selves, neglecting the continuing work that must be done to protect fragile learning identities against the pressures of poverty and disadvantage.

Hailey's life outside college also changed significantly after she returned to study. Most notably, she became involved with another young man and, although this turned out to be a short-lived liaison, it appeared to signal the end of her relationship with Peter. Although he now seemed to be taking a more independent role in childcare, looking after Leah for a few hours two nights a week and for part of the weekend so that Hailey could do coursework or go out, she talked about her relationship with Peter as very much in the past and looked forward to connecting more with other friends. Although in this interview Hailey described her relationship with Peter as over, a month later they were back together. She described college work less enthusiastically than before:

> I see Hailey at home. Peter is upstairs (I don't see him): they are back together.

> She is happy at college but feels as though she is getting behind with coursework. She has just failed a presentation she had to do but explains that it was group work and one member didn't pull her weight.

> She talks about Christmas, saying she has bought loads of toys for Leah and can't wait to see her face. She says she and her mum will not put the tree up until Xmas Eve and surprise Leah in the morning with lights and presents.
>
> (Field notes 23/11/2012)

This was the last substantial contact with Hailey before fieldwork came to an end; however, she kept in touch occasionally and, although detailed information is lacking, we were able to follow some of the broader outlines of her life. In November 2013, Hailey and Peter were still together; Peter had been working for a year installing office furniture, a job that took him to London and elsewhere in the country. Hailey was now in her second year at college, and looked forward to applying to the local university.

We must remember that all educational experiences are not equal and that, whilst Hailey's return to study led to a marked change in fortune, both the institution and the nature of study on which she re-embarked suited her interests and ambitions. Unlike Hailey, whose previous academic achievement provided a foundation for returning to college and possibly progressing to university, the majority of participants appeared trapped in a cycle of inadequate provision. Moving in and out of short-term training, often returning to the same providers for similar (or even the same) courses, few progressed to mainstream education or apprenticeships and often described their training as 'boring', 'repetitive' and 'pointless'. Others viewed it as something to pass the time when other options are unavailable; some felt forced onto certain courses for fear of benefits being removed or explained that the courses they really wanted to take were unobtainable as entry was too competitive or provision was full. Although practitioners in support services such as Connexions frequently emphasized that they understood the diversity of the NEET group, the advice they gave to Hailey did not always seem appropriate, and she appeared to have little confidence in what they offered. She explained that Connexions had played little part in her return to college, and in fact had repeatedly offered her places on short-term training courses which she regarded as 'for people who have got really bad grades'. However, Hailey acknowledged that Connexions had introduced her to the Care to Learn scheme, which was crucial in enabling her to return to study.

# 8
# Sean's Story

A frequent criticism of research into youth transitions is that it has tended to concentrate on the more extreme and sensational at the expense of the mundane and the average (Roberts 2011; 2012). To some extent this is understandable, and for academics and policymakers concerned with those most at risk, it is natural to concentrate on young people in very deprived areas or facing complex and multiple difficulties. Furthermore, as we found very early in our research, there is a paradox of access when attempting to investigate the lives of NEET young people. Those in very challenging circumstances are likely to be known to social services and are often subject to attendance requirements as a condition of receiving benefits. When access is negotiated through practitioners, these young people may therefore be easier to reach than those with less obvious needs. Because of this, we were able to include in our study young people from many of the various NEET subgroups described in earlier chapters, including young parents, care leavers and those with a history of youth offending. However, there are different degrees and forms of marginalization, and if young people outside these groups remained less visible to us, the scope and usefulness of our research would be diminished. Consequently we once again approached the local Connexions service and towards the end of 2011, it was suggested that Sean, a personable young man with relatively good GCSEs who had become NEET after leaving an apprenticeship programme, might be included in our study.

Sean was born in Greenford and was 16 years old when we first met him in November 2011. His mother and father split up when he was three, although Sean still has contact with his father. When he began taking part in the research Sean was living was his mother and stepfather who worked as a chef. His mother was at home looking after her younger children during the course of the fieldwork, although Sean said she had worked as a nursery nurse in the past. Sean had left school the previous summer with nine GCSEs at A*–C, and two BTEC qualifications.

> I got pretty good grades actually. I got a B in music; C in my core science and a B in my initial science; C in my English Language.... I got a C in my ICT. In my drama I got two Bs in BTEC and I've got grade C in my drama at GCSE. My two BTECs I've got an A* in practical but then it were C/D in my coursework which let me down a bit.
>
> (Interview 18/11/2011)

Although Sean failed English Literature – he had revised but 'it didn't make any sense to me' – he also gained a good GCSE in food technology, grade B in the coursework and A* in the practical. He had not disliked school: 'like most teenagers, I had some good days and some bad days,' but, despite his qualifications, Sean felt he was probably better suited to more 'hands-on' work than academic study.

When he began taking part in the research, Sean had a steady girlfriend, who worked as an apprentice at a local firm of accountants. He also had a well-established circle of friends, most of whom were at college, in apprenticeships or working.

> I'll be out seeing my friends most of the time and we'll be out playing football or some other sport. Sometimes my girlfriend will come over and I'll spend time with her or I'll take her out with friends and try and incorporate them both rather than having them both complaining. It gets really awkward sometimes.
>
> (Interview 18/11/2011)

During his last year at school, Sean did a two-week work placement at Greenford College and did some voluntary work for the RSPCA; he had a number of other interests and could play bass and drums. Sean had clear career ambitions when he left school and began an apprenticeship programme in catering run by Middlebridge College soon after he finished year 11. His work placement was at a restaurant in Greenford.

> I just have a passion for food and I like cooking it, and I like tasting it. It's just something that really appeals to me but I wouldn't mind being a chef but I wouldn't particularly want to be a head chef or own the business because I'm no good with paperwork or anything like that. I just find it too boring and I wouldn't want to own me own

business. I'd rather be working for someone else but still be doing
something that I like.

(Interview 18/11/2011)

## Marginalization and labour market entry

Sean appeared to have an intrinsic interest in the food industry, but his
ambitions in this direction had also been influenced by his stepfather.
There were no vacancies at his stepfather's workplace, and although
more generally we found social and family networks to be of great
importance in our research, Sean was not prepared to accept work in
which he felt unable to take a sustained interest.

> Obviously you don't want to be stuck in a job that you're not enjoy-
> ing. It might be OK for a year or two maybe while you get on your
> feet and get stuff sorted but you don't want to be in it for too long
> because it will just drive you crazy. My granddad set up his own fam-
> ily business as an electrician but the reason I didn't want to go into it
> was because I'm just not interested at all in electronics.

Sean also had quite conventional longer-term ambitions:

> At the moment it would be just with a nice little house some-
> where ... with a car and working as a chef in a local restaurant paying
> well so I can live comfortably without having to stretch my money.
> And just being able to settle down and not having to worry about
> anything.

(Interview 18/11/2011)

Despite these ambitions, Sean's apprenticeship was short-lived; he began
the programme in May 2011, but had left by the end of July. Initially,
Sean worked at the restaurant for about 40 hours a week, but it soon
became clear that he was expected to work much longer hours. After a
few weeks Sean found he was doing 14–16-hour days, six days a week.
Sean found the long shifts – preparing food, cooking, laying tables and
cleaning – exhausting. He talked about going into 'robot mode' and
being unable to cope with college alongside his placement. He also
recalled having concerns over hygiene in the restaurant, which he later
reported to his college tutors.

> I was feeling ridiculously tired every day and [a friend] said
> that, legally, they aren't supposed to let us work more than

40 hours-a-week anyway and I sort of realized that it was a little bit dodgy, and I just couldn't hack it anymore with the hours we were doing so I had to tell them I were quitting...they weren't really too bothered...they paid me and they let me go.

(Interview 18/11/2011)

Initially, Sean accepted the longer hours as he knew apprenticeship placements were scarce and feared he would not be able to secure an alternative placement – which, in fact, proved to be the case. By the time Sean left the restaurant, a series of domestic disputes meant that he had also left the family home, and Sean said his lack of a permanent address prevented the College from offering him another work place-ment. A closer examination of Sean's life reveals that difficult family circumstances presented significant barriers to his subsequent attempts to get back into the labour market. These barriers were connected to two related issues: family conflict and poverty.

Sean is one of seven children: he has three young siblings, one of whom, Natasha, was a baby when fieldwork began, and three older brothers – all of whom lived outside the family home. Living in overcrowded conditions had a significant effect on Sean. Whilst he attended primary school and started secondary school in Middlebridge, the need for a larger house meant that Sean's education was dis-rupted by a change of school when he moved with his family to a larger house in Greenford. The domestic disputes in which Sean later became involved appeared to relate mainly to the childcare duties he was expected to carry out, looking after his younger siblings. When he left home, Sean spent four months without a permanent address, 'sofa surfing'.

Lisa: Was it a fall out between you and your parents?
Sean: Yeah. There were disagreements in the house and I had to look after the kids a lot of the nights and I just wasn't able to go out or do anything. So I had to look after the kids constantly while they were going out all night...and coming back some time in the morning leaving me up with a little girl and stuff.
Lisa: So that was the summer that you left school and that meant you couldn't go to college so were you applying for stuff?
Sean: I was applying to colleges and stuff like that but none of them could really take me. And the same with jobs; no one could take me on apprenticeships.
Lisa: Is that what they told you?

Sean: Yeah. Because I didn't have a permanent address where they could send things.

Lisa: So you couldn't use your parent's address?

Sean: No, because we'd fallen out and stuff and I basically didn't think I'd go back at all and we had no contact between us at all apart from once when my great granddad died and my mum did ring me to tell me that he died and when the funeral stuff was.

Lisa: So how did you get back on track then?

Sean: I texted one day asking how the kids were and stuff and they said that they were fine and I should come over and see them and then it just went from there. So I started going over a couple a days a week to see them and I ended up moving back there which is where I am at the moment.

Lisa: And are you happy with that?

Sean: It's alright...I get the kids to school at nine o'clock and then I just tend to stay out during the whole day so I'm only really there from when I wake up and when I go to sleep, to be fair. So I suppose it's alright but I'm not really there enough to feel the atmosphere or anything.

(Interview 18/11/2011)

In various ways, family poverty affected Sean's life and shaped his future ambitions. Financial pressures played at least some part in Sean's initial decision to follow an apprenticeship rather than other forms of education and training.

I would go into training but the reason I want to do an apprenticeship more is that with the training you get the qualification but with the apprenticeship the pay also helps with your travel there and back whereas if it's just the training you don't always get the funding and, depending on where it is, you've still got to pay for yourself.

(Interview 18/11/2011)

Money worries also seemed to close off higher education as an option for the future.

Sean: I'm not looking, personally, to go to university because, one, I wouldn't be able to afford it and, two, I wouldn't want to be in debt and having to pay it back years down the line. I'd rather just get a job by going to college or something. A lot of universities have just been messed around and you hear of all this bad stuff that goes on.

Lisa: About the debt that you can get in?
Sean: Yeah because they are putting the prices up as it is and the amount of debt that you could get in. Ok, you don't have to pay them back until you're in a job paying more than 25,000 a year but still the thought of being in debt is worrying so I'd rather not. I know the trouble that me dad got into when he couldn't afford to pay the mortgage when me dad got made redundant the first time, and so just being in debt is something that I don't want to get into.

Financial hardship also had more immediate effects for Sean. After returning home, Sean began a nine-month period of short-lived engagement with various training courses. On a number of occasions Sean said that his parents were struggling to manage bringing up a young family, and were placing considerable pressure on him to bring money into the household. This manifested itself in different ways, but Sean was under significant pressure to enrol on any training programme to qualify for a training allowance. Although he had no interest in the subject, Sean began an IT training course just before Christmas 2011. Perhaps unsurprisingly, he left the course a couple of months later and also moved out of the family home, to live with his girlfriend's family in Greenford.

It was a mutual decision to move out from his mum's to ease things financially. Sean can now claim benefits (Income Support), and his mum has one less mouth to feed. Sean gets £90 every two weeks, he pays £40 rent to his girlfriend's mum every fortnight, and pays a £10 'top up shop' every two weeks; the rest is spent on bus fares and toiletries.

(Field notes 09/03/2013)

Sean then began a sustained campaign to find paid employment, visiting various employers in Middlebridge and Greenford, dropping off his CV and making personal enquiries. However, lack of money was still a problem. The costs of bus travel meant that most of Sean's job searching was carried out on foot. Although employers and careers advisers often say they prefer online recruitment, Sean found that such methods were not as effective as he had expected.

I've noticed a lot of things don't get updated that much and there have been a couple where I've rung up, and they've said that the job was filled three months ago so I don't see why it should still be on the site. So the site doesn't get updated that often...

A lot of the time it's just like 'apprentice chef' and sometimes it will say the company but a lot of the time it just says 'apprentice chef' and I can't always remember which ones I've applied for and which I haven't so it can be quite hard.

(Interview 23/05/2012)

When Sean eventually found a job as a trainee grill chef, travel expenses were again a significant issue.

Sean is worrying about his start date. He explains that he cannot start straight away as he has no money for a bus pass to get there, he will have to wait for his next benefit to come in. He says it is too far to walk and says he told an employer once that he couldn't start straight away due to transport costs – and he was told to be there or lose the job.

(Field notes 09/03/2012)

Although Sean did not have a sophisticated understanding of the local labour market he was aware of some of the causes of youth unemployment. Sean's opinions about the relationship between education and employment run contrary to those proposed by human capital theory, and reflect concerns about the social congestion caused by increasing levels of educational attainment alongside static or declining opportunities for employment (Brown 2013).

Lisa: Have you heard on the news about how a lot of young people are unemployed and ...
Sean: Yeah, it were on the news the other day that ... we are now the place with most unemployment, and especially with young people.
Lisa: And what is your take on all that?
Sean: One of the major problems is that ... they don't go on ... what qualifications you've got but they go more on your experience and references and stuff; and that does make it a lot harder for us younger people because we haven't been out there as much; we haven't got all the experience, which makes it a bit bad when you've got people coming out with A-levels and all these degrees and stuff, and they can't get a job or there's someone that, OK, they may have all the experience and stuff but they don't have any qualifications. So unless we are given jobs and given the chances to go out there we're not going to be able to get anywhere and this country can end up getting worse than it already is.

Perhaps understandably, Sean felt quite frustrated at his situation. He was also concerned about how potential employers would view his leaving his apprenticeship programme, although he believed that he had gained something positive from the apprenticeship:

> Sean: I did learn a lot more... from what I already knew because it was a fully functioning restaurant and before I didn't know how to tell when a steak was done properly and I didn't know all the ins and outs of food hygiene. I knew the basics but I did learn quite a bit in the short time I was there.
>
> Lisa: So if someone was to ask you about it what would you say? If you were in a job interview?
>
> Sean: Well, I'd tell them why I did it there and the valid reasons why I left – and all about the hygiene problem that they had with the rat infestation and not doing owt and that. So I'd tell them about it but I'd stress that it weren't anything to do with me and it were already in that state when I got there and that it did get shut down for the right reasons. But I wouldn't tell them this unless I were asked directly because places don't want to take on people who have worked somewhere as bad as that.
>
> (Interview 18/11/2011)

Sean's motivation was remarkably durable and he spent substantial periods of time job hunting whilst he was NEET. He was positive about the support he received from Connexions.

> ...they went through everything like what happened and why I wasn't in education or anything and they said 'right, sit down and we'll fill all your forms out and stuff', and they sent them off for me and they helped out with my CV and stuff. Yeah, they helped a lot.
>
> (Interview 18/11/2011)

## Work matters

In May 2012, Sean was offered a job as a trainee grill chef at the Middlebridge branch of Pietro's, a large restaurant chain. Sean got this job after seeing it advertised in the restaurant window – something which he described as 'a stroke of luck' – and there is no doubt that his experiences at Pietro's were markedly different from those he endured on his apprenticeship. Certainly, the objective terms and conditions were significantly better. Although he was only 17 when he began his new job, Sean was paid the minimum wage for a 21-year-old – £6.19 per hour. He was contracted to work for 16 hours per week, although Sean said this could be extended to 20 hours once he turned 18. Although Sean sometimes did overtime – which he was keen do as he wanted the money – the company abided by age-related restrictions governing not only the number of hours he was allowed to do in the restaurant, but also the timing and continuity of the shifts he was permitted to work. Pietro's also provided new staff with a structured programme of training and appeared to offer its employees opportunities to progress within the company. A number of supervisory staff had worked at the restaurant for extended periods of time and had been promoted through the ranks. Training was provided on-site, and this branch had designated training facilities above the restaurant. It also operated a 'buddying' system, whereby each new recruit was mentored by a more experienced colleague in the first few weeks of employment. Once Sean passed his initial training, he would get red stripes (on the plain t-shirt which forms part of his uniform). The higher the worker's status, the more decorated the shirt would become.

Everyone has to go through the basics when they first start... to see how you get on and that, but as you go through it you learn all the organization spec and all the stuff you need to learn like all your temperatures, your hot and cold temperatures. And... e-learning which you get tested for after, and that is all about health and hygiene and the safety side... you have to pass that... otherwise you've got to... redo it all. And then you do a test, dependent on your job role which will basically show all of your knowledge and you've got to get at least 80% on that otherwise you've got to retake it... You have to know the whole process because if you don't, and the food isn't cooked properly and it goes out then somebody might get food poisoning and that's not good for business...

... It (the training) generally goes on for up to three months. The job at the moment isn't definite until the end of the three months. You can be put into what is called a Pietro official employee and I'm just taking my test and, with being a griller, I've just got to do a grill test on how stuff should be made; how often temperatures should be taken and, like, you are supposed to study it all and know it by heart and you need to get above 85 per cent and then you can become a proper Pietro employee.

(Interview 23/05/2012)

Sean found his work environment congenial: the restaurant had a vibrant atmosphere and the staff seemed to get on well with each other. Latin-American music was played during opening hours, and there was a young, energetic ambience; a number of students from Middlebridge University were on the staff. The kitchen and restaurant were open-plan, and customers could view meals being cooked. When Lisa visited Sean at Pietro's towards the end of 2012 he seemed happy – both in his work and with the direction his life was taking more broadly. He talked about making a career at Pietro's over the next few years, and about how a number of staff had worked their way up to become supervisors and managers. Sean also looked foward to becoming a 'buddy', which would entail higher pay and helping to train others – although he did not see himself as an entrepreneur, running a business. He seemed more focused on developing his role as a chef and talked about people who had worked for Pietro's in the past and who had subsequently gone on to work in Michelin-starred restaurants. Sean seemed impressed by this and expressed an interest in doing this himself at some point. He also seemed positive about the training he undertook when he first started work there.

> Yeah, it was good because rather than being thrown into the deep end they said this is how you do it and then I was left to try it for myself and that's a lot easier to learn.
>
> (Interview 27/11/2012)

Workplace relations seemed cordial and Sean appeared to get on well with his colleagues and had also been out with workmates socially on a couple of occasions.

> Yeah, I've not really got any problems with anyone and I get all the help that I need. If anything needs explaining or if there is anything I'm doing that is wrong I get told.
>
> (Interview 27/11/2012)

Sean felt his job was a step above working for a fast-food restaurant, as it was about the 'dining experience' rather than a quick 'bite to eat'. His friends concurred, which helped give him pride in his work. External perceptions appear to have an influence on a young person's decision to pursue certain forms of employment and play an important role in shaping attitudes to work once in post.

[w]hen people know that I work at Pietro's it's like 'oh that's really good' or another thing I get is: 'oh you get free this and free that'. Whereas if you are working for McDonald's they think you're a prat, sort of thing. Pietro's is probably a bit more recognized and working for Pietro's is seen as a nice place...So if you work for Pietro's it's sort of seen as a good thing which is not the same if you work at McDonald's.

(Interview 27/11/2012)

In many ways, Sean's life changed for the better in the months after he began working at Pietro's and, by the end of 2012, he had become financially self-sufficient and found his own place to live. His relationship with his mother and stepfather had also improved significantly: Sean said his mother had commented on how he is 'growing up', and he talked about how he ensured all his bills were paid before spending anything on luxuries. Generally, he felt pleased with what he had achieved:

I've gone from doing nothing, although I was looking for jobs...And I've gone from where I'd moved out and had nothing [he lived with his girlfriend and her mother for a few months after the relationship with his own mother and stepfather broke down] to now having a job and my own place. So I've done quite well really...

(Interview 27/11/2012)

Sean was still working at Pietro's when fieldwork ended in spring 2013, and it appeared that he was beginning to make a successful transition into adult life and the world of work. But, despite leaving school with good qualifications, realistic career ambitions and a positive attitude to work, his journey has not been easy. Sean's personal circumstances presented him with some significant barriers to participation. Factors related to poverty, which both derived from and exacerbated difficult family circumstances, constrained Sean's ambitions and expectations, as well as the range of opportunities available to him. Although Sean's agency and cultural capital enabled him to grapple with disadvantage, the quality of the opportunities available to him was a significant factor in his trajectory. Although Sean's early difficulties could be interpreted as representing a transitional stage through which many young people travel, different contingencies could have extended the period during which he 'churned' between training and retraining programmes, and intermittent spells outside the labour market. However, Sean's story also suggests that better quality work can make a difference. Whilst Sean did not respond well to negative labour market experiences, he began to flourish – both in the workplace and in life more broadly – when he obtained a job consistent with his ambitions and expectations and in which he was treated reasonably. Sean's experiences reiterate the point made elsewhere in this book, that young people's attitudes and behaviour are as much a response to the circumstances facing them as they are a result of individual traits and dispositions.

# 9
# Family, Community and Welfare

As we have seen earlier in this book, young people's participation in education, training or employment is related in complex ways to their individual circumstances and their location within broader social structures. Whilst educational achievement is a central factor in inter-generational patterns of advantage and disadvantage, young people's experiences of education and the labour market are themselves influenced by these patterns. Rather than acting independently, educational and social achievement form part of a network of factors involved in social reproduction and, more specifically, in processes of marginalization and social exclusion. Burchardt et al. (1999) identify a range of such factors, including individual characteristics such as health and educational qualifications; life events such as job losses or partnership breakdown; characteristics of the neighbourhood in which an individual lives; and institutional factors such as welfare and benefit systems. Before discussing the remaining case studies, this chapter considers more closely the social and cultural matrix in which the experiences of marginalized young people are formed, with particular attention to the ways in which family life, local neighbourhoods and welfare systems interact with and influence educational achievement and prospects for employment.

## Families, social class and ethnicity

In Chapter 3, we explained how being NEET is particularly associated with deprived family backgrounds and must be seen as part of wider processes in which advantage and disadvantage persist from one generation to another. Within these processes, the material and financial resources to which families have access, their educational attainment and the nature of their social networks play important roles. Such factors are powerfully expressed in terms of Pierre Bourdieu's analysis of social, cultural and economic capital (Bourdieu 1986) discussed in Chapter 1. Bourdieu's analysis is a specific conceptualization of how social class operates in the transmission of advantage between generations. Whilst the tendencies towards greater individualization of social risk identified by Ulrich Beck (1992) have led some researchers to seek alternative conceptualizations, based on identity and biographical projects or more sophisticated blends of individual and structural processes (Farrugia 2013), social class remains the most powerful basis for understanding intergenerational disadvantage in modern capitalist societies (Erikson and Goldthorpe 2010). Empirical research consistently demonstrates that class background is a major factor in a range of outcomes, including health, educational attainment and other influences on the chances that a young person will experience one or more aspects of social exclusion. Social class also shapes the likelihood that protective factors will operate, either to prevent more advantaged young people with specific risk factors from entering vulnerable categories or to provide greater resilience to periods of exclusion. The trajectories of young people from middle-class backgrounds are often problematic (Power et al. 2003); however, fractured middle-class transitions can more easily be alleviated by financial and cultural resources. Thus, whilst leaving education at an early age poses a risk to young people from all backgrounds, this risk is greater for working-class young people.

Figure 9.1, based on data from the Youth Cohort Study (YCS[1]), illustrates the composition of the NEET population by social class. This composition is shown, firstly for anyone who had been NEET for any length of time by the age of 18, and secondly for those who had been NEET for more than 12 months by age 18. From the first distribution we see that a significant proportion of young people who have been NEET are from higher social classes; however, the second distribution shows that lower social class backgrounds are more strongly represented amongst those who have experienced long-term exclusion. As we have seen, this is largely because young people from higher social classes are more likely to remain in education, and being outside full-time education at 18 is associated with a significant risk of being NEET for all young people. Thus, although it would be inaccurate to picture NEET young people as almost exclusively from disadvantaged backgrounds, those experiencing the deepest exclusion – and therefore more likely to be deemed problematic – are drawn disproportionately from the poorest circumstances.

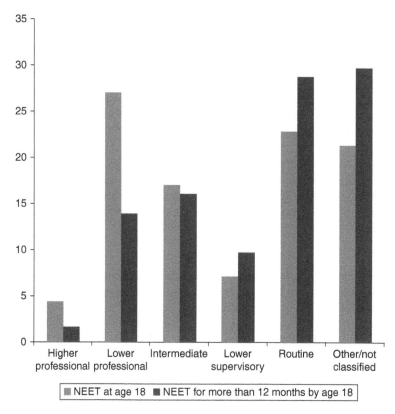

*Figure 9.1* Composition of NEET populations by social class for young people in England aged 18 in 2009
*Source*: Authors' analysis of data from DfE/ONS (2010).

In our research, practitioners tended to associate NEET young people with poor family backgrounds, particularly families in which relationships between parents or between young people and their parents had broken down:

> Obviously a lot of them are from really, really poor backgrounds. The majority of them are white... Family issues are a big thing and it's usually a case where they've run away or they've been chucked out of home. Or... they've been witnessing domestic violence but sometimes they are the victims [or] even the perpetrator... A lot of the time you will find that a parent has alcohol or substance abuse problems... Crime is a big issue but, again, that will come back to family

circumstances... Independent living is quite a common thing which then dictates the finances because finances just runs through it all.

(Connexions manager, 8/10/2010)

In some cases, however, family backgrounds were not seen as the immediate precipitating factor in becoming NEET. Lack of progress in post-16 education, for example, was also regarded as important, and could often result in a young person leaving college:

I actually developed a programme at college which was a flexible start programme [for college leavers]... and we picked up an awful lot of young people who had gone to sixth-form college... and [from] school sixth forms where young people had stayed on to do A-levels but then realized this was not for them.

(Manager for 14–19 provision, 30/09/2010)

In qualitative research, social class is often conceptualized in terms of distributions of social, cultural and economic capital or in terms of identities and cultural formations. However, in large-scale quantitative analyses which help us to understand overall trends in the social structure, class is traditionally thought of in terms of employment and the relations between employees and their work. The employment status and work history of the parents and step-parents of participants was therefore of interest to us. This was not straightforward: some young people had little contact with their parents in recent years and could not remember what jobs they had done; others gave confused and contradictory accounts. However, we were able to build up a picture of largely working-class employment, of churning between different jobs – particularly in recent years – and periods of unemployment. Self-employment was not unknown, usually in manual work or delivering materials. Some young people had siblings who were employed. Ten participants had parents or step-parents currently in work; these jobs were largely manual or routine white-collar employment, such as construction worker, lorry driver, mechanic and chef for men, and for women learning support assistant, clerical assistant, factory worker and care assistant. Becky's stepfather worked as 'a manager' in a large supermarket. Five of these young people had both parents currently in work. An eleventh participant, Saheera, said in a late interview that her father owned a restaurant, although she had not mentioned this before. Jed's parents had owned various small businesses, which seemed to have been serially unsuccessful, but were now both unemployed. Cheryl's mother was studying at university; she had lost contact with her father. Eight other participants had no parent in work (most of these young people had contact with only one parent), although Cayden's uncle – who had acted as his foster parent – had been a prison officer. For the remaining three participants it was not possible to gain any reliable information on the employment status of their parents or step-parents.

For some of the practitioners we interviewed, being NEET in Fernside and Northdale was perceived as largely an issue relating to young white people, particularly where becoming NEET had been associated with specific barriers to engagement, such as youth offending or early parenthood. However, it was recognized that there could be significant ethnic and gender inequalities in levels of engagement with support services such as Connexions; practitioners also pointed out that for some groups, such as those with learning difficulties or disabilities, there was greater representation of ethnic minorities.

> It's definitely boys. I have – between Fernside and Northdale – 103 boys and 21 girls and most are White. Of the boys, 83 are White, seven Asian and two Black and 11 mixed race. And of the girls, 20 are White and one mixed race. So it is very much a White, boy culture. Whether the girls are cleverer and don't get caught remains to be seen.
>
> (Connexions personal adviser working with young offenders, 13/10/2010)

These comments do not necessarily mean that there was under-representation of certain minority ethnic groups in the work of practitioners in Fernside and Northdale. National data suggests that NEET rates for young people from African-Caribbean, Bangladeshi and Pakistani backgrounds are roughly comparable to those for young White people (see Figure 9.2); one would therefore expect services to be accessed in similar proportions to the representation of these ethnic groups within the overall population. In Fernside and Northdale, NEET rates in August 2010 – when our research began – were around 10 per cent[2] for young people from Pakistani and White British backgrounds, whilst for Indian and Bangladeshi backgrounds rates were somewhat lower. The highest rates were 13 per cent and 18 per cent, respectively, for young people from African-Caribbean or mixed White and African-Caribbean backgrounds. However, cohort size must also be taken into account; these latter two groups together accounted for 3 per cent of the 16–18 cohort, whilst only 0.1 per cent were from Bangladeshi

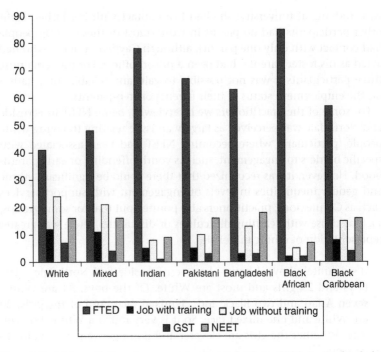

*Figure 9.2* Main activity of young people aged 18 in 2009 in England, by ethnicity
Source: DfE/ONS (2010).

backgrounds. The largest ethnic groups were White British (68 per cent), Pakistani (11 per cent) and Indian (4 per cent). The experience of practitioners is therefore understandable in terms of the relatively low numbers of young people from minority ethnic backgrounds in the NEET population as a whole. Nevertheless, there is substantial evidence that certain groups of families are less likely to engage with service providers, and this is particularly the case for those living in poverty and for some ethnic minorities (Katz et al. 2007, p.8). Whilst it is important to recognize the heterogeneity both within and across minority ethnic groups (Lloyd and Rafferty 2006), various factors appear to be involved in levels of engagement, relating both to the nature of the services provided and to family circumstances (Page et al. 2007). Families from minority ethnic groups are disproportionately at risk of living in poverty and having poor working conditions, which can affect the time and resources available to engage with services; cultural differences may also affect how the role of services provided by local authorities and other agencies is viewed in relation to problems within the family. However, service providers themselves may lack the expertise effectively to engage with certain family backgrounds, resulting in people from minority ethnic backgrounds becoming disillusioned with the provision available to them (Page et al. 2007, pp.12–13).

Differences and similarities between NEET rates for different ethnic groups highlight complex interactions between social, cultural and economic factors, which shape patterns of participation. Although average levels of educational achievement amongst young people from Pakistani, Bangladeshi and African-Caribbean backgrounds are lower than for young White people (DCSF/ONS 2009), they are more likely to participate in full-time post-compulsory education. However, young people from minority ethnic backgrounds are less likely to engage work-based learning (DCSF/ONS 2009), and there is evidence that those from Asian and African-Caribbean backgrounds are more likely to have negative perceptions of lower-status forms of work-based learning (Foskett and Hemsley-Brown 2001).

Lower educational participation rates for White young people do not necessarily imply greater vulnerability than those from ethnic minority backgrounds, although as we have seen young White people from working-class backgrounds are often regarded as a particular concern. The relationships between different forms of participation and their distribution across ethnic groups highlight the need to interrogate closely the nature of employment prospects and educational provision for all young people. In particular, unemployment rates are higher for certain ethnic minorities, and also show significant change over time, both against the overall rate of unemployment and relative to other ethnic minorities. During labour market depressions in 1984, 1993 and 2009–2010, Black unemployment was between two and three times the overall rate. Whilst in 1984 and 1993 the Black and Asian unemployment rates were similar, in 2009–2010 the rate for Asians was substantially smaller, albeit significantly higher than the overall rate (see Table 9.1). Young Black people entering the labour market without qualifications have been particularly vulnerable in these difficult times (Bell and Blanchflower 2010, p.8).

As in our E2E research in the same local authorities, some practitioners identified cultural barriers to taking part in certain forms of provision amongst young people from Asian Muslim backgrounds. Particularly for girls, provision that was too far from home or

*Table 9.1*   Unemployment rates, ethnicity and qualifications (%), 1984–2010

|                  | 1984 | 1993 | 2007 | 2008 | 2009–2010 |
|------------------|------|------|------|------|-----------|
| Overall          | 11.8 | 10.4 | 5.3  | 5.8  | 7.7       |
| No qualifications | 13.9 | 14.6 | 10.2 | 10.6 | 14.9      |
| 16–17            | 21.3 | 24.0 | 26.4 | 25.5 | 32.0      |
| 18–24            | 18.0 | 17.6 | 12.1 | 12.9 | 17.4      |
| Black            | 20.8 | 27.2 | 12.2 | 12.5 | 17.3      |
| Asian            | 19.3 | 20.2 | 9.6  | 9.8  | 11.5      |
| Black < age 25   | 31.5 | 44.9 | 33.7 | 33.4 | 38.6      |

*Source*: Labour force survey (Bell and Blanchflower 2010, p.8).

involving more 'masculine' subjects were seen as problematic for their families:

> But we can have youngsters come onto [Foundation Learning] and E2E previously who are from good homes but they've just got into a bad crowd or they get involved with gambling, drugs or alcohol and all manner of things. It's a very mixed bag. We get a lot of Asian young girls on E2E who are not able to progress then because their parents put barriers in place. And, again, that can be geographical.
>
> (Manager for 14–19 provision, 30/09/2010)

Generalizations about Asian Muslim culture as inevitably constraining and constituting a barrier to participation for young people from such backgrounds must be treated with caution. Page et al. (2007, p.12) argue that such stereotyping can contribute to lower levels of engagement with service providers. Moreover, Shain (2003) challenges conceptions of an isolated and isolating culture which is inimical to the development of girls in particular. She argues that Asian girls are not passive victims of oppressive cultures; the emerging identities of young Asian Muslim girls, like other young people, are shaped by multiple factors rather than being the deterministic outcome of monolithic and limiting perspectives. Other researchers also emphasize the complexity of interactions between social, cultural, religious and historical factors which, operating within the broader context of class and community deprivation, help to shape the identities and experiences of young people from Asian Muslim backgrounds, and in particular the educational aspirations of families for their daughters (Abbas 2003; Ijaz and Abbas 2010; Shah and Iqbal 2011). In the case of Shabina, one of the two Asian Muslim girls in our research, some aspects of her family life appeared to fit with images of a limiting culture; her brother in particular attempted to control her behaviour, and on one occasion Shabina was unable to attend a birthday treat arranged by her friend Saheera because she had been 'grounded' after being seen with her boyfriend. Shabina's brother did not want her to attend college, even in her home town of Eastville. However, Shabina's family ultimately relented, and after leaving school she began attending a Level 1 course in social care at a college 11 miles from her home, and located in a large city – a decision agreed with her parents. Shabina – who in fact never became NEET – had been identified by her school as 'at risk' due to various instances of disruptive behaviour, and felt that to succeed, she needed to avoid her former friends:

> Well, to be honest with you, it's the closest college that we've got where I don't know too many people... my mum and dad are seeing how I've progressed here and as they can see that improvement in how I'm doing they don't mind me coming here... I should be getting paid the EMA but I don't know why they are not sorting it out. Every time I go to sort it out she says to me 'you need to bring in this statement or that statement'... My brother pays for my expenses.
>
> (Interview 02/02/2012)

After some initial difficulties – college staff complained about Shabina's attendance, but she claimed that she had medical appointments – Shabina settled into her course and then progressed to Level 2 in childcare. However, rather than progressing to a Level 3 programme in this field as she had originally intended, Shabina applied in August 2013 for a Level 2 Beauty course.

## Neighbourhoods and deprivation

Deprivation has both individual and communal dimensions. It is, of course, perfectly possible for isolated pockets of deprivation to exist in otherwise affluent communities, affecting one or just a few families in specific circumstances. From this perspective, deprivation is conceptualized as a relative lack of key resources – not only economic as in relative conceptions of poverty, but also social, cultural and emotional. Peruzzi (2013) analyses childhood deprivation in terms of economic factors such as low income, housing tenure, overcrowding and lack of material goods, together with family socio-demographic risks including having a teenage mother, being in care and frequent changes of residence.

Cusworth et al. (2009, p.8) use similar indicators of deprivation, and also include factors such as being able to take holidays away from home, pursue leisure activities and entertain friends or relatives. Studies such as these demonstrate the links between childhood and adolescent deprivation, and later experiences of social exclusion. However, whilst both forms of deprivation are implicated in the persistence of disadvantage, the influence of the home environment appears to act differently to the grosser features of economic deprivation, being mediated primarily via deviant behaviours in adolescence (Peruzzi 2013, p.29).

Deprivation is not distributed uniformly; clustering effects tend to group poor people together, and it makes sense to talk of deprived communities as well as individuals. There is a substantial literature on growing up in poor neighbourhoods, much of it focusing on the question of whether spending one's formative years living in deprived communities has an impact on life chances independent of other variables, such as family poverty or individual characteristics. In other words, 'do poor neighbourhoods make their residents poorer?' (Brännström 2004, p.2515). Alternatively, do people with multiple disadvantages become concentrated in certain neighbourhoods either because of shared circumstances which made them poor in the first place – such as de-industrialization – or because people with greater resources move out as neighbourhoods decline, whilst poorer people either remain there or are forced by lack of resources to move in? A number of mechanisms have been proposed which might support the idea that neighbourhood factors exert an independent effect. For example, the greater prevalence of problematic behaviours in poorer neighbourhoods could provide negative 'role models' for young people; cultural and recreational resources may be lacking in poor areas, and schools may be less effective; job opportunities may be limited; or there may be environmental factors such as the presence of factories, busy roads and other undesirable features (Mayer and Jencks 1989; Wodtke et al. 2011). According to some accounts, particularly those associated with underclass theories, the poorest neighbourhoods become breeding grounds for a cultural malaise, in which underclass behaviours are not only transmitted between generations, but also spread between families – the *contagion model* of neighbourhood effects (Mayer and Jencks 1989). However, the evidence for independent neighbourhood effects is inconclusive; whilst studies such as Wodtke et al. (2011) find a significant influence of protracted exposure to concentrations of disadvantage on US high school graduation rates, other research finds little impact. Part of the reason for this may be contextual sensitivity; factors such as those identified by Burchardt et al. (1999) interact in such complex ways that cancellation effects may occur. The absence of neighbourhood effects found in an analysis of data from Stockholm during the 'golden era' of the Swedish welfare state (Brännström 2004) may be attributed to this kind of cancellation.

Other research on deprived neighbourhoods seeks to understand how locally embedded social networks in poor neighbourhoods form part of the processes whereby poverty and class-based inequalities are reproduced (MacDonald and Marsh 2001; MacDonald et al. 2005; Green and White 2008). Such studies take a holistic view of the interactions between people and places, taking into account the enabling and constraining features of local resources – whether social, cultural or economic. The characteristic focus of these studies on place, class and social exclusion emphasizes the difference between subjective and objective geographies of opportunity, and shows how young people's transitions in poor neighbourhoods, rather than being based on orthodox discourses concerning the need to develop human capital, are powerfully shaped by experiences closer to home. Social networks are particularly important for processes of social reproduction, and a consistent finding from research into poor neighbourhoods is the role of family, friends and neighbours in reproducing and recycling low-paid, often insecure jobs. For Steph, a family acquaintance provided the opportunity of employment in a supermarket café. Similarly, Jess obtained work at a school for the disabled through a family contact:

> I got a phone call [from] someone I've known since I were little and she's always known that I've wanted a job since I left school, and she rang me up … she said come in and give it a couple of weeks and then she started putting my hours up … I go on the till; clean; do various things.
>
> (Steph, interview 09/03/2012)

> Jess has since applied for a job at a school, a guy who works there knows her dad and she found out that there was a job going but she is still waiting for her CRB[3] check to come through before she can officially start. She … says she loves it; she has cousins with disabilities and has had experience caring for them.
>
> (Jess, field notes 16/03/2011)

Close friends Becky and Jasmine obtained work as carers, hearing about the opportunity from the carer of Becky's boyfriend. However, even employment gained through informal social networks can be subject to regulatory requirements which make it costly to obtain:

> Becky has a paid job at H-Care – a service that takes care of the elderly…Jasmine is also in the process of applying for this, they heard about the job from Gary's carer (he has ADHD and is autistic). It pays £7.50 an hour, £7.80 on weekends and £11.20 on bank holidays…Jasmine has been told she needs to get a CRB check – for which she has to pay £58. She needs a birth certificate, an additional cost; she has no money (for food) until Thursday and so must wait until then.

Jasmine needed financial assistance from her mother and from a housing charity to afford the cost of the CRB check. As we have already seen, Jasmine did not stay long in this job, at least partly because of its stresses; whilst the pay was relatively high for someone of her age and experience, she was not paid for travelling between clients and the work was demanding, with long hours and little tolerance of Jasmine's own health problems.

Inequalities in material and cultural resources have often been identified as leading to contracted spatial horizons for people living in poor communities. Green and White (2008) describe the barriers experienced by young people whose attachment to place sometimes overshadows the possibility of seeking education or jobs beyond the immediate locality, whilst MacDonald et al. (2005, p.880) report on the 'closing down' of social networks as the few people able to find work elsewhere moved out, leaving most of their participants surrounded by other socially excluded individuals. However, attachment to place is not purely a subjective phenomenon, and transport costs, travelling time and the geographical distribution of educational and employment opportunities are also important. As we found in our research, local education provision can be complex and unevenly spread. The nature and availability of education and training also depends to some degree upon national and local funding priorities, which can affect scattered smaller providers disproportionately. Travelling to work could involve lengthy journeys, as Jaylene found after moving house increased the time required to reach the charity shop where she worked four days a week as a volunteer:

> It's quite hard because I get four buses a day, but before I were getting two buses a day…I leave my house at 9.45 to get a bus down town

and I get a bus from [the town centre] at about ten and get up here for about half ten. So it's about forty-five minutes.

The great majority of young people in our research lived in areas of significant deprivation, and had spent most of their lives in such locations.[4] Eleven participants were located in areas which were amongst the 10 per cent most deprived in England, and a further six in areas included in the next decile. Only one participant lived in an area in the least deprived 50 per cent. Even in the less severely deprived areas, young people would often experience poor housing. Accommodation for participants living alone included both local authority housing and private renting, although some still lived with parents. There was concern amongst practitioners that young people living alone in privately rented accommodation are vulnerable to exploitation by landlords; consequently, educational provision for these young people included housing rights and responsibilities. Living 'independently' carried various risks if young people failed to meet their responsibilities, and in the course of our research some were served with eviction orders, warned about anti-social behaviour or taken to court for non-payment of council tax. The behaviour of landlords could also be problematic, and some participants spoke about failure to carry out repairs and unfair charges at the conclusion of tenancy agreements.

In our study, we found somewhat greater geographical mobility than was the case for MacDonald et al. (2005). Partly because of the number of care leavers in our sample, participants had often lived in various places, sometimes in quite distant parts of the country. Care leavers were also found places to live by social services, and such accommodation could be relatively distant from other places where they had lived. Participants sometimes moved because of overcrowding or to live with the families of boyfriends or girlfriends; as we have seen in Sean's case, this could involve moving from one town to another within Fernside and Northdale. However, such movements were limited: very few participants who talked about moving to other parts of the country actually did so, and it was uncommon for rehousing to involve a move of more than a few miles. More often, participants remained in broadly the same neighbourhood. Social networks were also limited by financial resources: friendships that could not easily be maintained by public transport soon withered. The movements that did take place did not involve significant changes in the type of neighbourhood where participants lived. These were, perforce, areas where housing was cheap. If participants found themselves surrounded by different people from time to time, these people were, in the words of MacDonald et al. (2005), also 'just like them'.

Overcrowding was a problem for some participants. Sara hoped for local authority accommodation by the time her baby was born, as both her parents and those of her partner had no room:

> His mum has got five kids. I'm not going to be on the streets [though] because my mate has got a two-bedroom house and I'll help her pay her bills and that's probably the biggest favour anyone has ever done for me in my life... I want a nursery and everything but if [we can't get a council place] we'll live with my best mate.
>
> (Interview 24/03/2011)

Some participants were reluctant to cross certain boundaries, even where relatively short distances were involved. The reasons for this are varied but can restrict opportunities; knowing and being known in an area could be problematic when social conflict occurred, transforming familiar territories into spaces of dispute. Jaylene, for example, would not travel to Eastville, even to pursue a benefit claim, as she feared she was known there as a 'grass', having on separate occasions reported abuse by her father and violence by her boyfriend to the police.

## Young people, families and schooling

As we have seen, low educational achievement is one of the most important risk factors associated with young people becoming NEET. In turn, low achievement is often explained in terms of two related concepts: educational disadvantage and educational disaffection. Educational disadvantage is defined in terms of systematic differences in educational experiences or achievement between different social groups: for example, achievement differentials relating to gender, ethnicity or social class will place certain groups at a disadvantage relative to others. Disadvantage may arise as a consequence of individual characteristics, such as having a learning difficulty or disability, or from family circumstances – for example, being placed in care. However, individual or family circumstances are themselves related to broader structures of disadvantage within society, and young people from poorer backgrounds are more likely to have statements of special educational need or to have been in care (Cassen and Kingdon 2007). Of particular significance for the young people in our research is the educational disadvantage associated with being in care. Although the percentage of looked after young people achieving 5 GCSE passes at grades A*–C improved significantly between 2008 and 2012, rising from 16.4 per cent to 31.2 per cent, the performance of other young people showed an even greater improvement, so that the attainment gap increased slightly from 43.3 per cent to 45.6 per cent. When English and mathematics passes are included, the gap widens: in 2012 only 11.4 per cent of young people in care achieved the benchmark of 5 A*–C passes including these subjects (DfE 2012a).

Whilst educational disadvantage refers to inequalities arising from individual characteristics or from social and family circumstances, disaffection is a more controversial – and contested – term in which subjective and ideological components may be identified. In its most extreme forms, disaffection may be manifested through persistent truancy or disruptive behaviour; less visible forms of disaffection, such as varying degrees of disengagement from educational activities, may also be involved. Particularly in policy statements, educational disaffection is represented more or less straightforwardly as depending on and revealing the attitudes and orientations of young people towards their schooling, which in turn are formed within families and communities, or through a 'soft bigotry of low expectations' on the part of teachers (DfE 2010, p.4). According to such accounts, disaffection is largely the result of low aspirations and anti-school attitudes, often transmitted between generations and sometimes blighting whole communities.

The deficiency of this kind of explanation is that it neglects the complex relationships between aspirations, achievement and broader social and economic circumstances. Kintrea et al. (2011) argue that this model, which has acquired almost hegemonic status within policy discourse, rests on three related but questionable assumptions. Firstly, that low aspirations cause low achievement; secondly, that some people from poorer backgrounds have depressed aspirations; and thirdly, that raising aspirations will help to break this cycle, and lead to improved outcomes for young people from deprived backgrounds. However, as these authors point out, whilst there might be some truth in these assumptions, the argument that low aspirations *cause* low achievement is not really tenable. It is equally possible that young people who do less well at school lower their sights for the future. In this case, low aspiration or negative attitudes towards education are consequences of low achievement, not its cause (Kintrea et al. 2011, p.12). Indeed, Goodman and Gregg (2010) find that aspirations are generally high, and that the real issue may well be as much about ensuring that high aspirations are achievable as in raising aspiration *per se*.

Finlay et al. (2010) draw similar conclusions: the problem is not with the aspirations of young people, but with their expectations, based on what they see around them. However, generalizing about aspirations can be misleading, whether such generalizations portray young people as full of ambition, or without it. Kintrea et al. (2011) draw attention to the diversity and complexity of aspirations, showing that places with similar levels of deprivation can be quite different in their social composition and the life experiences of residents, although within specific areas place, family and school factors seemed generally consistent in their effect on aspirations, which although relatively high were not unrealistic. These authors suggest that many young people in deprived areas have high aspirations precisely because of the scarcity of good jobs, realizing that to compete in depressed labour markets high levels of education are necessary, albeit not sufficient. There was no evidence from their study that young people see unemployment or criminal activity as preferable to work. Such findings are consistent with our own research, in which participants held quite mainstream attitudes, values and ambitions. However, we did find evidence that some parents were not as supportive as they could have been, and were sometimes ready to condone poor attendance or even withdrawal from school. For some participants, home life was so difficult that just attending school was an achievement:

> My mum didn't bother to send me to school and she just stayed in bed and I had my brother to look after.
>
> (Becky)

> I was being bullied at [high school] and so my mum brought me out of school plus I had a knee injury which was a result of being at high school. My mum [tutored me at home] . . .
>
> (Katie)

Archer et al. (2010) show how both practitioners and young people conceptualize some of the factors leading to disaffection in terms of 'the pull of the street' (p.26). In these discourses, the street takes on the role of both a place – the immediate environment – and a cultural space, with values and practices seen as placed in opposition to those of the school. Both enticing and a source of fear, this idea of 'the street' could also be discerned amongst the reasons for disrupted schooling offered by our participants:

I should have stayed another year but because there were some problems... it weren't because of bullying because I didn't get bullied it was just that I didn't like it. I preferred to be at home with my mates because my mates were all older than me...

(Sara)

I started getting into a bad crowd [when I was about 12 or 13]... so my mum and dad got me put in care and I went to school somewhere else. I were drinking and taking drugs as well and doing all sorts.

(Isla)

Although factors such as peer cultures and parental apathy or collusion may have been significant at the time, participants also learned from their experiences and in some cases contrasted their younger and older selves. Perhaps the last word on this point should go to Sara:

Well, at the time all my family and friends said it was alright not to go to school. And now my brother is going to be the same and I'm telling him now to keep his head down. But I help him with his homework and stuff. So I tell him to keep his head down because I don't want him to end up like me with no GCSEs.

(Interview 24/03/2011)

Although simple causal models of disaffection are inadequate, persistent truancy or exclusion from school are nevertheless important factors contributing to low educational achievement and becoming NEET after leaving school. Figure 9.3 shows differences in attainment between excluded pupils and persistent truants, and those with less problematic school careers. However, exclusion and truancy should not be seen solely in terms of an individual's rejection of the values and authority of the school; as Munn and Lloyd (2005, p.205) explain, 'Exclusion for disruptive behaviour is perhaps the most explicit form of rejection by a school of its pupils', and the practice of exclusion needs to be seen in the context of how the school system as a whole positions individual pupils, their communities and the schools serving them. James and Simmons (2007, p.368) propose that disaffection should be conceptualized in terms of a relationship between a young person and an educational activity or institution, emphasizing the role of both parties in the construction of value, as well as the varied nature of disaffection. The trajectories of excluded young people differ according to

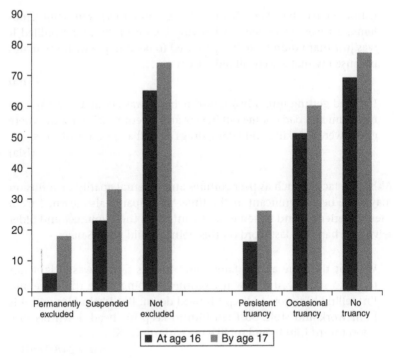

*Figure 9.3* Young people achieving Level 2 at age 16 and by age 17, by school exclusion and truancy
*Source*: DCSF/ONS (2009).

their engagement with support services, the qualities of staff in post-exclusion destinations and the existence of supportive family networks (Daniels and Cole 2010, pp.126–128). However, particularly with those who have repeatedly been excluded, challenging family circumstances may be a major factor in exclusions and can be further exacerbated by the fact of exclusion itself – sometimes with minimal educational provision for many months (Pirrie et al. 2011, pp.535–536). This suggests that excluded young people who lack family support will be at risk of further educational disadvantage.

Exclusion rates are much higher for boys than for girls, for pupils with special educational needs, for those receiving free school meals and for certain minorities – notably African-Caribbean pupils. Children in care are also more likely to be excluded than those who are not (DfE 2012b). However, such variations do not necessarily imply that discrimination against particular groups of pupils is institutionalized, or that children belonging to these groups are inherently more likely to offend against the school ethos. It is possible, for example, that inequality and other circumstances external to the school affect their behaviour within it, increasing their chances of exclusion. Nevertheless, there is some evidence that similar actions attract different responses from the school, depending on the social background of the young person involved (Munn and Lloyd 2005). Moreover, the promotion of competitive markets within education has made schools more reluctant to invest in pupils with a history of underachievement, truancy and school exclusion. Concentration on those closer to achieving good grades at the expense of the most disadvantaged can further reinforce disaffection (Shildrick and MacDonald 2007). The discourse of worth in relation to disruptive pupils identified by Munn and Lloyd (2005, p.213) can reinforce feelings of worthlessness or unfair treatment in those not deemed worth saving. In our study, the experience of sanctions or exclusion appeared largely a prosaic part of everyday life:

> I didn't want to go back to any school because I knew they wouldn't let me back into that school because of my behaviour and attitude and attendance and stuff like that. I got kicked out of all my lessons. I didn't like the teachers and the lessons were just boring.
>
> [Steph]

Processes of differentiation and exclusion operate between schools as well as within them. Giddens (1998) sees middle-class self-exclusion from public services as a significant factor in social exclusion, whilst Whitty (2001) extends this general argument to education. The withdrawal of cultural and social capital from areas of state schooling deemed unsafe or inadequate for more privileged children undermines the schooling of poorer families. Class-based segregation between schools signifies more than just the absence of certain groups: it can have both subjective and objective outcomes, stigmatizing some schools and their communities whilst reducing their ability to meet target-driven outcomes, now so important for the reputation of a school. Whilst market-based educational reforms present self-exclusion as the legitimate exercise of choice and attribute educational underachievement to deficiencies in families, communities and schools, they institutionalize a set of practices and discourses which exclude poor families from more successful schools and construct swathes of state education as 'places on the margins' (Shields 1991; Reay and Lucey 2004; Reay 2007).

Although working-class children may construct counter-narratives which represent their schools more positively, and some middle-class parents make counter-intuitive schooling choices (James et al. 2010), for young people such as those in our study the pervasive discourse is that good schools, and by implication successful students, are located elsewhere. Nevertheless, the schools attended by most of our participants were not officially regarded as ineffective, despite facing challenging circumstances; in the performative terms of contemporary education policy, most were judged to be providing a 'good' education overall. Three participants – Jaylene, Jed and Sean – attended Fairlea High School, although Sean and Jed later moved on to other schools. Jaylene was excluded in Year 9 and completed her schooling in a Pupil Referral Unit.

> Fairlea High School is a … community school located in a disadvantaged area … The student population is diverse, including refugees, asylum seekers and those who are new to the economic union … and a large number of students join and leave the school during the academic year. The proportion of students with learning difficulties and/or disabilities is above average.
>
> (Ofsted Report 2008; Inspection Grade 2 (Good))

The school careers of the young people taking part in our research fell into three broad groups. The largest group, consisting of 11 participants, had completed their schooling and took GCSE examinations in Year 11. Of these, only one participant did not achieve at least one grade C, and some achieved a significant number of higher grades. However, few of these young people obtained sufficiently strong grades to enable immediate progression to Level 3 courses. This may in part be attributable to their often precarious engagement with schooling, for as our case studies show, even within this group disrupted education was common. For the second largest group, exclusion or truancy from mainstream schools had effectively ended their full-time education, sometimes as early as Year 9. Of eight participants in this group, few had taken GCSE examinations and only one (Steph, who was on 'permanent study leave' for part of Year 11) had achieved grade C or higher. In most cases, they attended a Pupil Referral Unit after being excluded or maintained contact with their school through expedients such as online tutoring or part-time attendance. Such arrangements appeared largely ineffective:

> [I went part-time because] I didn't like school and then I were arguing with my mum and stepdad all the time … I went for three [GCSE

exams] and I got kicked out of one of them and I just sat there in another one because I just didn't have a clue and then in the other one I fell asleep.

(Becky)

The remaining five participants attended schools for pupils with special educational needs. Four of the five had low reading ages. In two cases – Cayden and Alfie – this was because of learning difficulties identified at an early age; however, for Sid and Karla, their attendance at special schools was related at least partly to behavioural problems. Of this group, only Karla achieved any GCSEs – a grade C in English and lower grades in two other subjects. Vernon, the other young person in this group, attended a school which catered largely for children in care who had behavioural, emotional or social difficulties. Vernon ceased attending in Year 10, and Sid was excluded in Year 11.

## Benefits and welfare to work

For young people such as those who took part in our research, welfare and benefit systems are a crucial arena of struggle between the individual and the state. As policymakers quickly became aware in the late 1980s, following the removal of entitlement to unemployment benefit from young people under the age of 18, withdrawing benefits sacrifices an important mechanism of social control and may entail losing the ability to monitor problematic youth and channel them into state-approved activities. The NEET discourse may be seen as one response to this problem, and Fergusson (2013) proposes that policies on welfare and participation function as a mode of governance, enabling surveillance and promoting self-entrepreneurship in exchange for financial support. Strathdee (2013) identifies three strategies employed by the state to reintegrate the disengaged. Motivational strategies are designed to encourage young people to adopt dispositions favourable to contemporary economic conditions and include the provision of individualized support, such as personal advisers.[5] Punishing (or work-first) strategies aim to reduce welfare dependence by making benefits conditional on undertaking mandated activities (such as looking for work). Finally, bridging strategies attempt to create links between job-seekers and employers. Later in this section, we will encounter examples of these strategies as participants negotiate the somewhat labyrinthine complexities of benefit systems, training schemes and work experience.

The benefits available to participants varied with age and circumstances, but potentially included Jobseekers Allowance (JSA), Income Support, Disability Living Allowance, Housing Benefit and the EMA – replaced during the research by 16–19 Bursaries. In some circumstances, Income Support could be paid to young people in education. Participants with children could also claim Child Benefit. Except in extreme need,[6] young people under the age of 18 could not claim JSA; those who reached this age during the research often reported a change in experience, from a relatively benign regime in which engaging in learning was prioritized, to a more adult world in which getting a job – any job – took precedence over other ambitions. This was not necessarily unwelcome, but some participants found it disorientating (Thompson et al. 2014). JSA claimants must sign a Jobseeker's Agreement setting out the type of work they are looking for, the days and times they are available and the steps they will take to find employment. They are required to 'sign on'[7] at the Jobcentre at least every two weeks to review their job search activities. Various sanctions may be applied to young people who fail to comply with the conditions for receipt of JSA, and their benefits may be reduced, suspended or disallowed entirely. Young people receiving Income Support are required to attend 'Learning Focused Interviews' at the start of their claim at certain times thereafter, such as when learning programmes end. As with JSA, sanctions may be applied if young people do not attend these interviews.

The requirement to demonstrate that they were actively seeking work exasperated some participants, who felt that such demonstrations were largely meaningless. Jaylene was in voluntary employment for two days a week at a charity shop, but to retain her entitlement to JSA she was also required to look for work, whilst Karla felt that the jobs she had been offered were inappropriate:

> You just print some things off the computer that they have in the Jobcentre. When you go down you show them what you've been looking for…it works for me. But you are meant to be seen every week. I don't have a CV but I can get one although I can't be bothered getting one right now.
>
> (Jaylene, interview 19/04/2012)

> Well, if I don't get this job then they'll kick me off the dole…Because they've offered me jobs but I wouldn't take them because it's not something that I've done. [Jobs] like working as a mechanic…[I've no experience]…But they said I still had to apply for it and I said why

because I don't actually want to do it. They said I had to get my CV and send it in and if I didn't they would cut my benefits... I've asked them if they could find me a course on midwifery because that's what I want to do.

(Karla, interview 23/03/2011)

It was difficult to assess the extent to which welfare processes supported young people in finding sustainable work or training. There was evidence that some practitioners went out of their way to help and encourage participants, and in some cases the Jobcentre could offer viable opportunities. The job Karla refers to above was in elderly care, and at six pounds an hour would have provided £900 per month, as well as the opportunity to gain NVQs (National Vocational Qualifications). However, a few days before the application deadline, Karla had not submitted her CV as requested, and claimed that she could not afford the postage to do so. Two weeks later, she began a ten-week pre-Foundation Learning course. To some extent, Karla's inability to pursue her job application could be seen as supporting the idea that youth unemployment is largely about individual deficits and the propensity of some young people to live on the state:

They don't know how to purchase a ticket; they don't know how to read the timetable; they don't know how to use the train station or the bus station... It's like if they've got a tenner in their pocket they think 'Wow, I'll get this and that' rather than thinking 'Oh, I've got this to pay and that to pay'. Although some of them have spoken to me about them getting better at that... These kids are streetwise and they can soon pick up how to get money out of the state and we need to give them a skill that integrates with their streetwiseness, if you like.

(Jobcentre adviser 04/02/2011)

However, there is also the possibility that these young people *are* in poverty, and *do* care about the type of work or training they undertake: that they want a sense of control, as well as support. Either way, it was obvious that in many cases employability programmes did not fulfil their stated purposes, of making young people more able to find work. It was certainly clear that many participants were extremely frustrated with their experiences of the benefit system, and apparently chaotic self-management could often be attributed to external pressures. We must also remember that many young people from more stable backgrounds display similar behaviours but have access to reserves of social capital, which tend to compensate for individual deficits. The overwhelming impression was of practitioners struggling to reconcile their role of supporting young people in a hostile economic environment with their responsibility to monitor and discipline on behalf of the state. Kelsey recounted her meeting with an adviser like this:

> Oh, that's doing my head in; absolutely doing my head in! I'm meant to bring, right, this form to say what day I go on college course; where it is; the times and to say that I'm attending it all the time. And I didn't bring it so I didn't have one so I had to fill in this other one which said... And I had to fill in this form and bring it in but I lost it anyway. And I've lost my CV as well.
>
> (Interview 25/02/2011)

By creating the conditions under which such discourses can emerge, benefit conditionality contributes to the construction of the use-less subject, the antithesis of the self-entrepreneur embedded in neo-liberal prescriptions of post-industrial identity. Abstracting young people's behaviours from the social relations in which they occur, this antithesis represents self-responsibility and self-organization as *purely* individual characteristics; characteristics through which 'class inequality is reproduced and refigured, individualised as a marker of personal volition and inclusion' (Skeggs 2004, p.60).

The concept of marginalization highlights the fuzzy boundary between exclusion and inclusion, and encourages us to think about inequalities within participation and the consequences for excluded young people of re-engaging in work or training. In their study of deprived communities on Teesside, Shildrick et al. (2012a) show how supply-side and demand-side factors interact, sometimes to the detriment of future employability. Whilst poor mental or physical health, alcohol or drug dependency, and a lack of 'soft skills' may be responsible for difficulties in finding decent work, they may also be aggravated by poor quality employment. For some of the participants in our study, interaction between supply-side and demand-side factors, particularly when welfare-to-work programmes are included, could be seen as exacerbating their problems. Jasmine, a lively, articulate young woman who was 18 when our fieldwork began, led a tempestuous and incident-filled life. Although still in frequent contact with her mother, she lived alone in a council flat, attending various employability programmes, working for short periods and often experiencing difficulties in her relationships with friends and her mother. Jasmine's mental and physical health was not good, and she suspected that she suffered from bipolar disorder. Superficially, these problems might be seen as responsible for her difficulties in finding work or suitable training. However, Jasmine's encounters with employers, welfare systems and training providers often left her in distress. The following extract indicates the effects of these encounters:

> Jasmine ... is 'feeling really shit' as she has no money ... and doesn't know what to do. She is supposed to sign on once a fortnight, but had to leave her last signing-on session as she had a panic attack. Jasmine tried to explain this to the Jobcentre staff ... [who] informed her that she must get a doctor's note ...
>
> Jasmine posted her doctor's note around 4pm on Friday. It would take three working days to process. Taking into account Bank Holiday Monday, today (Thursday) was the third day and she was hopeful that money was in her account so she could get some gas – she has no heating and the house is cold. She pulls at her clothes and says 'I've no clothes, they're all too baggy!' Jasmine has a doctor's appointment later today about her mental health, she says she 'can't face it' as she has had no sleep for days (she looks tired). She is also supposed to attend an employability programme – Jasmine says this is a waste of time as all she does is update her CV ... Her mum has told her she needs to stop thinking others will help her out and to stand on her own feet and keep these appointments.
>
> (Field notes 10/05/2012)

Jasmine was later taken to court over an unpaid council tax bill, a hangover from one of her periods of work. Although she claimed to spend over £20 on cannabis each week, Jasmine felt that she needed 'a spliff' to overcome her anxieties and help her to sleep.

The feelings of not being listened to, of lack of control, that were recurring themes in our research, are well expressed by Jed:

> There are quite a lot of people trying to support me but they're not giving me the right sort of help ... I asked my Connexions worker if she could get me onto a Food and Hygiene course and she said 'Why don't you do this and then halfway through it you can do that Food and Hygiene course' ... I do feel supported in a way but not in the right way ... If people would listen. Do you know like it's supposed to

be my review and I can say and do whatever I want in my review but I don't even get a chance to speak. My review officer has been with me a few years and I haven't been able to get a word in ... [She] would say 'What's happened, Jed?' and I get to say something like 'I had a fight with my dad', and they say 'Oh, we heard about that' and I'm thinking 'Well let me finish!' But when I try and do that she says 'Let me finish Jed before I forget.'

Welfare systems appeared most effective when they were consonant with young people's aspirations. For young mothers wishing to return to study, the Care to Learn scheme was particularly valuable. As we saw with Jackson's experiences in Chapter 5, support from practitioners that was linked to the skills and experience young people already had, and the kind of work they wanted, was valued – although not always forthcoming.

# 10
## Isla's Story

Isla was 18 years old when she began taking part in our research in February 2011. We first met her through an employability programme run by Fernside Council's Looked After Children (LAC) team when Lisa was observing Cayden – a young man whose story we recounted earlier. Like Cayden, Isla had spent time in foster care but the biographies of these two young people are quite different. As we pointed out in Chapter 3, disaggregating the NEET category into more specific sub-groups such as care leavers, young parents and young offenders can be helpful in understanding the complexity of what is, after all, a policy construct rather than a coherent social group. However, Isla's story also illustrates the limitations of this approach. Not only were Isla's circumstances and needs quite unlike Cayden's; her story also shows how NEET sub-categories overlap in ways that shift with time. For both the young people themselves, and for practitioners working with them, the differing and perhaps conflicting priorities arising from complex needs and circumstances can intensify the challenges associated with each category taken individually, thus increasing the risk of further exclusion.

Isla was born in Eastville and comes from a large and complex family. Her mother and father live together but both have children from previous relationships; Isla is one of seven siblings, although only one sister shares with her the same birth mother and father. Isla attended primary school and began her secondary schooling in Eastville, but left the area when she was placed in care at the age of 13 after 'falling in with the wrong crowd', becoming involved with drink and drugs. She was removed from the family home and placed with foster parents in Costingford, a market town in the East Midlands, where she completed her schooling. Isla moved to a second set of foster parents after her first foster mother became ill, following the death of a family member.

Unfortunately, her second foster placement also broke down. In Isla's account, her foster mother was an alcoholic and attempted to blame Isla for various domestic problems. Initially, social services were sceptical of Isla's claims but eventually believed her:

> It was in a meeting and they [the foster parents] were telling everyone that I were bad and stuff and I said 'No, you started drinking and if they don't believe me then go to the house and look in the fridge because there were all, like, cider bottles and stuff there' ...
>
> After I moved out she ran away from her husband and her kids and stole all the money and jewellery, and she were just missing for weeks, but they are back together now so I think she's sorted herself out.
>
> (Interview 25/02/2011)

During her time with these foster parents, Isla became pregnant, although the pregnancy ended in a miscarriage. She was then placed in bed-and-breakfast accommodation[1] but this arrangement also ended unhappily after two months.

> It were horrible, because I didn't have a door key to open my room and this guy, he seemed alright, and I were talking to him and everything, broke into my room and stole some jewellery that I were going to take to a gold collector; and he stole my Nintendo DS with all my games on it; and then he denied it were him; and the social worker said they were going to get money back for me so I could buy another DS and some games. But I didn't want to live there anymore....
>
> (Interview 25/02/2011)

Isla then returned to the family home in Eastville. Her parents had kept in touch with her when she was in foster care and apparently both parties were pleased to be reunited. Although Isla was in care for a much shorter period than Cayden, it is clear that her experience of the care system was quite unsatisfactory. Another notable difference between these two young people is that Isla is more academically able than Cayden and passed eight GCSEs (including five at grade C or above) when she was at school in Costingford. Isla was attending an art and design course at a college in the Midlands when she left to move back to Eastville.

## Learning on the margins

Isla's return to Eastville signalled a change in her career ambitions and she enrolled on a Level 1 hairdressing course with Blaze Academy, a private training company, shortly after coming back home. Isla passed this course and then progressed to an apprenticeship with another provider. But, like many of the other participants in our study, Isla's period of apprenticeship was short-lived:

> It were a three month trial run but I were poorly from the second week I were there and I went in for a week being really poorly and my voice had gone; and I kept coughing and when I was washing people's hair they were complaining because I had to keep covering my mouth when I was coughing, and it weren't really hygienic. So my boss said if I was poorly I shouldn't come in but I wanted to keep my place there. The next day I rang up and said I wasn't coming in today because I was going to the doctors... and they said 'Let's just call it quits'. So, basically, they sacked me for being poorly... I started signing on after that.
>
> (Interview 25/02/2011)

Thereafter, Isla's relatively successful educational trajectory took a downward turn and, although she had passed the course at Blaze Academy, there were problems with obtaining her certificate, which prevented her from progressing to a higher level course in hairdressing. This proved to be an intractable problem, and Isla had still not received her certificate by the end of the year.

> They still haven't given me my certificate yet so I might have to do Level 1 again. It's been over a year now and they keep saying the same thing – 'Oh, we'll get back to you' and stuff like that.
>
> (Interview 18/11/2011)

Eighteen months after we first met her, Isla was beginning another Level 1 course in Hairdressing and Beauty Therapy, the only way she could access the Level 2 course she wanted to do. Whilst it was quite common for participants in our research to repeat courses, this was usually because they had not completed them, or because the courses were not designed to provide access to higher-level vocational routes. Isla's case was quite different; whether it was due to misunderstanding on her part – perhaps a piece of coursework left unfinished or an attendance requirement unfulfilled – or inefficiency on the part of the training provider, it appears unlikely that there was any major obstacle to Isla obtaining a clear explanation of what she needed to do to receive her certificate. Much has been written on the mobilization of capitals in educational contexts, and policy initiatives that accentuate the role of parents in schooling have made the workings of these capitals more visible (Reay 2004). Whilst economic capital has always had a defining influence, the power of cultural and social capital has increased as the importance of parental involvement and choice has grown. Although often conceptualized in terms of differences between middle class and working class families, the contrast between Isla's difficulties and Hailey's return to college highlights the role of family social and cultural capital *within* classes in dealing with educational institutions. Unlike in Hailey's case, there seems to have been no attempt by Isla's parents to intervene on her behalf, and her own capitals were insufficient for the task of dealing effectively with authority.

Isla took part in other forms of training during our fieldwork and, as we have mentioned, we first met her on a course organized by Fernside's LAC team. All the young people attending this programme had spent time in care, and these learners constituted a diverse group. It is nevertheless surprising that Cayden – a young man with learning difficulties who we were told would probably never work by his Connexions advisor – was on the same course as Isla, who left school with several good GCSEs, and seemed to have fairly clear career ambitions. The programme emphasized confidence, generic 'life skills' and well-being.

> There is a slow start to the morning, the young people are just chatting and eating... Bryn eats his sandwich, screws up the wrapper and asks, 'Do you reckon I can get it in from here?' – he tries to throw the paper in the bin but just misses. He then gets up to put it in the bin by the door... The young people sit on soft chairs that surround the walls of the room. There are no tables, other than one with drinks and biscuits... No-one needs pens or paper.

> Heather gets anxious that Barry is not going to turn up – he is running the morning's session. The young people said it was good [last time] so they're having him back... Heather tells me [about] her back-up classroom plan which is to do a treasure hunt around town looking for specific items. When the continental markets were on she asked a group to buy a food they hadn't tried before, barter for the price – buy it cheaper, come back and talk about their experiences and share the food with the group.

> Barry arrives on time to deliver his session on anti-social behaviour. Barry asks everyone what their interests are; he says this is key to getting them involved in something... He addresses the group, 'What

do you think anti-social behaviour is?' Bryn responds, 'Being a knob head' and Barry says, 'Well, that's not a bad assumption'...

Barry moves on to ASBOs [Anti-social Behaviour Orders], Kim says, 'Yeah, but people don't always stick to them.'... Kim asks 'If you stay on a bus but go through areas that you're banned from is that allowed as long as you don't get off?' Barry says this is a good question, and says, 'You can build in rules on the order, so if you need to get to a certain post office to collect your giro, you can'...

Kim is dominating most of the content, the others are starting to get a bit restless, there's a lot of shuffling of feet, Sharon gets up to the bin, gets a biscuit from the table... Kim says, 'I'm just bored.' Heather interrupts at this point and the session finishes. She says they need ten minutes to do paperwork then they can leave.

(Field notes 03/02/2011)

Practitioners delivering employability programmes were often anxious to emphasize that they were not 'teachers'. This was related partly to a desire to dissociate themselves from the discipline of the school environment, but also to the nature of these programmes, which focused on practical skills related to the everyday lives and assumed needs of the young people taking part. A few weeks later, Isla was attending a similar course, operated by a voluntary sector provider.

Tim will be leading the session... The course is called 'A place of your own'. It runs over six sessions and today is the first day. Tim starts the session by explaining the ground rules, he says he is not a teacher and has no desire to be one... He says as far as he is concerned they are here on a voluntary basis and can leave if they choose to – although this is not strictly true as the young people would lose attendance payments if they didn't turn up.

Tim moves the tables closer together and we all stand up around them. We do a warm-up game. We have to pass a clap around the table as fast as we can, then we are offered the option of changing the direction of the clap, then we can send the clap to anyone by giving eye contact. The group seem to enjoy this, they laugh and find it difficult in places...

We then spend some time filling in forms. There are some groans around the table. Tim says they need to do this whatever course they are on, and it's best to get it out of the way. The first form asks questions such as 'Do you know why you might lose your flat/house?' ... They will revisit this at the end of the course with the aim of seeing some improvement in what they know.

The next section asks 'Why are you here? What do you want to learn on this course?' There are then five bullet points they need to answer. Bryn cracks a joke about only being here to get paid; Tim thanks him for his honesty and looks at Carly who has written 'How to get furniture', 'To decorate' and 'Pay bills weekly' – he says these are good examples of what they might write. He suggests writing a minimum of three...

(Field notes 02/03/2011)

Learning is often conceptualized as an individual psychological process, but learning cannot be separated from its social context – the institution or setting in which it occurs, and the relationships between the educational setting and the external social world. Within the setting, learning involves a range of interactions; for example, between learners, between tutors and between learners and tutors. Learning can therefore be seen in part as a set of social practices, which influence both curriculum content, and the way it is delivered. Drawing on the work of Pierre Bourdieu, James and Biesta (2007) argue that the cultural context in which education takes place is not merely a backdrop to the individual acquisition of knowledge and skills: learning is a social and cultural phenomenon in its own right. For them, institutions embody a *learning culture*, constituted by 'the social practices through which people learn' and the actions, interpretations and dispositions of participants are closely intertwined (James and Biesta 2007, p.23). In our research, and also in previous studies we have conducted, the learning cultures associated with provision for NEET young people appeared to reflect certain assumptions about these young people and the particular forms of learning appropriate for them, much of it informally structured and attempting to compensate for earlier experiences of education through high levels of emotional labour on the part of tutors.

The role of care and nurture in education has been vigorously debated in recent years. For authors such as Ecclestone and Hayes (2008), it has had a pernicious effect, devaluing knowledge and placing the self, and subjectivity, at the centre of 'therapeutic' educational practices. However, as Hyland (2009) reminds us, a caring and nurturing approach to pedagogy can be positive, especially in settings such as the one above which, involve learners who have experienced difficult social and personal circumstances. Furthermore, many – perhaps most – young people attending courses such as the one described above have had negative experiences of formal schooling, and as we saw in Chapter 9 this applied to the participants in our research. Being 'not like school' is commonly cited by young people as a feature they appreciate in programmes attempting to re-engage them in education (Russell et al. 2011b). From this point of view, creating an environment which attempts to provide graduated access to more formal learning appears eminently sensible. Initially, young people often appreciate these approaches; for Isla, there was some value in both the process and content of the employability programme:

> It has been [useful] because it's more things on my CV and when they put me on a placement it just gives me a bit more experience in hairdressing and it shows me what it's going to be like... all of it's good really because I received more certificates in drug awareness and alcohol awareness; anti-social behaviour, first aid... and we do something else as well but I can't remember what it was now but it's more things on my CV and it looks better, don't it?... [The course isn't long] but they are doing a residential as well which I think will be good because it will be fun working with people you don't really know and that's the other thing I think has been good.
>
> (Interview 25/02/2011)

As with a number of other participants, Isla's initially positive attitudes cooled when, after failing to complete an employability programme due to morning sickness, she was invited to repeat the course:

> I don't know whether I want to do it or not because I've done it before and I'd just like to go straight back into hairdressing, I think. But I'll go to the meeting and see what they say... [If I don't want to do it] I'll just say that I don't know if it's right for me this time because of Oscar and everything. I'll probably just want to go straight on to doing my hairdressing and then I can be qualified for that and then I can get a job then when he's in school or whatever.
>
> (Interview 18/11/2011)

Much of our data suggests that such provision, whilst purporting to provide a ladder of opportunity, is a ladder with only one rung.

Whilst the reasons for the repetitive churning between very similar programmes which we saw with many participants are complex, one of the key factors appeared to be a lack of intellectual challenge and access to coherent, principled knowledge. Whilst team-building exercises, improving inter-personal skills, confidence building and similar activities are often worthwhile, there comes a point at which it is necessary to add more concrete skills and abilities to any soft skills or aesthetic qualities a young person has acquired.

Basil Bernstein's (2000) work on pedagogic discourses offers a useful way of conceptualizing the sort of learning to which marginalized young people are often exposed. Bernstein contrasts the relatively limited educational and social value of generic employability skills, which are often delivered in isolation from the social practices in which they originate, with more high-status forms of education and training based upon knowledge structures and often embedded in particular vocational contexts. For Bernstein, access to forms of education or professional training which develop and apply conceptual understanding is a democratic right, offering the social and cultural benefits of a fuller participation in society. Wheelahan (2007) goes further, arguing that such learning provides participants with greater analytical and explanatory power in vocational contexts than can be gained through focusing on procedural competences or generic employability skills. Research evidence appears to support these arguments. Progression from low-level pre-vocational training programmes, into either higher-level study or employment, is often low (Wolf 2011). In our study it was clear that many participants felt frustrated by their experiences on such programmes, and progression from Level 1 courses was a particular concern. Other studies draw similar conclusions (see, for example, Smyth et al. 2013).

## Motherhood, marginalization and loss

When we met Isla, she had moved out of her parent's house to live with her boyfriend, Lee, a young man who was, at that time, enrolled on an employability programme with another training provider. Isla was pregnant:

> I visit Isla at home...She has bleached her hair and shows me pictures of Lee, whose hair she has also bleached. Isla's pregnancy is starting to show. She says she is happy to stay at home and wait for

the baby's arrival – Isla describes herself as a housewife, although she says Lee does the cooking. Isla wants to go to college when baby is six months old so she can get a free nursery place.[2] She wants to complete her hairdressing qualifications.

Isla has been given a lot of second-hand things for the baby; she has a cot, some baby clothes and a high chair.

Lee is still on a course that is designed to help him find work – she says it is rubbish though.

(Field notes 05/05/2011)

Despite her difficult adolescence and the prospect of early mother-hood, Isla's aims and ambitions seemed quite conventional and, at least initially, were centred upon family life and an imagined future as a hairdresser. She saw Lee as working and sharing childcare and herself combining motherhood with qualifying as a hairdresser. Further in the future, her aims were less precise but included herself and Lee in work, with more children and a bigger house. Like Hailey, Isla contested the label of 'teenage mother' and thought that having a baby might make her more employable:

> Well not a real young [mother] because some teenagers have babies at, like, 15 now, don't they? I think I am still a teen mum but I'm not that young. I think a young teen mum would be about 15 but I'll be 20 next year so I won't be a teenager then, will I? ... [Employers will] think it's probably more important now I've got a baby because they will be thinking I need to get a job to get more money in.
>
> (Interview 18/11/2011)

At this time, Isla appeared to have the support of family networks, and her account of everyday life portrayed a hyper-conventional working-class culture:

> Monday I have a day off so I'd get up and tidy up... have something to eat and watch telly and go out. Wait till Lee comes home and probably go to his mum's for a bit; come back here and just chill out. Tuesday I get up about 7:30 and go to my course which finishes about half-one; have some dinner; come home and tidy up; have some tea with Lee. Sometimes we go to his mum ... [or] I'll go and see my sister at my mum and dad's [they all live quite close] ... [Lee] likes to go out on a Friday night so we'd probably go to the pub and have a

game of pool. Saturday... I'll probably nip to my mum's because my grandmother is there and then Lee and I will probably have a drink again because we always drink at the weekend. We'll sometimes go [out] for a meal... then Sundays we just relax and sometimes I'll go to my mum's for Sunday dinner or we go to his mum's. We're going to his mum's this Sunday.

(Interview 25/02/2011)

Isla gave birth to a son, Oscar, in September 2011 and, in some respects, she seemed to be settling into motherhood quite well when Lisa visited her some weeks later.

Isla has just finished bathing Oscar as I arrive, and he is dressed in a grey babygro. He is six weeks old. Isla says she is enjoying motherhood and is fine in the house, she says she gets to town with her friends, sleeps in until 11am, he is going four hours or so between feeds. Isla's in-laws take Oscar every Saturday so she is getting time to herself. Oscar falls asleep as I cuddle him. She asks me to take out his dummy as she wants me to see him awake. Isla feeds Oscar and gives him medication for thrush in the mouth.

(Field notes 03/11/2011)

There were, nevertheless, also signs that her domestic arrangements were perhaps not as child-friendly as they could have been; Isla had taken up smoking again, there had been disputes with the neighbours over noise and an accidental fire, and in addition to a new puppy – which was kept indoors to avoid fleas – Isla and Lee had a pet snake. When Lisa visited her three months later, some radical changes had taken place in Isla's life; Lee had been charged with affray after a domestic incident and Isla had taken out a court injunction against him. Isla said that her relationship with Lee had been deteriorating for some time, and since the break-up she had begun seeing another young man – 'kind of' – a few years older than herself. Although Lee was allowed to have Oscar for three nights a week, the baby's visits were supervised by Lee's parents:

Isla and Lee had been out to her cousin's twenty-first birthday party, and afterwards a male friend had slept on the sofa at their house. Oscar was at Lee's parents' overnight. Apparently, Lee threw a bowl off the table in a rage, and then stormed off to bed. Isla says she didn't go with him – she didn't want to go to bed with 'someone like that'. Later, Lee came downstairs shouting and bawling, and demanding that she leave the house. Isla says things escalated when she refused to leave – Lee started up a chainsaw and threatened to saw her legs off if she didn't get out. Isla ran barefoot to her neighbour's house and called the police ...

Isla says that Lee has been violent to her on a number of occasions: bruising her, throwing her around and so forth; he cut her head open once by throwing her into the washing machine ... Lee had threatened her with the chainsaw on other occasions, but had never actually started it up before.

Lee has been in trouble with the police for various offences including theft and racial abuse. Isla says he is currently serving a six-month suspended sentence, and this may affect the verdict when they go to court. She has to go to court in early March to give a statement ... and isn't looking forward to seeing Lee there, although she realizes she will have to see him again as he is Oscar's father. At first Isla wanted Lee to go to prison but she now feels this might not be a good thing, as he is likely to come out angrier than ever.

(Field notes 09/02/2012)

Events did not develop as Isla imagined and Lee was found not guilty when he went to court – a decision which she found incredible. Isla claimed that Lee persuaded a friend to say that she was lying, and that the neighbour whose house she fled to on the night of the alleged offence refused to get involved in the proceedings. Meanwhile, Isla's life seemed to become increasingly chaotic.

Isla's says she has been seeing another lad, but Lee threatened him and he now stays away from her. She says that she feels Lee is still controlling her from afar, not allowing her to see new people. In the early hours of one morning the police arrived, responding to a phone call, which she thinks Lee made. The police had been told she was having a party and taking drugs with the baby in the house. Isla was asleep when they arrived ... but the police still insisted on seeing Oscar asleep in his cot. Isla says she doesn't regret having Oscar but she does regret her involvement with his father.

(Field notes 09/03/2012)

Isla is sporting a bright pink plaster cast: she has broken her ankle. Isla says a girl spotted her in a car on Thursday night and mistook her for someone who had slept with her boyfriend. The girl dragged Isla out of the car, and Isla was taken by surprise and fell. She is staying at her mum and dad's to get help with Oscar. Isla says it is 'Doing my head in'. Her father is depressed; he has anxiety attacks; he won't leave the house; and he likes to set the house rules. Isla says she has to ask if she wants a shower and has to go to bed when they do. She says as soon as she can…she is going back home.

(Field notes 20/04/2012)

By the time Lisa visited Isla at her parents' house in early July she had lost the tenancy of the house she was renting. It seems that Isla held a number of parties at the house and that a neighbour complained to Isla's landlady that drugs were being used in and around the house – an accusation that Isla strenuously denied (Field notes 05/07/2012). By this time, Lee and his parents had applied for custody of Oscar and had also applied to receive his child benefit:

I text Isla to say I'm outside. She asks me to come round to the back of the house; she is looking well, her hair is well kept, cut and dyed dark…we sit in the garden on the back doorstep in the rain while she smokes…She says Lee just wants to make her life a misery, and he is doing anything he can to achieve this.

(Field notes 05/07/2012)

The following day Lisa accompanied Isla to a meeting with her solicitor. Gary, Isla's social worker, had expressed concerns about the company Isla was keeping and her solicitor, Corinne, warned Isla to prepare for the worst.

Corinne tells Isla to prepare herself for the fact that she might lose Oscar – even though she is the last person who wants this to happen. Corinne says it is his word against hers. She says that Isla needs to get police incident reference numbers, any medical records and letters from Sure Start to confirm her attendance at parenting groups…

Isla says she is struggling to get people to do statements as people fear Lee and what may happen. Others haven't got round to doing it. Corinne says Isla needs to be more pro-active…

Isla has a cigarette outside after we're done. We walk back to the car and I drive her home. I go into the house for a cup of tea, her dad asks how it went and I say that Isla has a number of things she has to do, like get hold of her social worker, find her crime reference numbers and ring her health visitor and Sure Start contact. Isla uses my phone to try and contact these people.

(Field notes 06/07/2012)

In the autumn, Isla attended an alcohol counselling course following concerns over her drinking; she said: 'I'm not an alcoholic but to make it look better for me in court I've got to look like I'm doing something.' She was also attending college, and was approaching completion of her Level 1 course in hairdressing. If she completed this course successfully, Isla would begin a Level 2 apprenticeship in November and would be paid £95 a week. Because college only occupied two days a week, Isla qualified for JSA and was receiving '50-something pounds a week... I don't know how they expect me to live off that.' However, she would have to give up her course if she was found work.

Isla's son was taken from her following a County Court hearing in December. Lee and his parents, who have experience as foster carers, were granted full custody of Oscar, although Isla was granted permission to have him for two nights each week. Isla says she was told that she didn't have the 'right mother skill set' to look after a baby.

I meet Isla at home, she is looking well and is sporting a new tattoo on her foot... she knows someone who does them for free. Her mum and dad are sat in their usual chairs, mum opposite the TV and dad perched by the kitchen door.

Isla is frustrated and upset by the outcome of the custody battle and her parents can't believe it either. Her dad tells me that none of Isla's statements were taken into account. I read Oscar's social worker's report. It says that she has concerns about the company Isla is keeping and her behaviour which, it argues, is related to this and Isla's past activities.

The statement expresses no concerns about Lee, although it mentions the domestic violence allegations and advises Isla go to a support group – which she says she will do... Isla says she wants to appeal for custody in six months.

(Field notes 07/12/2012)

During this period Isla had been able to complete her Level 1 course, and had progressed to the apprenticeship. She was also in the process of 'bidding' for social housing. Lisa's last contact with Isla was in March 2013: Oscar's custody terms were unchanged, but Isla was now in her own house near her parents' home, and continuing with the apprenticeship.

# 11
## Saheera's Story

Saheera, who lived with her parents, her brother and four sisters in Gadley, was one of the first young people to join the research project when she began taking part in the study in late 2010. She was introduced to us, along with her friend Shabina, whilst in Year 11 of an all-girls high school, after both were identified by the school as 'vulnerable to becoming NEET'. Saheera was 15 when we first met her, and from the outset it appeared that she, Shabina and other members of their peer group had overtly negative attitudes to school. The girls were often absent or late for classes: sometimes they were off-site during the school day, whilst on other occasions they could be found smoking in and around the school grounds during lesson times. Much of their behaviour was openly anti-authoritarian.

I enter a room where two girls, Saheera and Shabina, sit giggling away. I ask if they know why I'm here. Marion – who works as a learning mentor at the school – explains that I am doing some research on NEET young people. Marion had explained to the girls what NEET means before I arrived. I say I am looking to see what life is like for them as a young person, to find out what they like about school and what they don't like. I say taking part is voluntary so it is up to them if they want to get involved.

Shabina sets me straight immediately: she says, 'If you throw your bag on the floor and tell me to pick it up I'm not gunna, if you ask me nicely then I might – it's all about respect!' I say to her that I would never make demands on her like that; I say I understand, smile and explain that I'd like to work with them. Shabina says if it gets her out of school timetable she's in.

(Field notes 10/11/2010)

Relations with teachers were often difficult and Saheera and her friends were frequently uncooperative or disruptive when they did attend classes.

> The teacher passes Saheera her work...She doesn't look at it once throughout the class. Saheera spends the lesson eating sweets, talking on the phone and moving folders on the computer. Saheera sits with her feet up for most of the session. She comments on how her mum accuses her of being masculine but then says, 'I am a girl though'...
>
> (Field notes 25/11/2010)

> Shabina says she is going to skive the next lesson, maths, as she can't be bothered. Fahrina and Saheera skive it too. We go outside for another smoke, the girls all share one cigarette, Fahrina goes to her lesson a bit late and we go to the sports hall. We sit in the changing room after getting crisps and chocolate from the vending machine. Shabina asks me if I'll say we are still in interview if they get caught, I say no but if they leave now and return to class I'll say they were showing me around. The girls leave the changing room as they hear someone coming...We go outside and see two White girls who ask what we're doing. Shabina says 'Skiving maths' and the White girls say they are too...
>
> (Field notes 10/12/2010)

Much of Saheera's behaviour reflected what Archer et al. (2007) describe as some of the paradoxes of 'hyper-heterosexual' femininity, combining certain forms of traditional working-class resistance to schooling with a rejection of conventional forms of hetero-femininity. Initially, Saheera adopted what Archer et al. (2007, p.176) describe as a 'ladette' or 'tomboy' persona, smoking, swearing and at times swaggering along the school corridors. Staff at the school remarked that Saheera and her friends came and went as they pleased, although Marion, Saheera's learning mentor, suggested that the expectations of staff were part of the problem and Saheera was actually more engaged than she appeared. However, whilst neither Saheera nor Shabina fitted the compliant 'model student' stereotype sometimes found in teacher discourses about young Muslim women (Mirza and Meetoo 2013), Saheera's experiences appeared to be shaped, at least to some degree, by the attitudes and beliefs of teachers and family, as well as broader cultural expectations. Although towards the end of our fieldwork she modified her views to some extent, Saheera's attitude to continuing in education after she reached the minimum school-leaving age was initially almost wholly negative, and she expressed a desire to find a job rather than stay in education or training. This, in part appeared to be the result of pressure from her father, which in turn stemmed from the family's response to Saheera's behaviour in school; according to later accounts which she gave, her father and brother saw education as offering too much freedom, a freedom which in their view she had already used to engage in activities which damaged the family's reputation.

The loss of jobs in manufacturing has had particularly profound consequences for male employment, but young women have also been affected by these far-reaching changes. In Eastville, where Saheera lives, the textiles industry was traditionally a significant employer of both male and female labour but the woollen mills and workshops are now largely defunct. Practitioners were familiar with the nature of local labour markets and the difficulty of young people securing full-time work. Both before and after she left school, Connexions advisers and support staff at the school repeatedly encouraged Saheera to continue her education. However, Saheera resisted their suggestions resolutely.

The Connexions advisor, Julie, clearly knows what went on at Eastville College recently: Saheera had an altercation with a member of staff there when she attended an interview for a childcare course. Julie asks Saheera if she is still interested in Hair and Beauty and Childcare . . . Saheera says she would like to go straight into a job, but Julie explains that this won't happen as she needs training . . . Julie tells me that Saheera has no plans to stay on in the sixth form, which Saheera confirms. So they are looking for alternatives to full-time education.

(Field notes 10/12/2010)

Martin, the Connexions Advisor . . . takes off his coat and asks, 'what can I do for you?' Saheera says she wants a job. Martin says 'OK' and asks what in. Saheera immediately responds with 'retail'.

Martin asks if she would consider training and Saheera adamantly refuses. He asks why and she says 'I don't know, I just don't want to do it.' Saheera looks at me searchingly and I chip in, 'She is worried about bumping into certain family members.' Martin nods his head.

He says the centre is shut today so he has been able to take a folder that is full of training opportunities and apprenticeship placements.

He slides it across to Saheera and asks if she would like to look through it. She takes the time to read through most of it. The folder starts with training, and Martin jokes about sneaking that in for her to look at.

(Field notes 29/02/2012)

## Learning, labour market and resistance

During the 1960s and 1970s, the textiles industry drew substantial numbers of migrants into Fernside and Northdale from Kashmir and the Punjab and, although this work has now largely disappeared, there is a significant and growing Asian population across the two authorities. But, mirroring national patterns, the ethnic minority population is unevenly distributed, and there is a concentration of British-Pakistanis in certain parts of Gadley and Eastville. Reflecting this, the majority of pupils at Saheera's high school are of Asian descent. Later, we will examine how the cultural matrix within which Saheera's story took place contributes to and reinforces particular forms of Marginalization. But, as Shain (2003) reminds us, it is important not to stereotype the lives of Asian girls or to present them as passive victims of static cultures, and, in some ways, Saheera's experiences mirror those of many other young working-class people in contemporary Britain.

Marion, the learning mentor, who provides pastoral and pre-vocational support to girls deemed to exhibit challenging behaviour, described Saheera as follows:

Marion: Socially she's lovely. Again she's very loyal to her friends. She's a difficult one is Saheera, because even with her it's more about lethargy because she just can't be bothered. And even on a one-to-one situation trying to get her settled down is extremely hard because she can't be bothered – what's the point? All she wants to do is to leave school and get a job to save money [towards] a flat.

She doesn't want to do anything after school unless it pays. So she would be quite happy doing an apprenticeship and I think she would actually be alright because I think she'd lend herself better to that environment and I think she'd be OK.

(Interview 17/03/2011)

Lisa: What is she like academically?

Marion: Again, she is middle of the road and there's no reason why she shouldn't do well but I'm more concerned about her grades than I am about Shabina's. I've got a feeling that it's going to be one of those cases where, when it comes to exam day, I'm going to be picking them all up in the minibus. She'll get a D in Art; she'll be getting a B at work skills although she's on a U at the minute because I've had no work from her at all. She should get a distinction for childcare. And she's done nothing for Citizenship – she's only attended three lessons…In maths she's been asked to leave and I don't think she's been entered for her resits. She got a G. For reading studies I'm actually sat with her in class to try and make her work. And that's it.

Whilst Saheera could not be described as a diligent student, she was not without ability and her desire to find a job was a common theme for most of the young people who took part in the research. This was a preference Saheera expressed throughout her last year at school and after she left education, at least for a time. However, her attempts to find work were highly localized – she would not consider travelling to Middlebridge or Greenford let alone the nearby city of Monkdown – and centred upon retail and other areas of low-pay service sector employment. They were also carried out through largely speculative methods in which, like other participants, Saheera called into shops and retail outlets with her CV, including a shoe shop where she had done work experience. She would still not consider returning to education and reiterated that 'I just wanted a job':

> Lisa: And what had been your experience as you've been dropping your CV off?
> Saheera: I got fed up because Matalan kept saying no because I was too young and Clark's just said no. I think the staff were a bit off and I was told to give my CV to the manager but I don't think they gave it to him because nobody's got in touch with me….
> Lisa: Have you heard anything from anywhere where you've dropped your CV off?
> Saheera: Only just calls telling me they've got enough people and they don't need any more.
> (Interview 03/08/2011)

Such processes are not uncommon in poor neighbourhoods where geographic mobility is often limited and job search tends to be localized and focused upon familiar forms of employment (MacDonald et al. 2005). However, evidence suggests that trying to find work in this way is often unproductive and tends to reinforce or, at best, reproduce existing patterns of participation and exclusion, even when individuals are successful in finding employment. But Saheera, like most of our other participants' who used informal job search methods, did not find work by approaching employers directly. She became NEET immediately after leaving school and remained so for the remainder of the fieldwork.

On one level, Saheera's age and the distance she was prepared to travel limited what was available to her.

> Ideally, Saheera wants a job in retail but she has been told in many places that she needs to be 18 before she'd even be considered. She asks me if I can help find her some local jobs, she only wants local as she has no transport. She will work in Heathfield, Gadley or Eastville only. I have a quick look online and send her some job applications through the post the next day. It seems there are no jobs in retail for young people under the age of 18. There is a week's placement at HSBC, but I think this is unpaid, a catering position and a job at the local cinema.
>
> (Field notes 18/01/2012)

Many companies in Fernside and Northdale do not employ anybody under the age of 18. Moreover, young people like Saheera are not only in competition for jobs with other better-qualified young workers but also with older people, many of whom have been forced to compete for what were previously regarded as 'entry-level jobs' by a lack of other employment opportunities. There were, however, other barriers constraining Saheera's entry to the labour market.

Although, like other participants, Saheera's worklessness was related, at least in part, to changes in the local and national labour market, arguably her marginalization was also related, at least in part, to particular familial and cultural pressures, and certain expectations about the role and behaviour of young Muslim women – although it is important to emphasize that her attitudes and behaviour can be interpreted as resistance as much as conformity. Nevertheless, throughout the fieldwork, there were significant tensions between Saheera and male family members. Much of this seemed to relate to a clash of expectations between Saheera and her father, especially about marriage and relationships, but also about her behaviour more generally. Marion and Pat, the NEET co-ordinator at Gadley High School, both said that conflict between Muslim girls and male family members was not unusual for pupils at the school.

> Marion explains that she is unsure how much of the problem with the girls is about 'chicken and egg' – they both have domineering

males at home which may make them rebel, or are the males more strict because the two girls are rebellious?

Pat says they have a huge problem around forced marriages. She explains the difference between arranged and forced marriages, and says that forced marriages are very stressful for the girls…They have had some girls who have disappeared…some [girls] say they could be told to pack, supposedly to go to their aunt's house that night, and be taken away that same day out of the country to be married. Pat says she finds her job extremely frustrating.

(Field notes 10/11/2011)

Whilst such views may be seen as reflecting a dominant liberal discourse about the need to 'save' young Muslim women from the constraints of backward-looking cultural and religious practices (Mirza and Meetoo 2013), it did appear that Saheera's relationship with her father was a source of great difficulty for her throughout most of the fieldwork – and Saheera claimed that her father had assaulted her on a number of occasions:

Saheera tells me she is having problems at home and has informed social services that her father has been abusing her. She says he has hit her around the head and smacked her around the neck – Saheera says he does this because it doesn't leave marks and so her father cannot be arrested. She says social services have recently been to the house but she felt as though she was made out to be a liar because there was no visible evidence of the attacks. Saheera says that she asked social services if she should contact them as soon as she has marks, but that she was told it doesn't work that way. She says her dad laughed at her attempt at informing social services…

Saheera says things have got worse since she turned 16 and that she wants to move out of the family home to live with her 18-year-old boyfriend, who she has been seeing for a year. Her parents found out about him when they caught Saheera on the phone. I ask her about arranged marriages and she says her dad would like this to happen but that she doesn't want one…Her dad first agreed that she could move out, as long as her boyfriend's parents consent to them living together – even though her boyfriend currently lives alone. Saheera says she has thought about running away, and confirms that the school know about all this.

(Field notes 18/02/2011)

Following their father's wishes, Saheera's older sisters had both married members of their extended family but Saheera resisted his proposal that she marry a cousin; and it appeared that Saheera's father was angered, at least initially, by her relationship with her boyfriend. Whilst it was not clear whether Saheera's father was aware of her smoking and drinking alcohol, or of the 'sleeping around' she described to Lisa, Saheera spoke of his disapproval of the company she kept and claimed that he often prevented her from leaving the house. Saheera said that her father did not allow her to travel on buses, insisting on dropping her off and collecting her from school in his car, and had tried to prevent her from going on work placement in Year 10. She talked a lot about her father being a 'respected man' in the local community, and according to staff at Saheera's school, her father had a reputation in and around Eastville for criminal activity. Over the course of the fieldwork it became apparent that Saheera's reluctance to use public transport or even walk to certain places on her own, and her unwillingness to go to college derived, to some extent, from her wish to avoid certain family members.

## NEET or not?

When Lisa visited the school in early May 2011, she was informed that Saheera and Shabina had both been put on part-time timetables in order to reduce the influence the two girls were having upon each other and other pupils around them. Marion, the learning mentor also informed Lisa that Saheera had married her boyfriend, Zahir.

> I struggle to find the house but she comes outside and meets me... Saheera is living in her husband's brother's house while he is away in prison. She says they will leave this address soon.

> Saheera says she is pleased she got married but that she had to organize it all in three days. Her dad has said she can visit the house to see her mum and sisters – but only when he is not there. Saheera says he is away in Pakistan at the moment. She went to see them but describes them as 'acting funny' with her, so she isn't sure she will bother in the future. She says Zahir is not over-protective and she can still see her friends.

> Saheera says her husband's family has a bad name and explained this is why her dad didn't want them seeing each other at first. She was

supposed to marry her cousin but said she didn't want to as he is ugly. Saheera said she had to face her uncle at the wedding, which was awkward.

(Field notes 23/05/2011)

At the time of their marriage, Zahir was an apprentice mechanic and he progressed onto full-time paid work thereafter. Although he later changed jobs, Zahir remained in employment for the duration of the fieldwork. Meanwhile, Saheera's motivation to find work faded.

Lisa: We've had the Easter break so have you been looking for jobs?

Saheera: No, I've given up.

Lisa: What are the main things people have said to you as to why you can't get a job?

Saheera: Underage – because if it's retail or something like hairdressing I've got to be over 18. The same with bar work...

Lisa: So what's your plan now then?

Saheera: I don't know. I've sent out some emails but I haven't got any replies yet.

(Interview 20/04/2012)

By the end of 2012, Saheera had moved to another house and her relationship with her parents appeared to have improved. Her father had helped Saheera and Zahir find a place of their own – at a reduced rent because Saheera's father knew the landlord. Like the house in which Saheera lived after she was first married, her new home was also close to her parents' house. Although the most significant dimension of spatial segregation in the UK has tended to be social class rather than race or ethnicity, there is some evidence of growing ethnic segregation in certain parts of the UK– for example, the high concentration of Bangladeshis in the East End of London and of Pakistanis in parts of Bradford and other areas of West Yorkshire and East Lancashire (Byrne 2005, pp.121–122). Such processes are evident in the part of Eastville in which Saheera and her family live, and are important not least in respect to differential patterns of access to public services such as health and education, as well as employment (Byrne 2005, p.117).

There had also been another important change in Saheera's life. When Lisa next interviewed her, in October 2012, Saheera told Lisa she was expecting a baby in December – two months before her eighteenth birthday. Her husband was working long hours at a nearby garage, but had agreed some time off when the baby arrived:

> Lisa: You know you're having a boy so was the pregnancy planned?
>
> Saheera: Yeah, it was. I thought that I couldn't get pregnant but when I went to the hospital I found out that I was pregnant.
>
> Lisa: Do you understand benefits like maternity benefits and what you're entitled to...?
>
> Saheera: I don't know fully what I'm entitled to. I just know child benefit and the maternity grant. That's all I know.
>
> Lisa: And do you think your husband is going to be pretty hands on?
>
> Saheera: He will be; he will help look after the baby.
>
> Lisa: Is your mum going to help you in any way?
>
> Saheera: Yeah, she's staying here for the last month [of the pregnancy]... After the baby is born my husband gets a week off and my mum will stay until she is perfectly sure that I know what I'm doing and then she'll just go back and she'll keep visiting regularly.
>
> Lisa: What do you think it's going to be like being a mum?
>
> Saheera: I'm looking forward to it but then I'm scared if I do something wrong.
>
> Lisa: Do you think that other people are judging you?
>
> Saheera: Yeah, because there are loads of people who are looking at me and thinking that I've just thrown my life away but I don't think I have. I still get to go out and do things. I was never interested in education and never have been... so I don't think I've thrown my life away.

Getting married at 16 and becoming a parent before the age of 18 is unusual in contemporary Britain, but the expansion of NEET as a descriptor for all young people under the age of 25 who are outside education and work draws in a range of individuals who would not traditionally have been regarded as unemployed. But the way certain individuals and their activity or inactivity are regarded is not independent of inequality and social status. Whilst Saheera could be described as 'long-term NEET', she was in fact a married woman with a husband who was constantly in work throughout the fieldwork. A young graduate living in comfortable and settled circumstances with a husband and baby is also technically NEET, but would be unlikely to attract concern from policymakers or practitioners. Similarly, 'taking a year out' before going to university, travelling overseas or engaging in other typically middle-class activities is often seen as adding to cultural and social capital, although young people undertaking these rites of passage would also be classified as NEET. These anomalies illustrate the tensions between the NEET category and social norms, but also show how many of the assumptions upon which it is based are bound up with status, inequality and social class.

The prospect of motherhood seemed to give Saheera a different perspective and she was more reflective about her relationship with her father.

Lisa: So it's a new experience for your mum and dad. And what did your mum and dad think about the whole pregnancy thing?

Saheera: My dad is chuffed, he's ever so happy...

Lisa: Right so you still see your dad but it's a kind of a difficult relationship?

Saheera: Yeah he goes into moods and we don't talk at all.

Lisa: And was there tension like that when you were growing up?

Saheera: No, he were alright. It was up until I were 13 or 14 we were really alright and we all got along well all the time.

Lisa: So what does your brother think? Does he see it as disrespectful?

Saheera: Yeah, he does. He told me that instead of disrespecting dad and going out and drinking and this and that I should have just sat him down and talked to him and said 'I want to go out; I want to do this...and told him that you've found someone instead of going behind his back and skiving off school and going to see him.' My brother, even though he is younger than me, was telling me that...

Saheera: I never used to go to school unless it were the lessons that I liked...

Lisa: And is that why your dad drove you to school and picked you up?

Saheera: Yeah, because if we wanted to we could walk it even though it was far or we could go on the school bus or go with mates or whatever and he never bothered. But if we were messing about and people were talking about us saying 'look at your daughter doing that' or 'look at your daughter doing this' and he didn't like it and so he started dropping us off and bringing us back.

Lisa: Probably your dad just wanted the best for you

Saheera: Yeah I know he did. I understand that now but I didn't understand it then. How was I to know that he wasn't just being a prick? But now I do understand because I'd do the same now. Now that I'm having a kid I understand that if my kid did the same to me I'd call that disrespectful. So I know where he's coming from now...

Saheera: My dad wouldn't have let me leave the house unless to go to education. I wouldn't be allowed to hang out with my mates. My dad hated those mates that I chose because their families had a bad reputation.

Lisa: So did you do that to rebel a little bit or was it just the way it happened?

Saheera: It was just the way it worked. If people sympathized with me I used to get on more with them but my dad just didn't like it. He used to say that he'd heard about their families so I wasn't to be friends with them.

(Interview 04/10/2012)

Whilst it was clear that Saheera had regrets about the past, especially her resistance to post-compulsory education, it was also evident that she did not see labour market participation as a priority, at least for the foreseeable future. Although she acknowledged that it may have been better to continue her education, she had little desire to go to college, or indeed to have another baby in the near future. Whilst such attitudes are hardly surprising for an expectant mother, it also appeared that Saheera saw few role models in her community. Speaking of the 'choice' her father had given her between getting married and going to college, she said:

I don't see many Asian women working and being married. I don't see that... [My mother] used to work until she was married but then she stopped and she didn't even bother going back.

(Interview 04/10/2012)

During this later phase of the fieldwork, it appeared that Saheera had rejected her former 'ladette' performance in favour of a more conventional femininity. Unlike Melissa, the young woman discussed in Archer et al. (2007), this did not yet enable Saheera to accept that a successful return to learning was either possible or desirable. However, in April 2013 Saheera reported that her baby had arrived, was often looked after by her mother, and that she had been contacted by Connexions and was interested in work.

# 12
# Cayden's Story

As we have seen, normative patterns of youth transition have extended during the last 40 years, and for most young people leaving home and acquiring the traditional signifiers of adult life have been considerably delayed. However, young people leaving care are exceptions to this trend, and accelerated transitions to adulthood are more likely for this group (Wade and Dixon 2006). Government policy has aimed to delay transitions and improve support for young people in the period leading up to and after leaving care.[1] But there is considerable variation in outcomes between local authorities and between different groups of young people; those with disabilities, mental health issues and offending behaviour tend to fare badly compared with care leavers with less complex needs. The number of children and young people in care in England has increased in recent years, with 67,050 children being looked after in 2012, an increase of 13 per cent compared with 2008. Consequently, the number of young people leaving care has also increased, and whilst the majority of these are aged 18 and over, some leave care at 16 or 17 (DfE 2012a; 2012c). Many of these young people return to live with parents or with other responsible adults; however, in 2011 a quarter of 16-year-olds and nearly 40 per cent of 17-year-olds moved into what is euphemistically know as 'independent living' but can instead be a frightening and isolating experience.

Many of the young people who took part in our study had spent at least some time in the care system, and nine were care leavers when our research began. One of these was Cayden, a young man who was 19 and outside education and employment when we first met him towards the end of 2010. Cayden did not take part in any form of paid work during the course of the research and, although he participated in an employability training programme and undertook two spells of voluntary employment, he was classified as NEET until fieldwork ended in March 2013. He remained on benefits throughout this time. Shortly after leaving school, Cayden dropped out of college and it would be fair to say that his commitment to finding paid employment fluctuated over the course of the research – although the pressure upon him to do so increased, particularly as he approached his twenty-first birthday. There are, however, important caveats relating to Cayden's motivation to work and, as we will see, it is clear that he is a vulnerable young man facing a number of personal and material disadvantages.

We were first introduced to Cayden through Connexions in November 2010. His personal adviser Heather informed us that he had learning difficulties and would 'probably never work'. Cayden never met his father and went into foster care when he was very young: his mother had two children from a previous relationship – both of whom also have learning difficulties – and Cayden said his mother 'couldn't cope' with him. At the age of four, Cayden went to live with an uncle and his wife and remained in their care until he was 16. Cayden's aunt and uncle then relocated to Scotland, something which Cayden said had always been their dream, and he moved into a supported housing scheme in Eastville run by St Alice's, a voluntary organization providing care and support services for people with learning disabilities, mental health issues and other difficulties. He said he chose to remain in Eastville, rather than move to Scotland. However, Cayden felt that he wanted more independence than was available to him at St Alice's and said he 'forced himself out' of living there. By the time we met him, Cayden had been living alone in a flat in Eastville for about a year – although he was still receiving help from Fernside's LAC team and other agencies.

Cayden went to a school for pupils with complex learning difficulties and had limited basic skills. He found reading, writing and some routine tasks difficult.

[I can read] a little bit but just little sentences... sometimes I can write but, like, copying is easy, but if I had a paper there and another paper there and I have to copy it that is hard like, or copying off the board. That is hard sometimes. But dot to dot is easy for me and I can, like, finish that in two minutes.

(Interview 13/01/2011)

Justin [Cayden's LAC Advisor] organizes a bus pass for Cayden. Cayden has no passport photograph though so I go with him to the bus station to get these done. He needs my assistance with this as he does not know how to work the machine. Justin gives us some money to do this. We need a £5 note and so I have to change a £10 note for two £5 notes at the bus station kiosk. With my and Justin's help, the bus pass is sorted.

(Field notes 13/01/2011)

Despite his learning difficulties, Cayden said that he liked school and he achieved numerous pre-vocational qualifications before leaving at the age of 16. These include certificates recording his ability to recognize and use shapes, numbers and words at a basic level and others which document his ability to carry out other tasks such as using coins, copying and drawing, and growing plants and flowers. During the course of our fieldwork, Cayden was awarded a certificate for completing an employability programme run by the LAC team in April 2011. Cayden had all his certificates stored tidily in a folder, although he commented that nobody had ever asked to look at them.

Like other categories and sub-categories of young people, 'care leavers' comprises a broad range of individuals with diverse experiences. However, they are considerably more likely to become NEET than the general population and in 2011, around 35 per cent of former care leavers in England were NEET at age 19 (DfE 2012c, p.14). Heather, who worked for the Fernside LAC team, outlined some characteristics she had encountered in young people who become NEET after leaving care.

Heather: [An awful lot] come through whose basic skills are lacking, and this might be true of the generic group, but I only know the NEET group. So an awful lot have very low basic skills and that, I presume, is because of their erratic school attendance; that's because a lot of them move around a lot and there's no stability...
So...they have to have the right learning environment if you are going to put them back into a school-based classroom situation. You have to develop innovative ways of teaching them.
Lisa: Does that tend to be more practically based?
Heather: Not always. I feel they can still thrive in traditional education. Although their situations have happened before they come to me, and we now have a supervision advisor in place that I fought [over] for five years because I was picking them up at 16...coming out of the education system, and I was having to do it all by myself because there was no one else trained to work specifically with these youngsters and now I've got somebody.

In addition to low educational attainment, other factors such as whether care leavers achieve settled accommodation, the nature of caring arrangements and the stability of care they have experienced are important influences on post-16 participation. Young people who entered care due to socially unacceptable behaviour were the most likely to be NEET at age 19 (DfE 2012c, p.18).

Heather runs an employability programme for care leavers and goes on to talk about some of the tensions associated with such provision, especially when training is delivered to young people in discrete rather than integrated groups.

> Somebody said to me once 'aren't you cocooning them all together? They've been institutionalized so much and you are putting them all together instead of mixing them in society'. And you can look at it like that but why does my employability course work? I think it works because they've got an understanding in that room that every one of them are in the care system. And if you talk about role models and the peer group then all it needs is for one person to say that they are going to college to do childcare and that will have an influence on the rest.
>
> (Interview 15/10/2010)

## Marginalization and complexity

The relationship between people with special needs and processes of inclusion and exclusion is complex, and it is notable that young people with learning difficulties are somewhat less likely to become NEET than other young people when they reach the minimum school-leaving age of 16. In some ways, particularly given the association between becoming NEET and low educational attainment, this may seem counter-intuitive. However, young people with learning difficulties tend to remain in educational settings for longer, receiving the specialist support offered in many schools, colleges and local authorities. Neil, who works for the Fernside and Northdale Learning Difficulties and Disabilities (LDD) Team, discussed this point:

> Neil: [T]here are four of us covering Fernside and Northdale and most of the resource of the team is within special schools. Fernside has got a fair few special schools and Northdale only has one local authority school and one private school. But the range of young people that we work with is very broad because in terms of those who have become NEET at 16, 17 and 18 – those that you might describe as 'traditional' special needs with moderate learning difficulties – they

are hardly represented in the NEET figures at all because, when there is the opportunity for them to stay in the sixth form, they usually do or they will, almost en masse, go to a college. There are two areas where there is a problem for us and for our clients, which is for those with social and emotional difficulties and they are the ones who aren't catered for well by provision.

Lisa: And they come under the LDD label as well.

Neil: Yes. They will have a statement for special educational needs for behavioural issues. So, for example, when, in Fernside, we were talking about 9% of the whole cohort being NEET, 4.5% of the whole LDD cohort was NEET, so we are doing well there. But, within that 4.5%, the vast majority are EBD [Emotional and behavioural difficulties] young people.

(Interview 13/10/2010)

Reflecting this pattern, Cayden did not become NEET at 16, and upon leaving school he joined an employability course at Eastville College, a programme designed especially for young people with learning difficulties. He only became NEET after he left college when 'things started to break down' after his mother died. This appeared to be a pivotal moment in Cayden's life and he had finished a programme of bereavement counselling shortly before he began taking part in the research. Although Cayden had not lived with his mother since he was a baby, she had maintained contact with him and Cayden was deeply upset by her death. This event appeared to precipitate his leaving college.

Despite his problematic circumstances, like virtually all the participants in our research, Cayden often said that he wanted 'a normal life' – including his own home, a family and a job. Initially, Cayden said he wanted to work in a nursing home and, in February 2011, after attending an employability programme run by the Fernside LAC team, he began a voluntary work placement at *The Avenue*, a care home for the elderly in Eastville. Amongst other duties, Cayden made tea, helped staff with lifting and handling, assisted residents with meals and spent time talking with them. He received no pay but was pleased to be given a 'free lunch'. The care home manager, Veronica, described Cayden as polite, punctual and as being able to show initiative. Initially, Cayden spent 12 hours each week at *The Avenue* but he was soon working longer.

Cayden: I'm on time; I do all the jobs they ask me to do; I like the job and I asked Veronica if I could come back again. And all the staff like me and all that, and the old people like me.

Lisa: You're good at talking to them and you've got patience.
Cayden: Yes. You really have to have patience for this job.

> We visit Nancy, an elderly lady Cayden has formed a relationship
> with ... She smiles and welcomes us into her room; Cayden pushes a
> trolley down with him to freshen her water. Nancy has seven grand-
> children ... she jokes about having an eighth grandchild in Cayden.
> He smiles, she tells him she is going home today and tells him where
> she lives, 'across the football pitch' – Cayden says he knows it and
> she says he is welcome any time.
>
> (Interview and field notes 16/02/2011)

Things seemed to be going well and it is interesting to compare Cayden's
performance at the care home with the views of his Connexions personal adviser, Heather, who did not think he would ever be capable of
working. After a while, Cayden formed the impression that he would
be paid for working at the care home – a prospect which, at least initially, seemed to motivate him. However, paid employment was not
forthcoming and, by July, he had left *The Avenue*.

> Cayden says this was because of his confusion over payment.
> Connexions said they [*The Avenue*] would pay him and then it tran-
> spired that they could not. Cayden says he needs a job that pays. He
> also tells me that his benefits are about to decrease, and that he needs
> to find paid work.
>
> (Field notes 15/07/2011)

It is difficult to assess the validity of Cayden's claim about being offered
paid work, and it is possible that at least some of the confusion about
this matter was related to his learning difficulties. But it also seems
that a lack of effective co-ordination between support services, such as
Connexions, the LAC team and the placement provider also contributed
to the misunderstanding. Leaving this aside, Cayden's decision to stop
working at *The Avenue* seemed to have a deleterious effect on his motivation to find paid employment, and when Lisa visited him in October
finding a job seemed to have slipped off Cayden's agenda.

> As I drive up to his flat I notice his curtains are drawn, the door is
> open as some workmen are moving furniture. He doesn't respond
> to the buzzer so I walk up to his room. He answers the door in his
> pyjamas, bleary eyed, clearly having just woken up. I apologize for
> waking him, he says 'it doesn't matter I'm not even bothered, I need

to get up.' He says he is supposed to be getting up between 8 and 9am but that lately he has been getting up later and going to bed later. He quickly gets changed and opens the curtains...He says he feels he isn't ready to get a job yet, due to his past – which is something he refers to a lot. He says, '...I don't know when I'll be ready to work yet, no point I'm happy seeing friends and all that'.

(Field notes 06/11/2013)

A few weeks later there had been little change:

I visit Cayden early today as he has an appointment with a nurse at the health centre later this morning; a woman called Diane is going with him...The room smells of smoke, which is unusual...he says he is not ready for work due to 'stress and all that'. Cayden says he has been on medication to help with his stress for some time now – he doesn't know quite how long. He says that 'Malc will be leaving me soon' (Cayden ceases to be the responsibility of the LAC team when he turns 21 in March)...Cayden apologies for missing our previous appointment. He says he slept in, he knew I was there but couldn't get up. He says he is sorry, and I tell him not to worry about it.

Cayden also seemed worried about forthcoming cuts to his benefits and talked about needing to get paid employment.

(Field notes 01/12/2011]

## Voluntary work, re-engagement and marginalization

In early 2012 Cayden began work as a volunteer in a retail shop in Middlebridge run by a well-known national charity. Tara, the shop manager, says 'He just walked in. He just said he wanted to volunteer and so, obviously, we got him started on the shop floor' (Interview 31/05/2013). Cayden seemed happy with his new job, even though it was unpaid.

Cayden is expecting me as I buzz his bell; he lets me in and leaves the door open. He is dressed in jeans and a jogging top. He has pierced his other ear and had a haircut...

As we approach Middlebridge, I struggle to find a car parking spot. We walk into town after parking the car and agree to eat in the Cooking Pot Cafe. Cayden has told work that he will be in later this afternoon – he says they are very flexible and happy for him to take time off. He says he can eat anything and not put on weight – he asks if he can have a Rocky Road cake, so I say yes. He says 'thank you' and clearly enjoys the cake. I ask what he eats for breakfast and he says 'healthy cereal or toast', I ask what he will have for tea and he says he will have mash, sausages and beef, as this is what needs using up.

We walk over to the shop. Cayden says the staff are nice, he has a female manager Tara, and a male one who he introduces to me as we enter. He looks busy so I say hello and leave shortly after, leaving Cayden to start his work. He says he deals with customers all the time ...

(Field notes 29/02/2012)

Initially, Cayden worked at the shop for four days a week (from ten until five) but he was soon working six days, and sometimes he came in to socialize on his day off. He dealt with customers, worked the till, cleaned and carried out odd jobs. The shop had 12 paid staff and also employed 21 volunteers, who apparently came from 'all walks of life':

There are some who want to come in because they are just sitting at home doing nothing. We've got the ones that come in for a couple of hours a day to give them something to do and it's really because they don't want to be sitting at home doing nothing. I've got one lad who comes from Yelcaster and I've worked with him for five years now and when I transferred over to Middlebridge he came with me, and he's now gone up to transport – which he would never have been able to do before – and he's passed his driving test. So he's come a long way in the five years that I've known him.

(Tara, Interview 31/05/2012)

Tara recognizes that Cayden is vulnerable and describes taking him under her wing. She sees welfare and counselling as part of her role running the store:

Tara: It's unofficial really but, obviously, as the manager of the store dealing with the majority of volunteers and the reason that they stay is the way they are treated and the way that the store is run as such, and people enjoy working here for whatever reason....
Right from the start [Cayden] just fitted in so well. He's like my little PA [personal assistant] and he follows me around everywhere I go and he has us in stitches of laughter, honestly!

Lisa: And what do you think he is getting out of coming here?

Tara: Friendship – a lot of friendship. Somebody to talk to; meeting people from different walks of life and of different ages, and he is a member of the team.

Lisa: Have you noticed any change in him since he's been here?

Tara: He's a lot happier... when he first came here he was quite down and he used to talk about the tablets that he took and he'd come to the back door, if I'd been outside, and he'd say 'oh I feel a bit down today, Tara' and I'd say 'oh come on let's go and take your mind off stuff.' And the other day I gave him worry angels and he's got some at the side of his bed and he said that they've taken his worries away from him now. He just doesn't seem as down and depressed, and he's happy coming to work and he'll tell me what's been happening with him...

Lisa: And how would you describe Cayden's personality?

Tara: Lovely. Sweet. Very naïve; thinks the best of people. Always jolly and smiling. Probably a worrier because he does worry about his brother and sister because he said to me one time that he shouldn't worry so much about his brother and sister.

Lisa: What is the future for Cayden – is he just going to carry on doing what he's doing now?

Tara: I don't know. He's quite happy with what he's doing. He's quite happy just coming in doing his time and talking to us. I think he was coming in just for the social side of it.

Lisa: And has Cayden spoken to you about wanting to stay here?

Tara: He won't be going anywhere. He's quite happy here.

Lisa: ... You've taken him under your wing a little bit.

Tara: I think yeah but everybody has. Everybody has a bit of a soft spot for him... There is nobody that doesn't get on with Cayden. And, like I say, there are different types of people in here but there is nobody that he annoys. You can't not like Cayden.

(Field notes 31/05/2012)

Tara also supports Cayden in more practical ways: she sometimes cooks for him or brings in food left over from family meals. She also helps Cayden to organize his finances and says Cayden needs this sort of support, and says nobody has been in to see him other than me. Tara says she runs a 'happy ship' and that Cayden fits in well. She says that he has gained in confidence and seems happier since he started working at the shop.

(Field notes 31/05/2012)

Here, it is worth pausing to reflect on how Cayden's experiences relate to broader discourses about the perceived benefits of voluntary work. Although charities are often well-placed to offer work experience, the relationship between voluntary work and paid employment is complicated. At one end of the spectrum, nowadays academic qualifications are often not sufficient to get the most prestigious forms of employment and a period of voluntary work can enhance a young high-flyer's CV, especially if presented alongside a range of other socially and culturally enriching activities. Meanwhile, for those seeking entry to policing, youth work and certain other occupations, applicants are increasingly expected to have done extended periods of voluntary work before even being considered eligible for entry to formal recruitment procedures. At the other end of the labour market, voluntary employment is often promoted as a way for disadvantaged young people to gain the work experience and life skills which will enable them to progress into paid employment (National Citizen Service 2013). However, whilst some OECD data seems to lend support to this idea (Quintini et al. 2007), voluntary work does not necessarily provide reliable access to more mainstream jobs for the most vulnerable young people. Cayden's experience illustrates this – although it appears that he gained significant social and emotional benefits from his time at the charity shop.

> Cayden: I don't get bored really here. I like doing all the different things here as well and I like the people here, and I like a laugh with them, and I've made new friends with them. I've made new social friends.
>
> (Interview 31/05/2012)

Cayden also met a young woman, Holly, who subsequently became his girlfriend, whilst he was working at the shop. The charity shop and the staff there seem to have become central to Cayden's life and he said he was planning to move from Eastville to Middlebridge to be nearer work.

> Cayden:... I've got a life and I'm going to move soon... I want to move and I'm having two weeks off when I move – probably in March or in February... I'm always coming here seven days a week. That is why I want to move.
>
> (Interview 11/01/2013)

In many ways, this represented progress for Cayden, and it is difficult not to be happy for him. However, in Cayden's case it seems quite clear that doing voluntary work was not facilitating the transition into more formal employment which policymakers often envisage. Whilst it must be acknowledged that Cayden gained in many ways simply from being with other people who treat him well, it is difficult to avoid thinking that, in some ways, he may also have been exploited. He was still working at the shop when fieldwork ended in spring 2013 but there did not appear to be any prospect of paid employment despite the long hours he continued to put in. These processes illustrate our argument that labour market participation does not necessarily mean an end to marginalization, and it seems unlikely that Cayden will realize his ambition of living a 'normal life' for the foreseeable future. More generally, it is also necessary to recognize that voluntary employment, like any other form of work, has the potential for both positive and negative consequences for participants. Cayden's time at *The Avenue* ended badly and it appears that, at least for some time, his experiences there reduced his motivation to find work. Nevertheless, volunteering remains a central part of his life, and in a recent contact Cayden informed us that he had moved with his girlfriend to Hartlepool, where he hoped to obtain further voluntary work with a branch of the charity he worked for in Middlebridge.

Perhaps the final lesson to draw from Cayden's experiences relates to the role of support services in working with marginalized young people. Practitioners working with unemployed youth are under considerable pressure to meet progression targets, which vary both according to the age of the young person and the vicissitudes of funding regimes and changing policy initiatives (Russell et al. 2010). Either way, what is deemed a positive outcome for a young person at the age of 16 may not be regarded in the same way later on, and, over time, Cayden came under increasing pressure to find paid work. This is something which Cayden clearly found daunting.

The support to which Cayden was entitled also changed over the course of the fieldwork, and officially he ceased to be the responsibility of the LAC team when he became 21. Practitioners are, however, not without agency and Malc from the Fernside LAC team continued to support Cayden after this point. Malc helped Cayden move to Middlebridge even though, strictly speaking, he was no longer expected to work with him.

> Cayden: Malc is happy. He's waiting for me until I move. He was meant to have left me last month really and he's going to wait for me until I move to see if I'm happy. Everyone knows what's

been happening in my life this year because I've told them. I'm still struggling a bit but I'm hoping I'm going to be happy in this new place. I'm a bit lonely and a bit stressed at my other place.

Lisa: Why?

Cayden: There is just no one around me. Like when I move to the other place there is a shared lounge space and I can meet people. I'm friendly with other people; I like to meet people really and that's why I'm working seven days a week. I like my own space sometimes but, yeah. That's why I'm getting me new flat and I'm happy for that.

Such commitment is commendable but not unusual. We have found similar relationships between support workers and marginalized young people in every research project we have undertaken. Although the way support services function is highly constrained by funding and legislative regimes, practitioners can and often do mediate the relationship between young people and the state, and their actions and behaviour can make real differences to individual young people's lives.

# 13
## Conclusion

In this book we have tried to provide some insight into the lives of marginalized young people and the challenges they face in a post-industrial liberal economy such as the UK. The fieldwork upon which the book is based allowed us to explore the participants' lives in a way which is not possible in most research projects, and to observe how young people's lived experience relates both to their individual circumstances and life histories and to the social, economic and institutional environment in which they are located. The longitudinal nature of the study gave us the opportunity to follow the unfolding contours of social change and to see how young people responded to the enabling and constraining effects of the social structures around them. Its findings have, we believe, allowed us not only to analyse policies and dominant discourses relating to NEET young people, but also to challenge some of our own attitudes, values and beliefs about the ways in which young people attempt to negotiate the journey into adulthood. One such belief was our initial hypothesis that *exclusion* was the problem: the belief that doing something must be better than doing nothing. If it were possible to reintegrate young people with learning, or in work with training, this must be preferable to the social isolation we saw affecting the lives of many participants. Although from our earlier research we were acutely aware of the limitations of re-engagement programmes, still it seemed that participation of some kind would provide a social interaction which could lead to more sustained engagement. However, as the research progressed it became clear that 'poor learning' and 'poor work', although sometimes providing short-term satisfaction, were by no means long-term solutions. Certain forms of inclusion seemed little better – and occasionally worse – than exclusion.

In his paper *Towards a Political Economy of Youth*, James Coté investigates the causes and consequences of the ways in which young people are positioned in relation to those (adults) with political and economic power, and draws attention to policies and discourses which perpetuate and promote inequalities which are inimical to the interests of the young, leaving them vulnerable to exploitation (Coté 2013, p.2). Coté suggests that, in the absence of such a perspective, youth studies may be rendered merely an apology for neo-liberalism. From the evidence presented in this book, we would not entirely agree that a political-economy-of-youth perspective is an essential feature of studies that seek to highlight the situation of young people in post-industrial economies. Whilst we concur with the emphasis on material conditions and recognize that neo-liberal policies have had a particularly pernicious effect on young people, we do not see the experiences of youth as constituting a separate segment of social life, but as classed, raced and gendered in ways that are contiguous with divisions and inequalities in adult life. Some young people, whilst exploited in terms of their own labour process or in relation to the age-based redistribution of wealth which Coté compellingly describes, can nevertheless draw on economic, social and cultural resources of which the participants in our study could only dream. If 'precariat' really is an appropriate term to denote people existing in marginal conditions of deproletarianization, the experiences of many young people in our study could tellingly be described as an 'apprenticeship to the precariat'.

There is, in any case, a need to examine the meaning of 'youth'. We have already discussed some technical implications of extending the NEET category to include those under the age of 25, or in some usages even to 30. More generally, this elasticity of youth appears to serve the broader purposes of the neo-liberal project. By aligning difficulties in a range of spheres, such as labour-market entry, housing trajectories and wealth accumulation, with *youth*, it becomes possible to individualize and neutralize inequalities affecting large numbers of people who would formerly have been accepted as adults. Just as the NEET discourse replaced the social problem of youth unemployment with the individual problem of disengagement, so the elasticity of youth attempts to transform processes of marginality affecting millions of adults into a temporal problem of social integration. It is also worth noting that one does not need to be in paid work to be exploited. Rather than accumulating further reserves of social and cultural capital, as in some high-status internships, it is difficult not to conceptualize the experiences of some of the participants in our research – in voluntary work, on apprenticeship programmes and in various forms of education and training – as exploitative. A whole industry geared to notions of servicing, maintaining and repairing marginalized youth, and where young people are effectively processed for profit, is now part of the landscape of education and work in twenty-first-century Britain.

## Academic research and the myths of policy and practice

There are long-standing debates about how academics should engage not only with policymakers and practitioners but also with business and civil society more broadly; and, whilst this is increasingly the case across academe, social and educational research has often been criticized as being too abstract or high-flown to be applicable to practice (see, for example, Tooley and Darby 1998). Whilst such tensions have always existed they are also related in part to the rise of neo-liberalism, and since the 1980s successive UK governments have increasingly striven to tie academic research to the perceived needs of industry and society (Harris 2007). Over time, such concerns have come to exert considerable pressure on academic life, and perhaps the clearest example of this is the way in which university research is now assessed and funded by the state. Although formal research assessment exercises have existed in the UK since the mid-1980s, the notion of 'impact' introduced in the 2014 Research Assessment Framework formalized the requirement for academic research to engage with business and the wider community – and university funding is now partly reliant upon this. Such requirements place considerable pressure on universities and on individual academics who are increasingly expected to demonstrate the utility and value of their research.

Whilst few would dispute that intellectual rigour should be at the heart of academic research, we also believe, following C. Wright-Mills (1959), that good social science should reach beyond the confines of the university and engage with wider public debate – and one of the purposes of this book is to do just that. We recognize that there is a place for research which aims specifically to develop and improve professional practice but, whilst this book aims to engage and to provoke social debate, it does not pretend to offer a blueprint for practice. Rather, it is our aim as academics to help set the intellectual climate in which policy decisions are made and in which practitioners go about their work with young people. The data presented in this book, and the participants' stories it tells, aim to bridge the gap between the particularity of the day-to-day experiences of practitioners, and the generalizations of quantitative research on their participation and non-participation in education and the labour market – although we draw on such research throughout the book to contextualize our findings and trace the broad social trends in which the lives of young people are played out. Drawing on the voices of participants as well as other research findings, we also challenge dominant policy discourses surrounding worklessness, employability and the relationship between the individual and the state. As we saw in Chapter 2, there is little evidence to support the thesis that cultures of worklessness are rife in the UK. Whilst multigenerational unemployment is common, this can be traced to the consequences of de-industrialization and other social changes over many years, including the effect of neo-liberal economic policies; most older people who are currently unemployed have worked in the past, and as the stories of our participants show, parents often shared the misery of being out of work with their offspring. True intergenerational worklessness, as the quantitative research reviewed in Chapter 2 indicated, is very rare, and this was reflected in our study over and again as we uncovered the work history of young people's parents. Moreover, many of the parents of our participants were in employment – usually low-paid and demanding work – and young people themselves often demonstrated high levels of commitment in work or jobseeking. Even when, as in Isla's case, parents appeared demoralized and moribund, there was little suggestion that contentment with a life on benefits was being inculcated within young people. It is unfortunate that cultural explanations of young people's marginalization had penetrated the discourse of practitioners to the extent we observed.

What, then, of a somewhat different argument that may be posed: accepting that welfare dependency is not transmitted as a widespread cultural form, is not the 'troubled families' thesis more convincing, at least for young people in more extreme circumstances? According to such an argument, although the number of such families is relatively small, their impact is large – on their own children, on neighbourhoods and on schools and other services. Government policy currently aims to 'turn around' 120,000 of the 'most troubled' families in England by 2015; estimates of the cost to the public purse vary, but one estimate for the London borough of Barnet is that each troubled family costs nearly £100,000 (DCLG 2013). In some ways, the research presented in this book may seem to support this argument; without doubt, some young people had very troubled lives, and family backgrounds that appeared to be chaotic and, in some cases, dangerous. Isla's story suggests that such experiences may be reproduced, however well-intentioned young mothers are, and therefore individualized explanations and interventions may be seen as legitimated by our findings. Based on the evidence presented in this book, we would strongly contest this interpretation. As we have argued throughout, it is wrong to abstract the kinds of behaviour ascribed to troubled families from their social and economic context, or to extrapolate these behaviours to other people affected by the same context. The poverty and deprivation experienced by our participants has been clearly demonstrated, and we believe that we have also shown that their circumstances can be traced, not to fecklessness, but to broader trends towards the marginalization of increasing numbers of young people and adults such as those described by Wacquant (2008), Standing (2011) and Shildrick et al. (2012a). In some ways, it is surprising to have to make such statements in the twenty-first century. The potential for poor working and living conditions to create alienation and moral breakdown was evident in the nineteenth century, and Frederick Engels was not the first to point out that educational disadvantage, poverty and insecurity are deeply implicated in *producing* the moral deficiencies that underclass theories and notions of troubled families advocate as their cause.

> The moral training which is not given to the worker in school is not supplied by the other conditions of his life; ... his whole position and environment involves the strongest temptation to immorality. He is poor, life offers him no charm, almost every enjoyment is denied him, the penalties of the law have no further terrors for him; why should he restrain his desires ... Symonds observes that poverty exercises the same ruinous influence upon the mind which drunkenness exercises upon the body.
>
> (Engels 1845/1892, p.115)

Seen in the context of neo-liberal ideologies which require the progressive dismantling of welfare states and the increasing commodification of public goods, attempts to individualize and isolate social problems are easily understandable. An alternative interpretation, and the one that we propose, is that the neo-liberal project has exacerbated tensions and inequalities already existing in older versions of capitalism and that restructuring neo-liberal democracies along more equitable lines is a minimum requirement for social progress. At the same time, we need to caution against overly deterministic interpretations of our findings. In our view, one of the essential features of ethnography is that it allows researchers to understand the richness and diversity of individual meanings and actions. Rather than seeking to impose a single interpretation on the data, the ethnographer aims to reveal the complex and contextually sensitive responses people make to the cultural matrix provided by the field. Whilst broad trends were apparent in our data, they need to be balanced against the very different ways in which young people described their situation, the courses of action they took and the identity work in which they engaged.

As a research team, we have a long-standing interest in the lives of marginalized young people. There is a degree of continuity between the findings reported in this book and previous research we have conducted, perhaps especially the ongoing tension between young people's goals and ambitions and the paucity of meaningful labour market opportunities available to them, particularly to the most vulnerable (see, *inter alia*, Simmons and Thompson 2011). However, the longitudinal nature of the research upon which this book is based also provided us with special insights into particular facets of young people's experiences of education and work. We were able to observe, over an extended period of time, how young people's individual and social circumstances, and particularly their labour market experiences, affected their orientations to employment; and whilst some participants' commitment to work was remarkably durable, perhaps unsurprisingly, repeated negative experiences – whether at the Jobcentre, on training programmes, or in the workplace – often affected their confidence and, over time, it was evident that the motivation and commitment of some participants to find employment decreased. In some instances, it gradually became evident that there was a mismatch between the stated attitudes and ambitions of certain participants and their day-to-day actions and behaviour. There is also no doubt that, at certain times, some of the young people who took part in the research engaged in forms of behaviour that were negative and problematic in a number of ways.

## Marginalization, employment and education

This leads us back to our use of marginalization – a principle we have mobilized to understand the experiences of our participants. Here we will reflect on how it helps us understand the lives of vulnerable young people in neo-liberal economies like the UK, and to understand the social and economic context in which they are located. There is no doubt that the concept of marginalization as we use it has some similarities to social exclusion, or at least certain versions of social exclusion which we have summarized earlier in the book. Whilst, as we have discussed elsewhere, the lives of the young people who took part in our study were all, to a greater or lesser extent, affected by poverty, it is clear that material disadvantages were not the only barriers to progression they faced. Participants often came from difficult family circumstances, had a history of negative educational experiences and faced various obstacles to accessing a range of social and cultural resources. Their experience of services intended to support and engage them was also sometimes problematic. Although often associated with poverty, it was evident throughout the research that, for all the participants, their predicament was about more than simply a lack of money. One way in which our analysis differs from either a redistributionist or an integrationist discourse of social exclusion is that our conception of marginalization goes beyond the duality of exclusion and inclusion. What is evident from our findings is that, especially for the most vulnerable young people, participation in education or employment does not necessarily lead to meaningful advancement. On the contrary, we argue that certain forms of engagement can lead to continued exclusion. Although most of the participants engaged in some form of education, training or employment during the course of the research, for the majority, their experience was a succession of temporary, low-paid work and training programmes of variable quality interspersed with periods of being NEET – and it became evident that, for some, this was a cycle which could, over time, sap their enthusiasm for education and employment.

As we discussed in Chapter 2, the way we use marginalization has many similarities to Wacquant's (1996) concept of advanced marginality, and certain elements of his argument are evident in our findings. For Wacquant, one of the key processes driving marginalization is the degraded position of waged labour. Whereas, in the post-war era, employment generally offered working-class people a way out of poverty, today work is part of the problem. There are, however, certain differences between Wacquant's position and the way we mobilize the concept of marginalization. Whilst we agree that the various forms of exclusion, stigmatization and social closure associated with marginality are not a result of backwardness but of mutations in post-Fordist neoliberal economies, we do not necessarily concur with Wacquant's other usage of the qualifier 'advanced' – that marginality lies ahead of us (Wacquant 1996, p.123). For us, it has arrived. Most of those who took part in our study engaged in various forms of employment during the course of the fieldwork but the nature of the jobs they were able to get did not necessarily lead to social inclusion. It is evident, as Wacquant

(1996, p.124) argues, that for many young people the 'integrative capacity' of employment is being eroded. We have often been asked the question – 'is doing something better than doing nothing?', but whilst a young person who is NEET would, at least at face value, seem to have little to lose by engaging in some form of education or work, the answer to this question is not straightforward.

There is evidence that some of the participants benefited significantly from taking part in the world of work. Although his initial experiences of an apprenticeship programme were negative, Sean's position improved after finding a job at Pietro's; and, whilst Cayden's involvement in voluntary employment was also mixed, it seems he at least benefited from the social contact provided by his work at the charity shop. For others, labour market insecurity and chronic 'churning' between various sites of participation and non-participation proved a frustrating and demotivating experience. Jasmine's brief spell of employment in the care sector, Isla's experiences in hairdressing and other participants' engagement in various other forms of work or apprenticeship mean that it is difficult to avoid turning to the classic Marxist concept of alienation to conceptualize their experiences of work. None of the young people who began an apprenticeship during the course of the research completed their apprenticeship programme, and employability courses rarely led to a suitable job or meaningful progression to further study. Danny, who experienced the training provision he undertook as dull, repetitive and, frankly, quite meaningless, provides a vivid illustration of some of the frustrations participants felt after repeated exposure to employability training. Whatever the strengths or limitations of particular programmes, there is no doubt that apprenticeships and similar forms of vocational training have been oversold as the solution to a range of challenges, but in particular the enduring problem of youth unemployment – although this phenomenon is rooted at least as much in a chronic lack of demand for young people's labour as in any deficits in their skills, abilities, attitudes and dispositions. It is important to remember that the success of any education or training initiative will always be limited without concomitant intervention in labour and product markets, and stimulation of the demand for employment (Sloman 2013). It is no coincidence that the state tends to intervene more proactively in the labour market in Germany, Denmark, Finland and other nations with relatively low rates of youth unemployment. Such economies also have more highly regulated and robust systems of vocational training linked to stimulating the demand for particular forms of knowledge and skill.

We do not wish to romanticize the problematic behaviour of some young people can be deeply problematic – for example, Danny's history of youth offending, his drug use and the various nefarious activities in which he engaged cannot be condoned. Nor can the turbulent relationships, the fickle friendships and anti-social behaviour exhibited by some of the other young people who took part in our research. However, whilst it is clear that an individual's behaviour and their attitudes and opinions can both contribute to and reinforce their marginality, we need to remember that the characteristics young people display are forged, to a significant degree, by the circumstances in which they are located. This is something which sociologists have argued for decades and, whilst there are different ways of conceptualizing this, academics like Albert Cohen (1955) and Robert Merton (1968) were writing about the responses of working-class youths to the inequalities inherent in capitalist societies as long ago as the 1950s and 1960s. Although we recognize that young people's lives are neither totally enabled nor wholly constrained by structural inequalities, the way we mobilize marginalization is as a set of processes to which vulnerable young people are subject, rather as deriving largely from individual deficits.

Calls such as those made by David Cameron (2013) to get all young people either 'earning or learning' have a certain populist appeal and, as we have discussed in Chapter 2, for most young people, spending extended periods of time outside education and work can have serious long-term consequences. However, our research suggests that participation in itself is not enough – good quality secure work, and education and training which provides participants with knowledge and skills relevant to their interests and ambitions can offer significant benefits, but our findings also show how poor quality provision and negative labour market experiences can have a deleterious effect upon young people and their progression. A key message from our research is that quality counts. In some ways, this should be obvious. Whilst, in the past, employability programmes such as YTS were often criticized as low quality – and there is little doubt that some employers abused such provision, using young people as cheap labour and offering little in terms of training or job opportunities in return – not all YTS programmes were exploitative. A wide range of employers were involved in such provision, and many took the development of trainees seriously, providing structured workplace learning, time off to attend college and additional pay over and above the minimum training allowance paid by the state; and often such employers would offer permanent employment at the end of a training placement (Simmons and Thompson 2011, p.49). Today, increasing the number of young people entering apprenticeships and traineeships is presented as a solution to a number of social and economic ills. But, whilst the best apprenticeships are highly prized and offer robust training and high-quality work experience, provision is variable to say the least. As we have seen from the experiences of the young people who took part in our research, getting an apprenticeship or – even more noticeably – moving into lower-status forms of training such as employability programmes may do little to alleviate their marginalization.

### Reclaiming the disengaged?

Twenty-four young people contributed to this book. Only Shabina never became NEET, and although her school career marked her out as 'at risk' she went to college the September after leaving school and continued attending to the end of the fieldwork and beyond. Nevertheless, Shabina's engagement with learning was at times precarious and her progress was limited. At the other extreme, no participant was constantly NEET throughout the fieldwork. Saheera, of course, was at school for part of this time, although she would have been classified as sustained NEET thereafter. One other participant, Vernon, came close to this description. A care leaver aged 20 when we met him in November 2010, Vernon had begun a foundation course in English, maths and animal care on leaving school, but after 12 weeks was 'kicked out' for fighting. When he began taking part in the research, Vernon had recently left a Level 2 course in Administration after becoming a father with his partner, Gilly. For some time thereafter, Vernon was unwilling to return to education as he felt that Gilly could not cope alone; however, after turning 21 and losing support from the leaving care team, Vernon decided to return to training. Vernon found that the agenda had changed – rather than being in education, he was expected to look for work. Struggling constantly with money problems, the fear of losing benefits and relationship problems with Gilly, who was pregnant for a second time, Vernon was unable to find work, but did attend a Learn Direct course in English and maths. In our last contact with Vernon, in November 2013, we found that he and Gilly had split up. Vernon was still unable to find work, and had moved with his new girlfriend to a town just outside Northdale, where he could be close to his father, who worked in a large supermarket.

For the remaining participants, their experience of being NEET was largely as we have described – a cycle of churning which, for the majority, offered little prospect of sustainable learning or employment. The most common destination on completion of training courses was to become NEET once more, and the next most frequent was another course. Rarely did an employability course lead to employment, even several months afterwards; indeed, sustained employment of any kind was rare. The reasons why training was largely ineffective have, of course, been explored in several chapters: fundamental changes in the labour market, economic and employment policy, and the nature of training figure large in these explanations, alongside the individual characteristics and circumstances of participants. One further point should be noted here, however. Although practitioners constantly reiterated the diversity of the NEET category, and emphasized the need to treat young people as individuals, in practice the availability of particular forms of training appeared to influence how young people were allocated to courses. Little note was taken of their prior educational attainment or, indeed, their aspirations – at least in the accounts of young people – and we identified earlier in this book the lack of control perceived by many participants. Although the notion of personalization has been in vogue with policymakers for some time, it is worth considering how such processes interact with the dynamics of social class. Whilst for more advantaged groups personalization can assist processes of self-actualization and augment broader educational achievement, for marginalized young people personalization is often subsidiary to pre-assembled 'solutions' which purport to make good deficits deemed to prevent re-engagement in work and society (Simmons 2009, p.141).

It is worth reflecting on what might be called the success stories amongst these 24 young people. At the end of 2012, we were still able to track the activities of 14 participants. Of these, Steph and Sean were in paid work in the catering industry, which appeared to offer the prospect of stable employment and some career progression, and Jackson had a three-year contract as a welder. Four participants were in full-time education: as we have seen, Hailey returned to sixth-form college and Isla was continuing with her training as a hairdresser, whilst Shabina had recently switched courses from childcare to beauty, both at Level 2. Becky was still following a social care course with a private training provider, and like Hailey thought about going on to university. It is difficult to anticipate the prospects of these young people, particularly those who aim for higher education. Enough has been said about education and the working class for us to realize that their transition to employment, and prospects for social mobility, may be anything but smooth. For those in work, it is salutary to consider that in the past, social reproduction was seen as problematic. Nowadays, in spite of much rhetoric about social mobility, for working-class kids to get working-class jobs is increasingly seen as a triumph of social policy. Whilst we would not fully accept the argument that young people as whole constitute a class in the making (Coté 2013), there appears little doubt that young people who lack access to substantial reserves of economic, social and cultural capital are increasingly at risk of long-term economic marginality; alongside progressive reductions in welfare provision, it seems likely that social marginality will also increase. If troubled families are a problem now, the policies being assembled to deal with them look set simply to increase their numbers. Indeed, it does not seem unreasonable to speak of 'the defrauding of young Britain' (Dorling 2013).

There is no doubt that de-industrialization and economic change has, since the late twentieth century, had a profound effect on young people and especially the nature and range of employment opportunities available to them. Evidence suggests that this has accelerated since the global economic crisis which began during 2007–2008 and which continues to shape much political and economic discourse in the UK, and elsewhere. We must, however, point out that economic circumstances are not naturally occurring phenomena and that the latest crisis of capitalism was the result of a series of conscious policy choices. Reactions to crises are also politically loaded and a series of policy decisions taken by the Coalition Government which took power as we began our research has intensified many of the long-term social and economic changes we have described in this book. Marginalization can, we argue, only be exacerbated by cutting back advice and guidance services, reducing financial support available to young people pursuing education and training, and the introduction of ever more draconian welfare initiatives. There is an urgent need for political intervention to address the structural forces which lie at the root of marginalization.

# Appendix

Table A.1  Young people who participated in the research project (*denotes subject of case study within this book)

| | Pseudonym | First meeting | Age at first meeting | Last contact[1] | Made contact through | Initially resident in: |
|---|---|---|---|---|---|---|
| 1 | **Shabina** | 10-Nov-10 | 15 | Aug-13 | Connexions/School | Fernside |
| 2 | **Hailey (*)** | 24-Feb-11 | 16 | May-13 | Employability course | Fernside |
| 3 | Cayden (*) | 18-Nov-10 | 19 | Apr-13 | Leaving care team | Fernside |
| 4 | Isla (*) | 03-Feb-11 | 18 | Apr-13 | Employability course | Fernside |
| 5 | **Saheera (*)** | 10-Nov-10 | 15 | Apr-13 | Connexions/School | Fernside |
| 6 | **Becky** | 24-Feb-11 | 17 | Mar-13 | Jasmine (participant) | Fernside |
| 7 | **Jasmine** | 09-Dec-10 | 18 | Mar-13 | Housing charity | Fernside |
| 8 | Jackson | 24-Jun-11 | 17 | Dec-12 | Outdoor activity project | Northdale |
| 9 | **Jaylene** | 18-Nov-10 | 18 | Dec-12 | Leaving care team | Fernside |
| 10 | Sean (*) | 03-Nov-11 | 16 | Dec-12 | Connexions | Northdale |
| 11 | Sid | 18-Nov-10 | 16 | Dec-12 | Leaving care team | Fernside |
| 12 | **Steph** | 24-Jun-11 | 17 | Dec-12 | Outdoor activity project | Northdale |
| 13 | Vernon | 18-Nov-10 | 20 | Dec-12 | Leaving care team | Fernside |
| 14 | Danny (*) | 27-Jan-11 | 17 | Oct-12 | Youth offending team | Fernside |
| 15 | **Sara** | 24-Mar-11 | 18 | Sep-12 | Parenting group | Fernside |

232

*Table A.1* (Continued)

| | Pseudonym | First meeting | Age at first meeting | Last contact[1] | Made contact through | Initially resident in: |
|---|---|---|---|---|---|---|
| 16 | Alfie | 19-Jan-11 | 19 | Jul-12 | Leaving care team | Fernside |
| 17 | Cheryl | 18-Nov-10 | 18 | Jul-12 | Leaving care team | Fernside |
| 18 | Jed | 25-Nov-10 | 16 | Jul-12 | Leaving care team | Fernside |
| 19 | Johnny | 18-Nov-10 | 16 | Jul-12 | Leaving care team | Fernside |
| 20 | Kelsey | 18-Nov-10 | 19 | Jun-12 | Leaving care team | Fernside |
| 21 | Jess | 02-Feb-11 | 19 | Dec-11 | Parenting group | Fernside |
| 22 | Jodi | 02-Feb-11 | 19 | Dec-11 | Parenting group | Fernside |
| 23 | Katie | 02-Feb-11 | 19 | Dec-11 | Parenting group | Fernside |
| 24 | Karla | 03-Feb-11 | 18 | Oct-11 | Employability course | Fernside |

# Notes

## 3 Young People Not in Education, Employment or Training

1. The British Cohort Study tracks over 17,000 people born in a single week of 1970. The Longitudinal Study of Young People in England followed 15,000 young people, born between 1 September 1989 and 31 August 1990, between 2004 and 2010.
2. The ratios given by Bynner are odds ratios.
3. Broadly equivalent to GCSE passes at grade C or above.
4. 2008 figures.
5. The data used in this study are from the LSYPE, the Labour Force Survey and the British Household Panel Survey.

## 5 Education, Training and Youth Employment

1. Ford's recent decision to relocate the production of the iconic Transit van to Turkey is perhaps emblematic of this enduring trend.
2. Elementary occupations include labourers, hospital porters, bar staff, packers and shelf stackers.
3. National Statistics Socio-Economic Classification. See Rose et al. (2005).
4. In October 2013 the publication of an OECD report on the literacy and numeracy skills of adults received widespread coverage in the media, with headlines referring to an 'education crisis' (Daily Mail) and to England's young people 'trailing the world' (BBC). See OECD (2013b).
5. In 2013–2014 the scheme involved a payment of £1,500 for each apprentice aged 16–24, up to a maximum of ten grants over the lifetime of the initiative.
6. Activity agreements were piloted in eight areas across England between April 2006 and September 2009. They were designed to encourage NEET young people into work or learning and provided an allowance of between £20 and £30 per week in return for participation in activities designed to support progression into education or employment.

## 7 Hailey's Story

1. Care to Learn currently provides up to £160 per week towards childcare costs for parents who are under 20 when they begin their course. It is not available to apprentices on a salary or to higher education students.

## 9 Family, Community and Welfare

1. The Youth Cohort Study of England and Wales is a series of longitudinal studies of young people which began in 1985. It was designed to monitor the

behaviour and decisions of representative samples of young people aged 16 years onwards as they make the transition from compulsory education to further or higher education, or to the labour market. To date the YCS covers 13 cohorts and over 40 surveys.
2. The rates given here are for 16–18-year-olds.
3. Clearance from the Criminal Records Bureau (now known as the Disclosure and Barring Service) is required for work with children and vulnerable adults.
4. The areas referred to are Lower Layer Super Output Areas (LSOA): homogenous small areas containing around 1,500 people (DCLG 2011). During the research, most participants lived in LSOAs amongst the 10 per cent most deprived in England and typically had lived in similar areas since birth.
5. Specialist advisers for 16–17-year-olds in receipt of benefits are available in Jobcentres (DWP 2011).
6. Extreme need includes circumstances such as physical or moral danger, estrangement from parents or serious risk to physical or mental health. Other eligible circumstances include being part of a couple responsible for a child, or severe hardship if JSA is withheld (DWP 2011).
7. That is, to sign a declaration that they have been actively seeking work, are still available for work and there has been no relevant change in their circumstances.

## 10  Isla's Story

1. Official guidance for local authorities on supporting care leavers states that bed-and-breakfast accommodation is considered unsuitable for 16–17-year-olds.
2. Isla needed to start a course before she was 20 in order to qualify for Care to Learn.

## 12  Cayden's Story

1. The legal framework for care leavers is provided by the Children (Leaving Care) Act 2000 (CLCA), which amended the Children Act 1989. Guidance to enable local authorities to meet their obligations under CLCA was revised in 2010.

## Appendix

1. Most recent contact, either face-to-face or telephone conversation. Some participants were in contact more recently by text.

# References

Abbas, T. (2003) The impact of religio-cultural norms and values on the education of young South Asian women. *British Journal of Sociology of Education*, 24(4), 411–428.

Ainley, P. (2013) Education and the reconstitution of social class in England. *Research in Post-Compulsory Education*, 18(1–2), 46–60.

Ainley, P. and Allen, M. (2010) *Lost Generation? New Strategies for Youth and Education* (London: Continuum).

Aldridge, H., Kenway, P., MacInnes, T. and Parekh, A. (2012) *Monitoring Poverty and Social Exclusion 2012* (York: Joseph Rowntree Foundation).

Archer, L., Halsall, A. and Hollingworth, S. (2007) Class, gender, (hetero)sexuality and schooling: paradoxes within working-class girls' engagement with education and post-16 aspirations. *British Journal of Sociology of Education*, 28(2), 165–180.

Archer, L., Hollingworth, S. and Mendick, H. (2010) *Urban Youth and Schooling: The Experiences and Identities of Socially 'at risk' Young People* (Maidenhead: Open University Press).

Armstrong, D., Istance, D., Loudon, R., McCready, S., Rees, G. and Wilson, D. (1997) *Status 0: A Socioeconomic Study of Young People on the Margin* (Belfast: Department of Higher and Further Education, Training and Employment).

Atkinson, A. (1998) Social exclusion, poverty and unemployment, in A.B. Atkinson and J. Hills (Eds) *Exclusion, Employment and Opportunity*. CASE Paper 4 (pp. 1–20) (London: London School of Economics).

Avis, J. (2004) Work-based learning and social justice. *Journal of Education and Work*, 17(2), 197–217.

Avis, J. (2007) *Education, Policy and Social Justice: Learning and Skills* (London: Continuum).

Barham, C., Walling, A., Clancy, G., Hicks, S. and Conn, S. (2009) Young people and the labour market. *Economic & Labour Market Review*, 3(4), 17–29.

Barnes, M., Brown, V., Parsons, S., Ross, A., Schoon, I. and Vignoles, A. (2012) *Intergenerational Transmission of Worklessness: Evidence from the Millennium Cohort and the Longitudinal Study of Young People in England*. Research Report DFE-RR234 (London: Department for Education).

Bauman, Z. (1988) *Freedom* (Milton Keynes: Open University Press).

BBC (2011) England riots: broken Britain is top priority, says Cameron. Available online at http://www.bbc.co.uk/news/uk-politics-14524834 (accessed 2 December 2013).

BBC (2013) What are zero-hours contracts? Available online at http://www.bbc.co.uk/news/business-23573442 (accessed 14 August 2013).

Beck, U. (1992) *Risk Society: Towards a New Modernity* (London: Sage).

Becker, G. (1994) *Human Capital: A Theoretical and Empirical Analysis with Special Reference to Education* (Chicago: The University of Chicago Press).

235

Becker, H. (1996) The epistemology of qualitative research, in R. Jessor, A. Colby, and R.A. Shweder (Eds) *Ethnography and Human Development: Context and Meaning in Social Inquiry* (pp. 53–71) (Chicago: University of Chicago Press).

Bell, D. and Blanchflower, D. (2010) UK unemployment in the great recession. *National Institute Economic Review*, 214, 3–25.

Bernstein, B. (1971) On the classification and framing of educational knowledge, In M.F.D. Young (Ed.) *Knowledge and Control: New Directions for the Sociology of Education* (London: Collier-Macmillan).

Bernstein, B. (2000) *Pedagogy, Symbolic Control and Identity: Theory, Research and Critique* (Revised edition) (Oxford: Rowman and Littlefield).

Beynon, H. (1973) *Working for Ford* (London: Allen Lane).

BIS (2013) *Participation Rates in Higher Education: Academic Years 2006/07–2011/12* (London: Department for Business, Innovation and Skills).

Boudon, R. (1974) *Education, Opportunity and Social Inequality: Changing Prospects in Western Society* (London: John Wiley).

Bourdieu, P. (1974) The school as a conservative force: Scholastic and cultural inequalities, in J. Eggleston (Ed.) *Contemporary Research in the Sociology of Education*, trans. by J.C. Whitehouse (London: Methuen).

Bourdieu, P. (1977) *Outline of a Theory of Practice* (Cambridge: Cambridge University Press).

Bourdieu, P. (1986) The forms of capital, in J. Richardson (Ed.) *Handbook of Theory and Research for the Sociology of Education* (pp. 241–258) (New York: Greenwood)

Bourdieu, P. (1987) What makes a social class? on the theoretical and practical existence of groups. *Berkeley Journal of Sociology*, 32, 1–17.

Bourdieu, P. (1998) Neo-liberalism, utopia of unlimited exploitation, in *Acts of Resistance: Against the Myths of our Time* (pp. 94–105) (Cambridge: Polity Press).

Bourdieu, P. and Passeron, J-C. (1990) *Reproduction in Education, Society and Culture* (London: Sage Publications).

Bowles, S. and Gintis, H. (1976) *Schooling in Capitalist America: Educational Reform and the Contradictions of Economic Life* (London: Routledge and Kegan Paul).

Brännström, L. (2004) Poor places, poor prospects? Counterfactual models of neighbourhood effects on social exclusion in Stockholm, Sweden. *Urban Studies*, 41(13), 2515–2537.

Breen, R. (2005) Explaining cross-national variation in youth unemployment: market and institutional factors. *European Sociological Review*, 21(2), 125–134.

Brewer, J.D. (2000) *Ethnography* (Buckingham: Open University Press).

Britton, J. (2012) The NEET population in the UK, in *Youth Unemployment: The Crisis We Cannot Afford* (London: Association of Chief Executives of Voluntary Organisations).

Brown, P. (1987) *Schooling Ordinary Kids* (London: Tavistock).

Brown, P. (2013) Education, opportunity and the prospects for social mobility. *British Journal of Sociology of Education*, 34(5–6), 678–700.

Brown, P., Lauder, H. and Ashton, D. (2011) *The Global Auction: The Broken Promises of Education, Jobs and Incomes* (Oxford: Oxford University Press).

Bukodi, E., Erikson, R. and Goldthorpe, J. (2013) The effects of social origins and cognitive ability on educational attainment: evidence from Britain and Sweden. *Barnett Papers in Social Research* (Oxford: University of Oxford).

Burchardt, T., Le Grand, J. and Piachaud, D. (1999) Social exclusion in Britain 1991–1995. *Social Policy and Administration*, 33(3), 227–244.

Byrne, D. (2005) *Social Exclusion* (2nd edition) (Maidenhead: Open University Press).

Bynner, J. (2012) Policy reflections guided by longitudinal study, youth training, social exclusion, and more recently NEET. *British Journal of Educational Studies*, 60(1), 39–52.

Bynner, J. and Parsons, S. (2002) Social exclusion and the transition from school to work: the case of young people not in education, employment or training (NEET). *Journal of Vocational Behavior*, 60, 289–309.

CACE (Central Advisory Council for Education (England)) (1963) *Half Our Future*. The Newsom Report (London: Her Majesty's Stationery Office).

Cameron, D. (2013) Speech given at the Conservative Party Conference, Manchester, 1st October.

Carspecken, P. (1996) *Critical Ethnography in Educational Research* (London: Routledge).

Casey, L. (2012) *Listening to Troubled Families* (London: Department for Communities and Local Government).

Cassen, R. and Kingdon, G. (2007) *Tackling Low Educational Achievement* (York: Joseph Rowntree Foundation).

Clark, D. (2011) Do recessions keep students in school? The impact of youth unemployment on enrolment in post-compulsory education in England. *Economica*, 78, 523–545.

Clifford, J. and Marcus, G.E. (Eds) (1986) *Writing Culture: The Poetics and Politics of Ethnography* (Berkeley: University of California Press).

Coates, R. (1966) *The Making of the Welfare State* (London: Longmans).

Cohen, A. (1955) *Delinquent Boys* (Glencoe: The Free Press).

Coleman, S. and Keep, E. (2001) *Background Literature Review of PIU Project on Workforce Development* (London: Strategy Unit, Cabinet Office).

Coles, B., Hutton, S., Bradshaw, J., Craig, G., Godfrey, C. and Johnson, J. (2002) *Literature Review of the Costs of Being 'Not in Education, Employment or Training' at Age 16–18*. Research Report RR347 (London: Department for Education Skills).

Coles, B., Godfrey, C., Keung, A., Parrott, S. and Bradshaw, J. (2010) *Estimating the Life-Time Cost of NEET: 16–18 Year Olds Not in Education, Employment or Training* (York: University of York).

Coté, J. (1996) Sociological perspective on identity formation: The culture-identity link. *Journal of Adolescence*, 19, 417–428.

Coté, J. (2013) Towards a new political economy of youth. *Journal of Youth Studies*, iFirst article. 17 (4), 527–543 Crawford, C., Duckworth, K., Vignoles, A. and Wyness, G. (2011) *Young People's Education and Labour Market Choices Aged 16/17 to 18/19*. Research Report DFE-RR182 (London: Department for Education).

Cremin, H., Mason, C. and Busher, H. (2011) Problematising pupil voice using visual methods: findings from a study of engaged and disaffected pupils in an urban secondary school. *British Educational Research Journal*, 37(4), 585–603.

Curtis, K., Roberts, H., Copperman, J., Downie, A. and Liabo, K. (2004) How come I don't get asked no questions? Researching 'hard to reach' children and teenagers. *Child and Family Social Work*, 9, 167–175.

Cusworth, L., Bradshaw, J., Coles, B., Keung, A. and Chzen, Y. (2009) *Understanding the Risks of Social Exclusion across the Life Course: Youth and Young Adulthood* (London: Social Exclusion Task Force).

Daniels, H. and Cole, T. (2010) Exclusion from school: short-term setback or a long term of difficulties? *European Journal of Special Needs Education*, 25(2), 115–130.

DCLG (Department for Communities and Local Government) (2011) *The English Indices of Deprivation 2010* (London: DCLG).

DCLG (2013) *The Cost of Troubled Families* (London: DCLG).

DCSF/ONS (Department for Children, Schools and Families & Office of National Statistics) (2009) *Youth Cohort Study and Longitudinal Study of Young People in England: The Activities and Experiences of 17 year olds: England 2008* (London: DCSF).

Denscombe, M. (1995) Teachers as an audience for research: the acceptability of ethnographic approaches to classroom research. *Teachers and Teaching: Theory and Practice*, 1(1), 173–191.

Denzin, N. (1994) The art and politics of interpretation, in N.K. Denzin and Y.S. Lincoln (Eds) *Handbook of Qualitative Research* (London: Sage).

Denzin, N. and Lincoln, Y. (1998) *The Landscape of Qualitative Research: Theories and Issues* (Thousand Oaks, CA: Sage Publication).

Dewey, J. (1966) *Democracy and Education* (New York: Free Press).

DfE (Department for Education) (2010) *The Importance of Teaching*. The Schools White Paper 2010. Cm 7980 (London: DfE).

DfE (2012a) *Children Looked after in England (including adoption and care leavers) year ending 31 March 2012* (London: DfE).

DfE (2012b) *A Profile of Pupil Exclusions in England* (London: DfE).

DfE (2012c) *Care Leavers in England Data Pack* (London: DfE).

DfE (2013a) *Participation in Education, Training and Employment by 16–18 Year Olds in England*. SFR12–2012 (London: DfE).

DfEE (Department for Education and Employment) (1999) *Learning to Succeed: A New Framework for Post-16 Learning* (London: DfEE).

DfE/ONS (2010) *Youth Cohort Study and Longitudinal Study of Young People in England: The Activities and Experiences of 18 year Olds: England 2009* (London: DfE).

DfES (Department for Education and Skills) (2001) *Modern Apprenticeships: The Way to Work*. The Cassels Report (London: DfES).

Diamond, I. (2008) Foreword to TLRP report, Education, *Globalisation and the Knowledge Economy* (London: Institute of Education, University of London).

Dorling, D. (2013) The defrauding of young Britain. *New Statesman*, 1–7 November, 23–27.

Duckworth, K. and Schoon, I. (2012) Beating the odds: exploring the impact of social risk on young people's school-to-work transitions during recession in the UK. *National Institute Economic Review*, 222, 38–51.

Duncan Smith, I. (2012) Reforming welfare, transforming lives: Speech given at the University of Cambridge, 25th October. Available online at http://www.dwp.gov.uk/newsroom/ministers-speeches/ (accessed 7 August 2013).

Durkheim, E. (1903/1956) Pedagogy and sociology, in E. Durkheim, *Education and Sociology*, translated by S.D. Fox (New York: Free Press).

DWP (Department of Work and Pensions) (2011) *Delivering Services in Relation to Young Benefit Claimants from April 2011: Benefits Liaison* (London: DWP).

Ecclestone, K. and Hayes, D. (2008) *The Dangerous Rise of Therapeutic Education* (London: Routledge).

Engels, F. (1845/1892) *The Condition of the Working Class in England in 1844,* translated by Florence Kelley Wischnewetzky (London: Allen & Unwin).

Erikson, R. and Goldthorpe, J. (2010) Has social mobility in Britain decreased? Reconciling divergent findings on income and class mobility. *British Journal of Sociology,* 61(2), 211–230.

Eurofound (2012) *Young People not in Employment, Education or Training: Characteristics, Costs and Policy Responses in Europe* (Luxembourg: Publications Office of the European Union).

Farrell, C. and O'Connor, W. (2003) *Low Income Families and Household Spending* (Leeds: Department of Work and Pensions/Corporate Document Services).

Farrugia, D. (2013) Young people and structural inequality: beyond the middle ground. *Journal of Youth Studies,* 16(5), 679–693.

Fergusson, R. (2004) Discourses of exclusion: reconceptualising participation amongst young people. *Journal of Social Policy,* 33(2), 289–320.

Fergusson, R. (2013) Against disengagement: non-participation as an object of governance. *Research in Post-Compulsory Education,* 18(1–2), 12–28.

Fielding, M. and Moss, P. (2011) *Radical Education and the Common School: A Democratic Alternative* (London: Routledge).

Finegold, D. and Soskice, D. (1988) The failure of training in Britain: analysis and prescription. *Oxford Review of Economic Policy,* 4(1), 21–53.

Finlay, I., Sheridan, M., McKay, J. and Nudzor, H. (2010) Young people on the margins: in need of more choices and more chances in twenty-first century Scotland. *British Educational Research Journal,* 36(5), 851–867.

Finn, D. (1987) *Training without Jobs.* (Basingstoke: Palgrave Macmillan).

Foskett, N. and Hemsley-Brown, J. (2001) *Choosing Futures: Young People's Decision-making in Education, Training and Career Markets* (London: RoutledgeFalmer).

France, A., Bottrell, D. and Haddon, E. (2012) Managing everyday life: the conceptualisation and value of cultural capital in navigating everyday life for working-class youth. *Journal of Youth Studies,* 16(5), 597–611.

Francis, B. and Skelton, C. (2005) *Reassessing Gender and Achievement* (London: Routledge).

Franzen, E. and Kassman, A. (2005) Longer-term labour market consequences of economic inactivity during young adulthood: a Swedish national cohort study. *Journal of Youth Studies,* 8(4), 403–424.

Fuller, A., Rizvi, S. and Unwin, L. (2013) Apprenticeships and regeneration: the civic struggle to achieve social and economic goals. *British Journal of Educational Studies,* 61(1), 63–78.

Fuller, A. and Unwin, L. (2011) Vocational education and training in the spotlight: back to the future for the UK's Coalition Government? *London Review of Education,* 9(2), 191–204.

Fuller, A. and Unwin, L. (2012) *Written Evidence to the House of Commons Public Accounts Committee, Eighty-fourth Report: Adult Apprenticeships* (London: House of Commons).

Furlong, A. (2006) Not a very NEET solution: representing problematic labour market transitions among early school leavers. *Work, Employment and Society,* 20(3), 553–569.

Furlong, A. (2009) Revisiting transitional metaphors: reproducing social inequalities under the conditions of late modernity. *Journal of Education and Work,* 22(5), 343–353.

Furlong, A. and Cartmel, F. (2007) *Young People and Social Change: New Perspectives* (Maidenhead: Open University Press).

Gaffney, D. (2010) *The myth of the intergenerational workless household.* Available online at http://www.leftfootforward.org/2010/09/the-myth-of-the-intergenerational-workless-household/ (accessed 11 September 2013).

Gangl, M. (2002) Changing labour markets and early career outcomes: labour market entry in Europe over the last decade. *Work, Employment and Society*, 16, 67–90.

Geerdsen, L.P. (2002) *Are the Marginalised Truly Marginalised? A Study of Labour Force Attachment in Denmark* (Copenhagen: Danish National Institute for Social Research).

Geertz, C. (1973) *The Interpretation of Cultures: Selected Essays* (New York: Basic Books).

Germani, G. (1980) *Marginality* (New Brunswick: Transaction Books).

Giddens, A. (1991) *Modernity and Self Identity: Self and society in the Late Modern Age* (Cambridge: Polity).

Giddens, A. (1998) *The Third Way: The Renewal of Social Democracy* (Cambridge: Polity).

Gillborn, D. (2008) *Racism and Education: Coincidence or Conspiracy?* (London: Routledge).

Gillborn, D. (2010a) The colour of numbers: surveys, statistics and deficit-thinking about race and class. *Journal of Education Policy*, 25(2), 253–276.

Gillborn, D. (2010b) The white working class, racism and respectability: victims, degenerates and interest-convergence. *British Journal of Educational Studies*, 58(1), 3–25.

Goldthorpe, J.H. (with C. Llewellyn) (1980) *Social Mobility and Class Structure in Modern Britain* (Oxford: Clarendon).

Goldthorpe, J. and Mills, C. (2008) Trends in intergenerational class mobility in modern Britain: evidence from national surveys, 1972–2005. *National Institute Economic Review*, 205, 83–100.

Goodman, A. and Gregg, P. (2010) *Poorer Children's Educational Attainment: How Important are Attitudes and Behaviour?* (York: Joseph Rowntree Foundation).

Goodwin, J. and O'Connor, H. (2005) Exploring complex transitions: looking back at the 'Golden Age' of youth transitions. *Sociology*, 39(2), 201–220.

Goos, M. and Manning, A. (2007) Lousy and lovely jobs: the rising polarization of work in Britain. *The Review of Economics and Statistics*, 89, 118–133.

Goujard, A., Petrongolo, B. and Van Reenan, J. (2011) The labour market for young people, in P. Gregg and J. Wadsworth (Eds) *The Labour Market in Winter: The State of Working Britain* (Oxford: Oxford University Press).

Green, R. and White, A. (2008) Shaped by place: young people's decisions about education, training and work. *Benefits*, 16(3), 213–224.

Gregg, P. and Tominey, E. (2005) The wage scar from male youth unemployment. *Labour Economics*, 12, 487–509.

Habermas, J. (1975) *Legitimation Crisis* (Boston, MA: Beacon Press).

Hammersley, M. (1992) *What's Wrong with Ethnography* (London: Routledge).

Hammersley, M. and Atkinson, P. (2007) *Ethnography: Principles in Practice* (3rd edition) (London: Routledge).

Hargreaves, D.H. (1967) *Social Relations in a Secondary School* (London: Routledge and Kegan Paul).

Harris, S. (2007) *The Governance of Education: How Neo-liberalism is Transforming Policy and Practice* (London: Continuum).

Higgins, J. (2013) Towards a learning identity: young people becoming learners after leaving school. *Research in Post-Compulsory Education*, 18(1–2), 175–193.

Hillman, K. (2005) *Young People outside the Labour Force and Full-time Education: Activities and Profiles* (Camberwell: Australian Council for Educational Research).

Hillage, J., Johnson, C., Newton, B., Maguire, S., Tanner, E. and Purdon, S. (2008) *Activity Agreements Evaluation: Synthesis Report* (Nottingham: Department for Children, Schools and Families).

HM Government (2010) *Unleashing Aspirations: The Final Report of the Panel on Fair Access to the Professions* (London: Cabinet Office).

HM Government (2011) *Building Engagement, Building Futures: Our Strategy to Maximise the Participation of 16–24 Year Olds in Education, Training and Work* (London: HM Government).

Hodgson, A. and Spours, K. (2010) Vocational qualifications and progression to higher education: the case of the 14–19 Diplomas in the English system. *Journal of Education and Work*, 23(2), 95–110.

Hodgson, A. and Spours, K. (2011) Rethinking general education in the English upper secondary system. *London Review of Education*, 9(2), 205–216.

Hodgson, A. and Spours, K. (2013) Middle attainers and 14–19 progression in England: half-served by New Labour and now overlooked by the Coalition? *British Educational Research Journal*, DOI: 10.1002/berj.3091.

Hoggarth, L. and Smith, D. (2004) *Understanding the Impact of Connexions on Young People at Risk*. Research Report RR 607 (Nottingham: Department for Education and Skills).

Holmes, C. and Mayhew, K. 2012. *The Changing Shape of the UK Job Market and its Implications for the Bottom Half of Earners* (London: Resolution Foundation).

Hyland, T. (2009) Mindfulness and the therapeutic function of education. *Journal of Philosophy of Education*, 43(1), 119–131.

Hyland. T. and Winch, C. (2007) *A Guide to Vocational Education and Training* (London: Continuum).

Ianelli, C. and Smyth, E. (2008) Mapping gender and social background differences in education and youth transitions across Europe. *Journal of Youth Studies*, 11(2), 213–232.

Ijaz, A. and Abbas, T. (2010) The impact of inter-generational change on the attitudes of working-class South Asian Muslim parents on the education of their daughters. *Gender and Education*, 22(3), 313–326.

ILO (1982) *Resolution Concerning Statistics of the Economically Active Population, employment, Unemployment and Underemployment (October 1982)*. Available online at http://www.ilo.org (accessed 16 August 2013).

Institute of Careers Guidance (2011) *Uncertain Futures: The Impact of Cuts to the Careers Service on the Futures of Young People* (Stourbridge: Institute of Careers Guidance).

IPPR (Institute for Public Policy Research) (2011) *Rethinking Apprenticeships* (London: IPPR).

Istance, D., Reese, G. and Williamson, H. (1994) *Young People Not in Education, Training or Employment in South Glamorgan* (Cardiff: South Glamorgan Training and Enterprise Council).

Jackson, M. (Ed.) (2013) *Determined to Succeed? Performance versus Choice in educational Attainment* (Stanford: Stanford University Press).

James, D. and Biesta, G. (2007) *Improving Learning Cultures in Further Education* (London: Routledge).

James, D. and Simmons, J. (2007) Alternative assessment for learner engagement in a climate of performativity: lessons from an English case study. *Assessment in Education*, 14(3), 353–371.

James, D., Reay, D., Crozier, G., Beedell, P., Hollingworth, S., Jamieson, F. and Williams, K. (2010) Neo-liberal policy and the meaning of counter-intuitive middle-class school choices. *Current Sociology*, 58(4), 623–641.

Jeffrey, B. and Troman, G. (2004) Time for ethnography. *British Educational Research Journal*, 30(4), 535–548.

Jeffs, T. and Smith, M. (1998) The problem of 'youth' for youth work. *Youth and Policy*, 62, 45–66.

Jones, G. (1995) *Leaving Home* (Milton Keynes: Open University Press).

Jones, O. (2012) *Chavs: The Demonization of the Working Class* (2nd edition) (London: Verso).

Jones, S. and Riddell, W. (1998) Unemployment and labour force attachment: A multistate analysis of non-employment, in J. Haltiwayer, E. Mauser-Marilyn and R. Topel (Eds) *Labour Statistics Measurement Issues*, Vol. 60 (Chicago: University of Chicago Press).

Katz, I., La Placa, V. and Hunter, S. (2007) *Barriers to Inclusion and Successful Engagement of Parents in Mainstream Services* (York: Joseph Rowntree Foundation).

Keep, E. (2006) State control of the English education and training system – playing with the biggest train set in the world. *Journal of Vocational Education and Training*, 58(1), 47–64.

Keep, E. and Mayhew, J. (2010) Moving beyond skills as a social and economic panacea. *Work, Employment and Society*, 24(3), 565–577.

Kehily, M.J. (2009) What is identity? A sociological perspective, in ESRC Seminar Series: The educational and social impact of new technologies on young people in Britain, 2 March 2009, London School of Economics, UK. Available from http://oro.open.ac.uk/16372/2/What_is_Identity.pdf (accessed 17 February 2014).

Kintrea, K., St Clair, R. and Houston, M. (2011) *The Influence of Parents, Places and Poverty on Educational Attitudes and Aspirations* (York: Joseph Rowntree Foundation).

Korenman, S. and Neumark, D. (2000) Cohort crowding and youth labour markets: a cross-national analysis, in D.G. Blanchflower and R.B. Freeman (Eds) *Youth Employment and Joblessness in Advanced Countries* (Chicago: University of Chicago Press).

Lahelma, E. and Gordon, T. (2003) Home as a physical, social and mental space: young people's reflections on leaving home. *Journal of Youth Studies*, 6(4), 377–390.

Lash, S. (1992) *Modernity and Identity* (Oxford: Blackwell).

Lawy, R., Quinn, J. and Diment, K. (2009) Listening to 'the thick bunch': (mis)understanding and (mis)representation of young people in jobs without training in the South West of England. *British Journal of Sociology of Education*, 30(6), 741–755.

Lee, N. and Wright, J. (2011) *Off the Map? The Geography of NEETs: A Snapshot Analysis for the Private Equity Foundation* (London: The Work Foundation).

Lefebvre, H. (1987) The everyday and everydayness. *Yale French Studies*, 73: 7–11.

Levitas, R. (2005) *The Inclusive Society? Social Exclusion and New Labour* (2nd edition) (Basingstoke: Palgrave Macmillan).

Lewis, O. (1966) The culture of poverty. *Scientific American*, 215(4), 19–25.

Lipsky, M. (1980) *Street-Level Bureaucracy: Dilemmas of the Individual in Public Services* (New York: Russell Sage Foundation).

Lister, R. (2004) *Poverty* (Cambridge: Polity Press).

Lloyd, C., Mason, G. and Mayhew, K. (Eds) (2008) *Low-Wage Work in the United Kingdom* (New York: Russell Sage Foundation).

Lloyd, N. and Rafferty, A. (2006) *Black and Minority Ethnic Families and Sure Start: Findings from Local Evaluation Reports* (London: National Evaluation of Sure Start).

Lovell, T. (2004) Bourdieu, class and gender: 'The return of the living dead?' in L. Adkins and B. Skeggs (Eds) *Feminism after Bourdieu* (Oxford: Blackwell).

Low Pay Commission (2013) *National Minimum Wage: Low Pay Commission Report 2013*. Cm 8565 (London: The Stationery Office).

MacDonald, R. and Marsh, J. (2001) Disconnected Youth? *Journal of Youth Studies*, 4(4), 373–391.

MacDonald, R. and Marsh, J. (2005) *Disconnected Youth? Growing up in Britain's Poor Neighbourhoods* (Basingstoke: Palgrave Macmillan).

MacDonald, R., Shildrick, T., Webster, C. and Simpson. D. (2005) Growing up in poor neighbourhoods: the significance of class and place in the extended transitions of 'socially excluded' young adults. *Sociology*, 39(5), 873–891.

Macmillan, L. (2010) *The Intergenerational Transmission of Worklessness in the UK* (Bristol: Centre for Market and Public Organisation, University of Bristol).

Marcus, G. (1995) Ethnography in/of the world system: the emergence of multi-sited ethnography. *Annual Reviews of Anthropology*, 24, 95–117.

Marx, K. (1867/1976) *Capital: A Critique of Political Economy*. Vol. 1. (Harmondsworth: Penguin Books).

Marx, I. and Nolan, B. (2012) *In-Work Poverty*. GINI Discussion Paper 51. (Amsterdam: Amsterdam Institute for Advanced Labour Studies).

Mayer, S. and Jencks, C. (1989) Growing up in poor neighbourhoods: how much does it matter? *Science*, 243(4897), 1441–1445.

McCrone, T., Southcott, C., Featherstone, G., McCloud, S. and Dawson, A. (2013) *Research into Training for Young Adults Aged 19–24 Who are not in Education, Employment or Training* (London: Department for Business, Innovation and Skills).

McDonald, K. (1999) *Struggles for Subjectivity: Identity, Action and Youth Experience* (Cambridge: Cambridge University Press).

McDowell, L. (2000) Learning to serve? Employment aspirations and attitudes of young working-class men in an era of labour market restructuring. *Gender, Place and Culture*, 7(4), 389–416.

McInnes, T. (2012) *There is a difference between 'workless' and 'never worked'*. New Policy Institute. Available online at http://www.npi.org.uk/blog/work-and-pay/there-difference-between-workless-and-never-worked/ (accessed 11 September 2013).

McRobbie, A. (2004) Notes on 'What not to Wear' and post-feminist symbolic violence, in L. Adkins and B. Skeggs (Eds) *Feminism after Bourdieu* (Oxford: Blackwell).

Merton, R. (1968) Social structure and anomie, in R. Merton (Ed.) *Social Theory and Social Structure* (New York: The Free Press).

Mirza, H. and Meetoo, V. (2013) Gendered surveillance and the social construction of young Muslim women in schools, in K. Bhopal and U. Maylor (Eds) *(In)equalities: Race, Class and Gender* (London: Routledge).

Moore, R. (2004) *Education and Society: Issues and explanations in the Sociology of Education* (Cambridge: Polity Press).

Munn, P. and Lloyd, G. (2005) Exclusion and excluded pupils. *British Educational Research Journal*, 31(2), 205–221.

Murray, C. (1990) *The Emerging British Underclass* (London: Institute of Economic Affairs).

Murray, C. (1994) *The Underclass: The Crisis Deepens* (London: Institute of Economic Affairs).

NAO (National Audit Office) (2012) *The Introduction of the Work Programme* (Norwich: The Stationery Office).

National Citizen Service (2013) Available on-line at http://www.ncsyes.co.uk/ (accessed 13 October 2013).

Nayak, A. (2003) 'Boyz to men': masculinities, schooling and labour transitions in de-industrial times. *Educational Review*, 55(2), 147–159.

Nixon, D. (2009) 'I can't put a smiley face on': working-class masculinity, emotional labour and service work in the 'new economy'. *Gender, Work and Organisation*, 16(3), 300–322.

Nolan, B. and Whelan, C.T. (1996) *Resources, Deprivation and Poverty* (Oxford: Clarendon Press).

O'Connor, A. (2001) *Poverty Knowledge* (Princeton: Princeton University Press).

OECD (2013a) *Education at a Glance 2013: OECD Indicators* (Paris: OECD Publishing).

OECD (2013b) *OECD Skills Outlook 2013: First Results from the Survey of Adult Skills* (Paris: OECD Publishing).

Ofsted (Office for Standards in Education, Children's Services and Skills) (2013) *Lessons from the Foundation Learning Provision for the New 16–19 Study Programmes* (Manchester: Ofsted).

O'Neill, D. and Sweetman, O. (1998) Intergenerational mobility in Britain: evidence from unemployment patterns. *Oxford Bulletin of Economics and Statistics*, 60(4), 431–447.

ONS (Office of National Statistics) (2012) *Characteristics of Young Unemployed People, 2012*. Available online at http://www.ons.gov.uk/ons/rel/lmac/characteristics-of-young-unemployed-people/2012/index.html (accessed 11 September 2013).

ONS (2013a) *Poverty and Social Exclusion in the UK and EU, 2005–11* (London: ONS).

ONS (2013b) *Working and Workless Households 2013 – Statistical Bulletin* (London: ONS).

ONS (2013c) *Workforce Jobs by Industry*. Excel spreadsheet. Available online at http://www.ons.gov.uk/ons/rel/lms/labour-market-statistics/august-2013/table-jobs02.xls (accessed 9 September 2013).

ONS (2013d) Real wages down by 8.5% since 2009. Available online at http://www.ons.gov.uk/ons/dcp171780_305213.pdf (accessed 26 October 2013).

Osborne, G. (2011) Speech at the Welsh Conservatives Spring Conference, Cardiff, 4th March.

Padley, M. and Hirsch, D. (2013) *Households Below a Minimum Income Standard: 2008/09–2010/11* (York: Joseph Rowntree Foundation).

Page, J., Whitting, G. and McLean, C. (2007) *Engaging Effectively with Black and Minority Ethnic Parents in Children's and Parental Services*. Research Report DCSF-RR013 (London: Department for Children, Schools and Families).

Payne, J. (2003) *Choice at the End of Compulsory Schooling: A Research Review*. Research Report RR414 (London: Department for Education and Skills).

Penny, L. (2010) Girls, exams and employment: A race to the bottom, *New Statesman*, Available at http://www.newstatesman.com/blogs/laurie-penny/2010/08/young-women-girls-market (accessed 29 August 2013).

Peruzzi, A. (2013) *From Childhood Deprivation to Social Exclusion: Evidence from the 1970 British Cohort Study* (London: Centre for Longitudinal Studies, Institute of Education).

Pierce, N. and Hillman, J. (1998) *Wasted Youth: Raising Achievement and Tackling Social Exclusion* (London: Institute for Public Policy Research).

Pink, S. and Morgan, J. (2013) Short-term ethnography: intense routes to knowing. *Symbolic Interaction*, 36(3), 351–361.

Pirrie, A., Macleod, G., Cullen, M. and McCluskey, G. (2011) What happens to pupils permanently excluded from special schools and pupil referral units in England? *British Educational Research Journal*, 37(3), 519–538.

Power, S., Edwards, T., Whitty, G. and Wigfall, V. (2003) *Education and the Middle Class* (Buckingham: Open University Press).

Pyper, D. and McGuiness, F. (2013) *Zero-Hours Contracts. Standard Note SN/BT/6553.* (London: House of Commons Library).

Quintini, G., Martin, P. and Martin, S. (2007) *The Changing Nature of the School to Work Transition Process in OECD Countries*. Discussion Paper 2582 (Bonn: Institute for the Study of Labour).

Raffe, D. (2008) The concept of transition system. *Journal of Education and Work*, 21(4), 277–296.

Reay, D. (2004) Education and cultural capital: the implications of changing trends in education policies. *Cultural Trends*, 13(2), 73–86.

Reay, D. (2007) 'Unruly places': inner-city comprehensives, middle-class imaginaries and working-class children. *Urban Studies*, 44(7), 1191–1201.

Reay, D. and Lucey, H. (2004) Stigmatised choices: social class, social exclusion and secondary school markets in the inner city. *Pedagogy, Culture and Society*, 12(1), 35–51.

Rees, G., Williamson, H. and Istance, D. (1996) 'Status Zero': a study of jobless school-leavers in South Wales. *Research Papers in Education*, 11(2), 219–235.

Resolution Foundation (2013) *Low Pay Britain 2013* (London: Resolution Foundation).

Roberts, K. (2004) School-to-work transitions: why the United Kingdom's educational ladders always fail to connect. *International Studies in Sociology of Education*, 14(3), 203–215.

Roberts, K. (2009) Opportunity structures then and now. *Journal of Education and Work*, 22(5), 355–368.

Roberts, S. (2011) Beyond 'Neet' and tidy pathways: Considering the 'missing middle' of youth transition studies. *Journal of Youth Studies*, 14(1), 21–40.

Roberts, S. (2012) 'Just getting on with it': The educational experiences of ordinary, yet overlooked, boys. *British Journal of Sociology of Education*, 33(2), 203–221.

Rose, D., Pevalin, D. and O'Reilly, K. (2005) *The National Statistics Socio-economic Classification: Origins, Development and Use* (Basingstoke: Palgrave Macmillan).

Rose, N. (1998) *Inventing Our Selves: Psychology, Power and Personhood* (Cambridge: Cambridge University Press).

Rowntree, B.S. (1937) *The Human Needs of Labour* (London: Longmans Green).

Russell, L. (2005) It's a question of trust: balancing the relationship between students and teachers in ethnographic fieldwork. *Qualitative Research*, 5(2), 181–199.

Russell, L. (2013) Researching marginalised young people. *Ethnography and Education*, 8(1), 46–60.

Russell, L., Simmons, R. and Thompson, R. (2010) Playing the numbers game: Connexions personal advisers working with learners on entry to employment programmes. *Journal of Vocational Education and Training*, 62(1), 1–12.

Russell, L., Simmons, R. and Thompson, R. (2011a) Conceptualising the lives of NEET young people: structuration theory and 'disengagement'. *Education, Knowledge and Economy*, 5(3), 89–106.

Russell, L., Simmons, R. and Thompson, R. (2011b) Ordinary lives: an ethnographic study of young people attending Entry to Employment programmes. *Journal of Education and Work*, 24(5), 477–499.

Sandbrook, D. (2013) *Seasons in the Sun: The Battle for Britain, 1974–1979* (London: Penguin).

Scarpetta, S., Sonnet, A. and Manfredi, T. (2010) *Rising Youth Unemployment during the Crisis: How to Prevent Negative Long-Term Consequences on a Generation.* OECD Social, Employment and Migration Papers, No. 106 (Paris: Organisation for Economic Co-operation and Development).

Scottish Executive (2006) *More Choices, more Chances: A Strategy to Reduce the Proportion of Young People Not in Education, Employment or Training in Scotland* (Edinburgh: Scottish Executive).

SEU (Social Exclusion Unit) (1997) *Social Exclusion Unit: Purpose, Work Priorities and Working Methods* (London: Her Majesty's Stationery Office).

SEU (1999) *Bridging the Gap: New Opportunities for 16–18 year Olds Not in Education, Employment or Training*, Cm4405 (London: The Stationery Office).

Shah, S. and Iqbal, M. (2011) Pakistani diaspora in Britain: intersections of multi-locationality and girls' education. *British Journal of Sociology of Education*, 32(5), 763–783.

Shain, F. (2003) *The Schooling and Identity of Asian Girls* (Stoke-on-Trent: Trentham Books).

Shields, R. (1991) *Places on the Margin: Alternative Geographies of Modernity* (London: Routledge).

Shildrick, T. and MacDonald, R. (2007) Biographies of exclusion: poor work and poor transitions. *International Journal of Lifelong Education*, 26(5), 589–604.

Shildrick, T., MacDonald, R., Webster, C. and Garthwaite, K. (2012a) *Poverty and Insecurity: Life in Low-Pay, No-Pay Britain* (Bristol: Policy Press).

Shildrick,T., MacDonald, R., Furlong, A., Roden, J. and Crow, R. (2012b) *Intergenerational Cultures of Worklessness? A Qualitative Exploration in Glasgow and Middlesbrough* (York: Joseph Rowntree Foundation).

Simmons, R. (2009) Entry to employment: discourses of inclusion and employability in work-based learning for young people. *Journal of Education and Work*, 22(2), 137–151.

Simmons, R. and Thompson, R. (2011) *NEET Young People and Training for Work: Learning on the Margins* (Stoke-on-Trent: Trentham Books).

Simmons, R. and Thompson, R. (2013) Reclaiming the disengaged: Critical perspectives on young people not in education, employment or training. *Research in Post-Compulsory Education*, 18(1–2), 1–11.

Simmons, R., Russell, L. and Thompson, R. (2014) Young people and labour market marginality: findings from an ethnographic study. *Journal of Youth Studies*, 17(5), 577–591.

Simon, B. (1999) *Education and the Social Order 1940–1990* (London: Lawrence & Wishart).

Sissons, P. and Jones, K. (2012) *Lost in Transition? The Changing Labour Market and Young People not in Employment, Education or Training* (London: The Work Foundation).

Skeggs, B. (2004) *Class, Self, Culture* (London: Routledge).

Skeggs, B. (2005) The making of class and gender through visualising moral subject formation. *Sociology*, 39(5), 965–982.

Sloman, M. (2013) Training for skills in crisis – a critique and some recommendations. *Training Journal* LandD 2020 project paper.

Smith, A. (1776) *An Inquiry into the Nature and Causes of the Wealth of Nations* (London: Routledge).

Smyth, J., McInerney, P. and Fish, T. (2013) Re-engagement to where? Low SES students in alternative-education programme on the path to low-status destinations. *Research in Post-Compulsory Education*, 18(1–2), 194–207.

Spielhofer, T., Benton, T., Evans, K., Featherstone, G., Golden, S., Nelson, J. and Smith, P. (2009) *Increasing Participation: Understanding Young People Who do Not Participate in Education and Training at 16 and 17*. Research Report DCSF-RR072 (Nottingham: Department for Children, Schools and Families).

Spielhofer, T. Marson-Smith, H. and Evans, K. (2009) *Non-Formal Learning: Good Practice in Re-engaging Young People Who are NEET* (Slough: National Foundation for Educational Research).

Standing, G. (2011) *The Precariat: The New Dangerous Class* (London: Bloomsbury).

Strathdee, R. (2013) Reclaiming the disengaged: reform of New Zealand's vocational education and training and social welfare systems. *Research in Post-Compulsory Education*, 18(1–2), 29–45.

Thompson, R. (2011) Individualisation and social exclusion: the case of young people not in education, employment or training. *Oxford Review of Education*, 37(6), 785–802.

Thompson, R., Russell, L. and Simmons, R. (2014) Space, place and social exclusion: an ethnographic study of young people outside education and employment. *Journal of Youth Studies*, 17(1), 63–78.

Thomson, P. and Russell, L. (2009) Data, data everywhere – but not all the numbers that count? Mapping alternative provisions for students excluded from school. *International Journal of Inclusive Education*, 13(4), 423–438.

Tomlinson, M. and Walker, R. (2010) *Recurrent Poverty: The Impact of Family and Labour Market Changes* (York: Joseph Rowntree Foundation).

Tooley, J. and Darby, D. (1998) *Educational Research: A Critique* (London: Office for Standards in Education, Children's Services and Skills).

Townsend, P. (1979) *Poverty in the United Kingdom* (London: Tavistock Press).

UKCES (UK Commission for Employment and Skills) (2011) *The Youth Inquiry: Employer's Perspectives on Tackling Youth Unemployment* (London: UKCES).

UKCES (2012) *UK Commission's Employer Skills Survey 2011: UK Results* (London: UKCES).

Van Berkel, R., Møller, I. and Williams, C. (2002) The concept of inclusion/exclusion and the concept of work, in R. Van Berkel and I. Møller (Eds) *Active Social Policies in the EU: Inclusion through Participation* (Bristol: Policy Press).

Vincent, C., Ball, S. and Braun, A. (2010) Between the estate and the state: struggling to be a 'good' mother. *British Journal of Sociology of Education*, 31(2), 123–138.

Wacquant, L. (1996) The rise of advanced marginality: notes on its nature and implications. *Acta Sociologica*, 39, 121–139.

Wacquant, L. (2008) *Urban Outcasts: A Comparative Sociology of Advanced Marginality* (Cambridge: Polity Press).

Wade, J. and Dixon, J. (2006) Making a home, finding a job: investigating early housing and employment outcomes for young people leaving care. *Child and Family Social Work*, 11, 199–208.

Walford, G. (2009) For ethnography. *Ethnography and Education*, 4(3), 271–282.

WEF (World Economic Forum) (2013) *The Global Competitiveness Report 2013–14* (Geneva: WEF).

Wheelahan, L. (2007) How competency-based training locks the working class out of powerful knowledge: a modified Bernsteinian analysis. *British Journal of Sociology of Education*, 28(5), 637–651.

Whitty, G. (2001) Education, social class and social exclusion. *Journal of Education Policy*, 16, 287–295.

Whyte, W.F. (1943/1981) *Street Corner Society* (Chicago: University of Chicago Press).

Wilkinson, C. (1995) *The Drop Out Society: Young People on the Margin* (Leicester: Youth Work Press).

Williamson, H. (2010) Neet acronym is far from a neat description. *TES Cymru*, 5 March 2010. Available online at http://www.tes.co.uk/article.aspx?storycode=6038266 (accessed 11 September 2013).

Willis, P. (1977) *Learning to Labour: How Working-Class Kids Get Working-Class Jobs* (Farborough: Saxon House).

Wiseman, J., Roe, P. and Parry, E. (2011) *An Evaluation of the Apprenticeship Grant for Employers (AGE) Programme* (Birmingham: BMG Research).

Wodtke, G., Harding, D. and Elwert, F. (2011) Neighbourhood effects in temporal perspective: the impact of long-term exposure to concentrated disadvantage on high school graduation. *American Sociological Review*, 76(5), 713–736.

Wolf, A. (2011) *Review of Vocational Education*. The Wolf Report (London: DfE).

Wright-Mills, C. (1959) *The Sociological Imagination* (Oxford: Oxford University Press).

Yates, S. and Payne, M. (2006) Not so NEET? A critique of the use of 'NEET' in setting targets for interventions with young people. *Journal of Youth Studies*, 9(3), 329–344.

# Index

Note: The letters 'n' following locators refer to notes.

Printed and bound by CPI Group (UK) Ltd, Croydon, CR0 4YY